Africa and China

Africa and China

How Africans and Their Governments are Shaping Relations with China

Aleksandra W. Gadzala

ROWMAN & LITTLEFIELD
Lanham • Boulder • New York • London

Published by Rowman & Littlefield
A wholly owned subsidiary of The Rowman & Littlefield Publishing Group, Inc.
4501 Forbes Boulevard, Suite 200, Lanham, Maryland 20706
www.rowman.com

Unit A, Whitacre Mews, 26-34 Stannary Street, London SE11 4AB

Copyright © 2015 by Rowman & Littlefield
First paperback edition published 2018

British Library Cataloguing in Publication Information Available

Library of Congress Cataloging-in-Publication Data

Africa and China (Rowman and Littlefield, Inc.)
Africa and China : how Africans and their governments are shaping relations with China / Aleksandra Gadzala.
p. cm.
Includes bibliographical references and index.
ISBN 978-1-4422-3775-9 (cloth : alk. paper) -- ISBN 978-1-4422-3776-6 (electronic) -- ISBN 978-1-78660-656-3 (paper : alk. paper)
1. Africa, Sub-Saharan--Foreign economic relations--China. 2. China--Foreign economic relations--Africa, Sub-Saharan. 3. Africa, Sub-Saharan--Relations--China. 4. China--Relations--Africa, Sub-Saharan. 5. Africa, Sub-Saharan--Economic conditions. I. Gadzala, Aleksandra W. (Aleksandra Weronika), 1984- author, editor. II. Title.
HF1611.Z4C615 2015
337.67051--dc23

2015028234

™ The paper used in this publication meets the minimum requirements of American National Standard for Information Sciences Permanence of Paper for Printed Library Materials, ANSI/NISO Z39.48-1992.

Printed in the United States of America

Only ill-informed observers would see Africa's embrace of China as a zero sum game.
—Denis Tull, German Institute for International and Security Affairs, Berlin

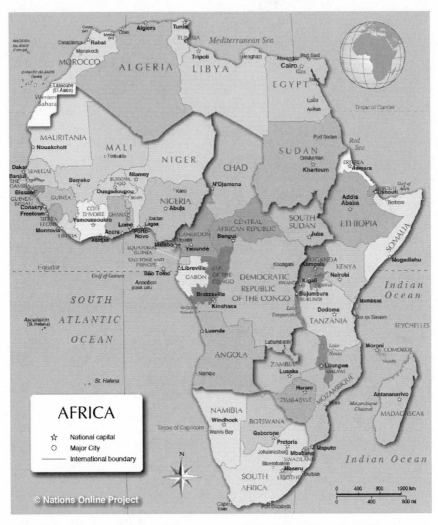

Map of the African continent with countries, main cities and capitals. (Source: Nations Online Project)

Contents

Preface

Since *Africa and China* was first published in 2015, bilateral relations between Africa and China have come more squarely into the limelight.

At the latest China-Africa summit in South Africa in December 2015, Chinese president Xi Jinping pledged $60 billion of support for African development – a big, sweeping commitment covering many areas and inextricably embedding China in Africa's long-term future. Between 2000 and 2014 Chinese trade with Africa grew from $10 billion to $220 billion. China's foreign direct investment stocks rose from two percent of U.S. levels to fifty-five percent over the same period; China now contributes around one-sixth of all lending to the continent. Beijing has diplomatic missions in fifty-two of Africa's fifty-four states; its first permanent overseas military base opened in Djibouti in August 2017, a reflection of China's increasingly assertive foreign policy stance and Africa's role in it. These advances have started to turn heads. In a recent report McKinsey & Company, a global consulting firm, found that China is among Africa's top four partners in terms of trade, investment stock, investment growth, infrastructure financing, and aid. "No other country matches this depth and breadth of engagement," it enthused. The technology media outlet *TechCrunch* similarly extolled Africa's ties with China as a "macro megatrend set to impact everything."

Africa's ties with China are more multilayered than is often recognized. What in the early 2000s began as Beijing's push for commodities and Africa's demand for infrastructure and financing has evolved to encompass peacekeeping missions, business and technology ventures, educational initiatives, and ideological jockeying. Each year some 10,000 African government officials are trained in Chinese approaches to a variety of issues ranging from agro-industry to economic policy, cadre management to media strategy. Africa's ties with China have also become more bottom-up than initially perceived, with Chinese provinces and African regions frequently playing the role of international actors. Certain Chinese provinces will often specialize in aspects of Beijing's Africa policy. The Gaza-Hubei Friendship Farm, for example, was created when grain-producing Hubei province signed an agreement with Mozambique's Gaza province, leading to several agricultural projects. The Ogun-Guangdong Free Trade Zone in Igbesa, Nigeria, began as a partnership between Guangdong province and Nigeria's Ogun state government. To a degree, China uses Africa almost as a testing ground for its international ambitions: Africa is Beijing's workroom of ideas.

These developments unfold against a backdrop of an ever-evolving continent. Inasmuch as Africa is for China a workroom it is not a blank canvas, and the realities of Africa's relations with China reflect Africa's own political, economic, security, and social conditions. Traditionally averse to intervening abroad, Beijing has had to learn this the hard way. When in 2014 Chinese workers were kidnapped in Cameroon and in 2016 Chinese peacekeepers killed in Mali and South Sudan, Beijing responded with shock and condemnation, vowing to "resolutely fight violent terrorist activities that hurt innocent lives." Though this was not the first time that Beijing encountered overseas risks, the attacks underscored the at times labyrinthine and opaque African environment and the sometimes unexpected outcomes that it can yield. As this book argues, Africa is not an entity that is acted *on,* but rather one with its own structures and agency – an agency, too, that is not singly concentrated but distributed across multiple state and non-state actors throughout the continent's fifty-four countries.

Since *Africa and China*'s initial release, Africa has seen an explosive uptake of mobile and other disruptive technologies, as well as the steady emergence of a credible consumer class – challenges of falling commodity prices, rising youth unemployment, and environmental and governance difficulties notwithstanding. By 2019 there will be an estimated one billion phones in Africa – almost one per person – of which some eight hundred million will be smartphones. Mobile phones are transforming Africa and emboldening previously marginalized non-state actors. Farmers use them to check market prices before selling to middlemen; consumers use them to compare product prices; those who until recently lacked access to financial institutions use them to perform traditional banking services, pay bills, send money, and save. Mobile phones are spurring access to healthcare and education, new forms journalism and, where possible, means of engendering government accountability. Local protests in 2014 in Kenya in opposition to the construction of China's East African Railway, for example, were almost entirely organized on social media and through text messages sent over mobile phones. This surge in mobile technology is giving Africans greater control over their circumstances and, in facilitating access to information and opportunity, is forging new and multiple centers of African non-state agency.

Many 'China-Africa' narratives still tend to overlook these everyday Africans as critical actors in Africa's ties with China. They focus instead on the activities of governments and large corporations. Governments and corporations are, of course, central players in the relations. Yet it is the bottom-up, grassroots interactions between ordinary Africans and Chinese that are likely to be most significant over the long-term – especially as more and more Africans are brought into the political and economic fold through advancements in technology. While Beijing's influence is undeniable, it is not unfettered and will certainly not go unchallenged. Part of what this book sets out to do is to drive home this point. To appreciate China's long-term engagement in Africa, it is important to first appreciate how Africa is evolving and changing, and how these changes spillover into wider domestic and international contexts.

I was initially compelled to write and edit this book to move beyond platitudes of 'China and Africa' and towards an understanding of the factors shaping Africa's foreign relations – with China, but not only. The book aimed then, as it does now, to unearth key decision-making settings and structures, and to highlight African agency and innovation. It aimed to showcase the salience of Africa's political, economic, and social realities for its relations with the global community, and to place deliberations over African foreign affairs on equal footing with deliberations focused elsewhere. With this paperback re-release the objectives remain unchanged and have only expanded in their scope. Since 2015 I have traveled even more frequently to Africa where I have worked with and alongside local technology entrepreneurs, smallholder farmers, renewable energy and media start-ups – those who broadly fall under the umbrella of 'social entrepreneurs' and are the very African 'agents' about whom this book is about. In re-releasing *Africa and China* now the aim is to divert attention from the macro to the micro and to bring these individuals more directly into the spotlight. Though many of the book's chapters continue to focus on state relations, the hope is that readers discover the local in the national and the global.

This book is about the ways in which Africans, their organizations, and their government shape relations with China. The efforts are not always successful, and the outcomes often uneven. This book is also about Africa today: its challenges, its entrepreneurialism, and the economic, social, demographic, and technological shifts driving politics and industry. At the end of the day, Africa's lived realities shape the relations we find so fascinating. Taking time to understand 'Africa' is important. In conversations about 'China and Africa,' 'Africa' must come first.

Acknowledgements

This book is the product of a long and winding road that began in 2006, in the first year of my Master's degree in Politics at the University of Oxford. What began as an initial focus on the development of the rule of law in post-apartheid South Africa gradually morphed into a thesis on Chinese migrants in the East African informal economies – a subject on which I have since published elsewhere. I am thankful to my supervisor back then, David Anderson, for giving me the freedom to pursue what was at the time an unappreciated, if not slightly eccentric, topic. For that independence, encouragement, and expert support, I am enormously appreciative.

David remained the bedrock of my graduate years at Oxford. In 2009 I embarked on my doctoral studies where focus turned to the theme of African agency in Sino-African relations, which this book takes up. This theme was explored in the Ethiopian context, during which many months were spent living and researching in Addis Ababa. It is there that most of the ideas contained in this took shape. Indeed, little of this project would be possible if not for the inspiration, insights, experiences, and cheering of those whose lives then meshed with mine, and who in many ways are the 'African agents' this book champions. Fellow researchers, professors, journalists, government officials, business professionals, shop and restaurant owners, taxi drivers, entrepreneurs – to them I owe much gratitude. I am also especially grateful to all who put me up (and put up with me!) in Addis Ababa, and in so doing not only eased the burdens of field research but created a home away from home.

This project could not have succeeded without the willing cooperation of this book's contributing authors, who gave of their time and talents - who tolerated countless revisions and the not-so-occasional nagging - and whose work has made the book what it is. My thanks goes to Mark Kaigwa and Yu-Shan Wu for their persistent enthusiasm; to Lucy Corkin for her unyielding patience; Mohan Giles and Ben Lampert for their diligence and professionalism; Calestous Juma for his commitment, and Barry Sautman for his kindness of word. Immense thanks to Ian Taylor for his expertise; Iginio Gagliardone for his thoughtfulness; and, finally, to Joshua Eisenman for his partnership and 'can-do' attitude. I would also like to express thanks to Marie-Claire Antoine at Rowman & Littlefield, who early on recognized this project's potential, and to Dhara Snowden for making possible its paperback release.

Numerous people, particularly dear friends in Oxford and Zurich offered bottomless encouragement and support. There are here too many to name, and surely they know who they are.

Finally, to my wild and wonderful family - and to my parents, in particular, thank you for giving me an insatiable curiosity and a passion for the written word that propels me daily. Ironically, perhaps, words fail to capture the depths of my gratitude.

Introduction

Aleksandra W. Gadzala

The marketplace neighborhood of Merkato in Addis Ababa swarms with shoemakers, shops, and shoe retailers dealing in sometimes ordinary and sometimes wildly colorful shoes and shoe accessories, many of which proudly display "Made in Ethiopia" labels. Walking through the crowded stalls and narrow market alleys, it's hard to imagine that nearly a decade ago Ethiopia's shoe manufacturing sector was in dire straits, overwhelmed by cheaply manufactured Chinese shoes that had flooded the market. Between 2000 and 2004, shoe-manufacturing profits had declined by as much as 30 percent as a previously loyal consumer base shifted to flashy and low-cost Chinese footwear. "It was not good," Tesfaye[1] tells me as we wind among the sewing machines abuzz on the factory floor of Anbessa Shoes, among Ethiopia's leading footwear manufacturers, located a mere two miles from Merkato. "We lost a lot of business; the risk was very high. But we innovated."

Anbessa's management figured out that despite the appeal of lower-priced Chinese shoes, most Ethiopians opt for shoes that they can buy once and wear for longer periods of time without having to frequently budget for the expense. With the help of the Ethiopian government, Anbessa in 2007 bought upgraded German production machines and started manufacturing specialty sheepskin leather shoes, leveraging Ethiopia's ninety million cattle, sheep, and goat population—among the largest in the world. Tesfaye tells me, "If we wanted to stay in the market, we had to find our competitive advantage." Anbessa Shoes today serves not only the local market but also exports its shoes to Germany, France, Italy, Canada, and the United States. Although still early days, Anbessa, it seems, has been able to sidestep Chinese competition and reestablish its foothold in the domestic market while expanding globally.

A TALE OF TWO BEDFELLOWS

Most Western media coverage of China's present-day engagement with Africa reads unlike that of Anbessa. Of China's engagement in the Ethiopian footwear sector, we are likely to hear about declining domestic outputs, rising Ethiopian unemployment, and bankruptcy. In wider circles, China is described as a twenty-first-century colonialist who is flooding African markets with its workers, plundering its natural resources, and encouraging entrenched patterns of authoritarianism. In most accounts, almost nothing is said of African states save little of the role they play in defining the relations: news of Chinese factories popping up in parts of eastern Africa fail to mention the role that local governments play in inviting such investments. Accounts of labor abuses in Chinese-operated mines ignore the fact that enforcement of labor policies usually rests with African governments and industry bodies. Stories like that of Anbessa are few and far between. Indeed, curiously marginalized in the "China-Africa" narrative is Africa. While this has started to change, for the average person mention of "China-in-Africa" still elicits images of a one-way domination, replete with metaphorical dragons advancing on an unsuspecting continent.

China's forays into Africa since the early 2000s are, of course, unprecedented. While less than 1 percent of American foreign direct investment (FDI) went to Africa in 2013, at least 3 to 4 percent of China's direct FDI went to the region. Chinese trade with Africa zoomed past $200 billion in 2012, a more than twentyfold increase since the turn of the century; in 2013, US trade with Africa was a mere $85 billion. Not a year goes by without multiple high-level Chinese visits to the continent, each bringing promises of new investments and more capital. The government in Beijing has established embassies in fifty out of the continent's fifty-four countries; it has exchanged military attachés with nearly twenty African states. Confucius Institutes, funded by China's Ministry of Education for the promotion of Chinese language and culture, have popped up in an estimated thirty African cities. In Zimbabwe, president Robert Mugabe has made the learning of Mandarin mandatory at all national universities. Beyond the diplomatic exchanges, too, an estimated one million Chinese today call Africa home: they live, work, and raise their families alongside African nationals. This historic movement of peoples from China to Africa—their behaviors, business ventures, and local interactions—will, as Howard French aptly notes, "do more to determine China's image, and perhaps China's broad relationship to the continent, than any carefully planned actions by the Beijing government."[2]

The immensity and diversity of these ventures has generated a lively if not at times uninspiring debate about whether Chinese activities in Africa stand poised to launch the continent into an era of unparalleled prosperity, or to hark back to days of colonialism gone by. The questions that fuel this conversation—Where is China investing? Why is China investing? Is knowledge spilling over to African populations? Why doesn't China employ more locals? Is China "here to stay"? What of African democracy? Is China exporting illiberal policies?—inevitably implicate China, its actions, and motivations. Yet Chinese action does not yield African inaction. Through various channels and in various ways, African individuals, organizations, and governments participate in the continent's multifaceted, tangled, and often confusing relations with China. How they participate, to what ends, and with what consequences is the subject of this book.

The recent history of the African continent is largely one of foreign occupation—of being acted upon, and subordinate to, alien powers. During the Scramble for Africa at the end of the nineteenth century, European powers staked claim to nearly the entire continent and carved up its boundaries in ways unrepresentative of precolonial ethnic or geographical identities. At meetings in London, Berlin, Paris, and other European capitals, statesmen bargained over their coveted spheres of influence with but limited knowledge of the African hinterland. Expressions of African agency today operate still within the constructs of these histories of state formation.

Yet even under the heavy hand of colonialism, African leaders were not idle. A fairly recent and understandably controversial wave of research suggests that Africans were active participants in the processes that led to their eventual subservience to European powers and their dependence on the international system. Jean-Francois Bayart's[3] writings have been instrumental in this regard, as have those of Bruce Berman and John Lonsdale, whose work on colonial Kenya shows that the processes that led to the formation of the Kenyan colonial state were not all alien. Berman and Lonsdale argue that matters of state control were in Kenya "mitigated by a rough compatibility between the needs of settler capital and the patronage exercised by African chiefs within a peasant sector which was expanded to solve the colonial administration's need for peace and revenue."[4] What emerges is a picture of a dualistic relationship in which European policy was as much a response to African strategies as were African strategies a response to the realities of colonialism. Whatever one may think of this proposition, it at minimum sets up an interesting intellectual exercise that prompts reconsideration of longstanding approaches to Africa's international relations, and an acknowledgment of the active role of African state and nonstate actors in shaping their history—past, present, and future. The chapters in this book invoke a similar exercise. Rather than asking what is China doing in Africa and how does Chinese engagement stand to impact African realities, we instead ask how and in what ways are African actors shaping these relations. It is high time that this question be asked.

Africa is at a critical juncture in its history. Advancements in infrastructure and technology, education, science, and medicine are opening up opportunities for many African countries to move beyond the shackles of poverty and take their seat at the table of middle-income states. Economic growth in sub-Saharan Africa rose from 4.7 percent in 2013 to 5.2 percent in 2014 on the back of increasing investments and strong household spending; over half of the world's twenty fastest growing economies are African.[5] Of course, growth and development are not the same thing. Yet more and more African governments are also starting to take a more proactive interest their country's economic development. In some cases the concern is sincere, and in others it is borne out of recognition that a failure to develop will deal a serious blow to their legitimacy.

Africa's population is poised to double by the middle of this century, from 1.1 billion to 2.4 billion. Much of this growth will be among young, working-age Africans, like this book's contributing author, Mark Kaigwa, who are industrious and entrepreneurial, and who neither feel restricted by the vestiges of the continent's colonial past nor dependent on others for their success. Individuals like Mark are part of a growing African civil society that is capitalizing on the opportunities created by Africa's widening international relations to advance themselves, and, in turn, the continent. Chinese activities in Africa are an irrevocable part of this process. Faced with the challenge of marginalization by Chinese manufacturers, for example, Anbessa's management took it as an opportunity. It restructured its corporate strategy and transformed itself into a global enterprise. Of course, not all businesses are so lucky—hundreds of African enterprises have folded under insurmountable pressure from China. Yet not all are doomed.

The persistent emphasis on China in its relations with Africa ignores what this book will establish as key actors in relations between the country and the continent, and the ultimate authors of its outcomes—Africans. The illusion in accounts of "China and Africa," still, is of a one-way domination and of a victimized, chaotic, and pliant Africa whose development somehow rests in the hands of China and the Chinese. Yet the relations are best understood as an interaction rather than a domination, and the issue of Africa's development is not China's issue any more than it is Argentina's or Iceland's: it is Africa's issue with Africans as the responsible agents. This book argues that by focusing too much on China we submit ourselves to tired tropes of a passive continent. But Africa and its people are not passive; they are active. The question is who is active, how, and why.

AGENCY ANONYMOUS

In making clear the position this book argues, I accept that this position is controversial. For decades many African governments have seemed content to place responsibility for their country's survival at the doorstep of the international community, and many Africans have by extension been reliant on the fruits of someone else's labor for their livelihoods. The case for African agency goes against a perceived history of indolence and dependency. That is why it will take an entire book of detailed case studies to consider whether, and to what extent, what this book will refer to as *African agency* truly influences Sino-African relations and their outcomes.

The question of agency in Africa's foreign relations is a surprisingly recent one. Agency as such has until lately also been little theorized about in international relations. Insofar as it has been considered, this has been in the context of the agency-structure problematic and its concerns with the nature of agents, structures, and their interrelations. Agent-structure theorists including Anthony Giddens, Alexander Wendt, and Martin Hollis and Steve Smith have sought to mediate between the extremes of structural determinism and methodological individualism implicit in the earlier theories of Marx, Althusser, and Emile Durkheim, who famously asserted that "the individual is dominated by a moral reality greater than himself: namely, collective reality."[6] Here, the debate has wavered between assertions that social outcomes are the outcomes of individuals—Margaret Thatcher's famous dictum that "there is no such thing as society"[7]—and counterclaims that the individual, as such, exists only in the structure of the relations of production. Colin Wight observes that while "methodological individualism postulates a social world devoid of social determinants [. . .] methodological structuralism presents a world devoid of creative agents."[8] Contemporary agent-structure theorists have gone a long way in reconceptualizing notions of structure. What has been missing, however, has been a discussion of what the term *agent* means, and what we mean when we say that someone or something—Africa—has agency.

On a basic level, agency implies the "capacity to do"—the possession of causal power.[9] Ian Taylor (in this volume) argues that "[a]s a concept, agency implies that individuals ('agents') are capable of directing their structurally formed capabilities in ways that are imaginative and inventive, for personal or communal advancement." Indeed, an agent's "capacity to do" is defined by the structures within which he or she is embedded; an agent is always an agent of something.[10] This notion informs most of the analyses contained in this book. Writing on the interactions between Chinese enterprises and African actors in Ghana and Nigeria, Giles Mohan and Ben Lampert (in this volume) describe how social networks and particular forms of patronage enable local Ghanaian and Nigerian patrons to dictate the terms on which Chinese enterprises operate. Aleksandra Gadzala's chapter in turn reveals how a circumscribed group of political elites in Ethiopia's government is able to influence the uses of Chinese investment. The institutional setting of the elites allows them to assert their agency in a different way and to a different degree than that exercised by local Ghanaian and Nigerian patrons.

Because agents are "differentially located"[11] in social structures, their exercise of agency is inherently disparate.

The definition of agents as "agents of something" prompts us to pause and consider the use of the term *Africa*. Is it correct to speak of a collective *African agency* in the context of its relations with China? Of what is "Africa" an agent—if it is an agent at all?

With the question framed in this way, we might be led to say that "Africa" is an agent of the international system—or an agent of the community of "developing countries" or "weak states" with which it is often associated. But this is a nonstarter. We may then be led to unify "Africa" under the banner of a shared colonial history. But what then of states like Ethiopia that escaped colonialism? Is Ethiopia somehow *un*-African? Beyond this we might point to instances in which African states have collaborated to jointly influence China's activities on the continent. Of this there are few examples, particularly in the realm of continental security where China is gradually becoming more engaged. But the history of such attempts is so far patchy at best, with China's involvement in the 2007 United Nations–African Union peacekeeping force in Darfur as perhaps the best example. To date, the African Union has nothing resembling a China policy.

Finally, we might speak of a singular African agency on the basis of the shared experience of Chinese engagement. In much of Africa, Chinese tactics are similar: oil-for-infrastructure contracts, special economic zones, cultural exchanges, "win-win" rhetoric, and claims of supposed domestic noninterference. Still, the diversity of this experience and the diversity in the way in which Chinese policies are attended to by African governments make ascriptions of a singular African agency a misnomer. Ultimately, relations between Africa and China are relations between China and individual African states; because no two states are the same, no two relations can be the same. From the case studies in this book we will see how historical, cultural, political, and social considerations color interactions between China and African countries. These considerations cannot be generalized across fifty-four entities but are the provinces of each one, respectively.

The contributions to this book identify two broad categories of African agents, reflected in the book's structure: state and nonstate agents. For agents of the state—political parties, institutions, government agencies, charismatic leaders, and connected elites—internal legitimacy is key to their influence over their relations with China. As Robert Putnam famously argued, foreign affairs is a "two-level game"[12] in which the ability of state actors to represent and carry forward domestic interests informs their ability to act in the international arena. In this regard, descriptions of the state in Africa generally fall into one of two categories. The first consists of "strong" states like Ethiopia that exert sweeping domestic political control. Although the state's legitimacy may be on shaky grounds, its reach is extensive and the government obsessed with the issue of territory; even the most remote and intimate agents are under the authority of centralized structures. Iginio Gagliardone's discussion of Chinese-funded advances in telecommunications technology in Ethiopia illustrates the various avenues through which leaders of strong states manipulate "members of the state apparatus in the peripheries into messengers of ideas and policies formulated in the capital."

In the second category, states are defined by their empirical "weakness," their lack of legitimacy, inability to extend authority, and their administration of services, which colors their exercise of agency in the context of foreign powers. Lucy Corkin's contribution on Angola's management of Chinese credit lines provides an illustrative example of such a state. Corkin, following Bayart, maintains that despite the ruling People's Movement for the Liberation of Angola (MPLA)'s "entrenched political position, the party has since independence faced constant threats to its monopoly on power; intraparty factionalism, rural resistance, and foreign intervention. It has sought to counterbalance these threats through repeated sanction of external interventions, which in circular fashion both uphold and erode its domestic legitimacy." For Angola, as for other "weak" African states, external recognition—recognition by China—is a key element in its ability to assert its sovereignty. Yet as Corkin is quick to point out, there are limitations to these strategies.

The second category of African agents addressed by this book is that of nonstate, or substate, agents: community organizations, labor unions, private enterprises, ethnic militancies, virtual networks, and other associations that either complement, and in some cases supplement, the state. Mark Kaigwa and Yu-Shan Wu's account of the influence of social media on the "China-in-Africa" narrative in Kenya and South Africa offers an interesting illustration of how citizens in both countries are turning to social media as a platform through which to engage their leaders on issues of policy, including policy on China. Social networking sites like Twitter and Facebook are increasingly used to vent frustrations or to organize rallies that are then played out on the streets. In making more general assessments, Ian Taylor suggests that frustrations generated by unrepresentative state structures create opportunities for alternative forms of agency—counteragency—to develop. The degree to which counteragency can be exercised, however, depends on the structures in which it is embedded. For example, while Kaigwa and Wu underscore the still-limited influence of social media in countries like South Africa where other avenues for political activism are well established, Barry Sautman's account of the "racialization" tactics used by Zambian opposition leaders to subvert China's Zambia presence shows the weight of such tactics when articulated from within positions of power. Yet even here the outcomes of this agency are not so clear.

The picture of African agency that emerges from this book is a messy one. Divergent state and substate agents bump up against each other in sometimes uncomfortable and contradictory ways. None act similarly or with an equal degree of influence. Some agents do not—cannot—act at all. The case for African agency is necessarily incomplete: the social positioning of many Africans significantly constrains their ability to influence affairs—global, with China, or domestic. These are the roughly three hundred million Africans who continue to live below the poverty line; who are led to migrate to escape conflict, famine, or to find gainful employment; and whose future, still, is a question mark. In making the case for African agency, we must be careful not to overstate our claim. Nevertheless, China's engagement with Africa has seen deliberate efforts on the part of African state and nonstate actors to define the relationship. It is only by focusing on those expressions of agency that we can tease out the intricacies of Sino-African relations and what they stand to mean for the African continent and its people.

THE AIMS OF AGENCY

Judgments of African agency implicate fundamental questions about the effects of that agency and who within Africa benefits from it. This is especially true in the case of relations between Africa and China: questions regarding if, and to what extent, the ties may facilitate Africa's economic and political progress are ubiquitous among many in development circles.

Many of this book's contributions suggest that the objective of regime survival is at the core of strategies pursued by most African state actors—what Ian Taylor (in this volume) terms "agency-as-corruption." "Where the state is the major source of wealth and fortune, agency for self-advancement is necessarily focused on capturing power within the state whereby [rents] can be appropriated." "Agency-as-corruption" and associated ambitions of regime survival take us back to the well-established issue of African leaders leveraging benefits accrued in the international arena (infrastructure finance, natural resources, aid) to bolster their domestic standing and advance other, personal objectives.[13] Here, the spread of benefits to the general public are often minimal at best. Gadzala's examination of Ethiopian policy, for example, sees the ideology of the country's political elites as playing a significant role in their dealings with China and other foreign powers. Investment deals are frequently structured to advance ideological ends first and economic development, as such, second. Both Corkin and Taylor similarly see the respective personal interests of Angolan and Nigerian elites as key to their interactions with China.

Viewed in this way, the analyses suggest that in trying to understand the ends in the name of which state agents exercise agency we must first begin to unpack the agents themselves. As Colin Wight aptly notes, agency is always "the activity of particular individuals acting within particular contexts."[14]

The identities, prejudices, and experiences of African state agents are central to how they act and why they do what they do when China is seated across the table.

So, too, with substate actors. Mohan and Lampert's contribution to this volume shows that African patrons often rely on locally embedded social, economic, and political resources to either support or block the activities of Chinese migrant entrepreneurs. Their location in particular patronage networks informs the motivations behind their actions as well as the actions themselves. Sautman's account of anti-Chinese sentiments in Zambia similarly points to the salience of context. While agency exercised by Zambia's leadership has generally had its intended consequences, the often-accidental character of mass anti-Chinese mobilizations has meant that they frequently fall short of their objectives. In this respect it is worth noting that a focus on agency neither implies that African agents today somehow have significantly more influence than they did at any other time, nor that the outcomes of this agency are always the desired ones. The authors to this book differ greatly in their analyses of African agency in contemporary China-Africa relations. Where they agree, however, is that the room for maneuver is expanding. The directions in which African agents ultimately maneuver will determine their future—and Africa's.

CHINA WHO?

A focus on African agency in Sino-African relations makes it is easy to take China for granted. So much is today said about the country that it is natural to assume knowledge of who, or what, China is. Yet in most cases this knowledge is rudimentary, and distinctions of the "China" that interacts with African state and substate agents are blurred.

It is a near tautology to say that China is complex. A peek under the hood of the Chinese model reveals a labyrinth of political structures that stretch from the highest levels of government to the lowest. At the center is Beijing, the Chinese Communist Party, around which extend many bureaucratic arms: party committees; government agencies; the People's Liberation Army and state security forces; enterprises, including state-owned oil, construction, and telecommunications firms; banks—the China Export-Import Bank, China Development Bank, Industrial and Commercial Bank, Agricultural Bank—and other financial vehicles, including sovereign wealth funds. The China Investment Corporation, China's largest sovereign fund and among the largest globally, and China-Africa Development Fund, the equity investment arm of China Development Bank, are today leading financiers of China's African investments, having together invested roughly $2.5 billion since 2011. Official China also includes the state media. As Gagliardone (in this volume) notes, "China has become an increasingly important partner in the shaping of African information societies, engaged both in laying down the infrastructures on which these are built and in the production of content and meaning."

Official China's reach extends to provincial and local agents. The dual processes of decentralization and internationalization that took place under Deng Xiaoping's policy of "reform and opening up" and later Hu Jintao's "New Deal" strengthened the foreign policy roles of Chinese provincial governments. While "[t]he central government remains the dominant actor in China's foreign relations [. . .] the provinces have raised their profile on the international stage and have made themselves important foreign policy players in the area of what could be called 'low-level politics.'"[15] China's relations with Africa today progress primarily from within provincial rather than national political and economic structures. Nearly all of China's provinces have an "Africa policy"; all coastal provinces do. As early as 2002, for example, the government of Zhejiang implemented a directive under which provincial state-owned enterprises with over $3 million invested in Africa would receive an up to $40,000 in government subsidy. In 2003, the province of Fujian similarly began issuing financial incentives for enterprises investing in the Nigerian and South African natural resource and construction sectors.[16]

Responsibility for the formulation and implementation of such policies rests with provincial governors and Communist Party secretaries; both answer to the central government and the Chinese Communist Party. The provincial Foreign Affairs Office and Foreign Trade and Economic Cooperation Commission are the leading bureaucratic institutions in the relations, and each, in turn, receives guidance from China's Ministry of Foreign Affairs and the Ministry of Commerce, respectively. Chen Zhimin and Jian Junbo observe that China's is a "multilevel" foreign policy in which the "levels intersect with one another in a variety of ways, and demand that decision makers operate in a number of political arenas simultaneously."[17] While Trade and Economic Commissions are accountable for local foreign economic relations, including the conduct of overseas due diligences and oversight of foreign construction projects, Foreign Affairs Offices are charged with implementing China's national foreign policy locally. This includes administering foreign consular and media affairs, arranging the overseas trips of local government leaders, and overseeing the foreign affairs activities of other provincial agencies.[18]

Around these core institutions unfolds a similar labyrinth of overlapping structures akin to that on the national level: provincial state-owned enterprises, financial vehicles, media outlets, trade associations, and cultural institutes. For example, Huajian Shoes, one of the largest shoe exporters in China with an over three-thousand-person-strong workforce in Ethiopia's Eastern Industrial Zone, is a subsidiary of Guangdong Rising Assets Management, a sovereign wealth fund owned by the government of Guangdong province. Guangdong Rising is supervised by the Guangdong State-Owned Assets Supervision and Administration Commission, which is supervised by the same institution nationally. When Huajian began its Ethiopian operations in 2011, the governing Memorandum of Understanding was signed between the governments of Guangdong province and Oromia region; then national leaders Hu Jintao and Meles Zenawi posed for the photo op.[19] By 2012 Huajian was operating two production lines, with new machines and six hundred workers producing shoes with "Made in Ethiopia" labels for export to the American market; by 2013, it was employing upward of three thousand workers and producing two million shoes.

Yet the "China" with which African state and substate agents interact is not only official. Elsewhere, Mohan and Lampert argue for the need to examine the growing presence of independent Chinese migrants who have settled in many African countries, and the informal African governance structures in which they operate.[20] Gadzala, too, elsewhere insists that the most significant implications of the relationship between China and Africa will be experienced by the continent's informal sectors in which hundreds of thousands of such migrants are today active participants.[21] What might be called "unofficial China" has penetrated every conceivable walk of life: entrepreneurs running small-scale shops and roadside kiosks; teachers, traders, smugglers, journalists, waitresses, farmers, prostitutes, taxi drivers, janitors. The everyday realities of the relations between African and Chinese agents take place beyond the spectacle of high-level meetings and handshakes and in the ordinary day to day.

What this tells us about African agency in Africa's relations with China is that it is convoluted; it occurs at a myriad of locations and with multiple determinants and effects. African agency is shaped not only by the distinctive contexts of African state and substate agents but also by the contexts of the Chinese agents with which they interact. Nationally, African leaders, politicians, and other agents of the state mesh with agents of China's state system whose actions are similarly determined by their institutional embeddedness, and who likewise act in pursuit of specifically defined ends. More locally, African agents across a range of trades assert their agency within shifting political, social, and economic realities of which "unofficial China" has become a principal driver. As in the case of Anbessa Shoes, these changing realities provide new openings for learning and growth. But they also constrain the agency of some agents, or demand that they alter how it is expressed.

BOOK OUTLINE

This book is divided into two sections. The first section, African State Agency, considers African agency in relations with China by looking at the national level. Chapters in this section of the book draw on the problems of corruption, patronage, power differentials, the limitations of state agency, and how state agents manage shifting external relations. The image of agency that emerges is rather dispiriting. Commonly held views of African governments as fraudulent and its leaders as self-aggrandizing are sadly reinforced. Yet the chapters also describe instances in which state agency has been broadly constructive, and point to openings for its positive expression. Joshua Eisenman examines the causes and consequences of trade between African states and China, and contributes a welcome window on Chinese agency in a volume otherwise focused on Africa. While Sino-African trade is often portrayed as politically motivated, Eisenman points instead to economic determinants of the patterns. "Shared autocracy," he argues, "appears unlikely to determine China's trade partners in Africa." The increase in China-Africa trade over the past decade has, however, prompted political reactions among various African governments and publics. Eisenman suggest that, increasingly, state and nonstate actors are pushing back against what they perceive as unfair practices. Yet this trend remains undermined by a number of problems, including weak governments, underdeveloped African economies, and China's persistent comparative advantage.

Ian Taylor advances a different interpretation of African agency, and he suggests that the agency domestically exercised by Nigeria's elites creates the political setting within which Chinese actors have to negotiate. In Nigeria, oil-sector corruption and often violent expressions of counteragency are the status quo. Indeed, interactions between Africa and China do not transpire in the abstract, but are situated in the wider context of relations between African states and their societies. These relations often place unexpected demands on Chinese interests. Considerations of Africa's political and economic realities, too, push back against notions of Africa as a carte blanche for Beijing and the Chinese. The continent is for China a complex terrain that it must still try to understand.

Iginio Gagliardone subsequently picks up the importance of context. Gagliardone's analysis of Chinese engagement in the media and telecommunications sectors in Ethiopia and Kenya reinforces the idea, advanced by Taylor, that China's influence of domestic African affairs is generally quite limited: the influence of African policies on China is often greater. Despite similarities in the tactics pursued by Chinese telecommunications firms Huawei and ZTE, for example, the outcomes differ: in Ethiopia, the telecommunications sector remains in poor shape. In Kenya, it is rapidly expanding. Gagliardone's chapter makes the additionally important point that by partnering with

African governments, China is either unknowingly or indifferently empowering one set of African agents over another.

Lucy Corkin's careful analysis of Angola's management of Chinese credit lines is one of the leading examples of an increase in the influence of African agency. Taking a historical view on the Angolan state, Corkin argues that the government has been able to successfully manipulate its resource relations with China so that it not only garners the greatest fiscal benefit but also wins political favor domestically. Taking up the story from Gagliardone, Gadzala claims that Chinese investments in Ethiopia are leveraged by the country's political elites to advance the aims of their ideology. While this does not necessarily suggest an increase in agency, as such, it is indicative of the government's astute ability to fashion relations with China to its advantage. This is true not only in its relations with China but with all foreign partners. Gadzala's contribution underscores the need to consider cognitive, historical, and ideological variables in examinations of relations between China and African states: when the party and government are one, a focus on institutions and power dynamics will alone not lead very far.

The second section of the book, African Agency Beyond the State, considers African agency from the perspective of Africa's emergent civil society. Here, the picture of agency is muddled. Civil society in many African countries is still nascent or is otherwise a de facto extension of the state; its growing pains are reflected in its interactions with China and other foreign powers. Interestingly, Giles Mohan and Ben Lampert argue that the sometimes vague arena between state and society is a key arena in which African agency is exercised. Drawing on fieldwork in Ghana and Nigeria, their contribution shows how African patrons use their state connections to negotiate, and often encourage, Chinese enterprises in the nonstate realm; ambiguity often gives way to creative interactions.

Barry Sautman's chapter captures the complexities inherent in assertions of African agency beyond and within the state. Sautman rightly points out that agency does not necessarily translate into influence, nor does it always have its intended consequences. Efforts by Zambia's opposition parties and parts of its civil society to "racialize" and penalize "the Chinese" have had the effect of severing the country's social fabric more than affecting Chinese practices in the country. Moreover, a disproportionate emphasis on China has distracted from holding other domestic and foreign agents similarly accountable. When not carefully handled, agency, Sautman points out, can be counterproductive.

Mark Kaigwa and Yu-Shan Wu offer a refreshing and forward-looking analysis of agency expressed by segments of Kenyan and South African civil society. Drawing on their own experiences as young African professionals and active participants in the continent's technological renaissance, they argue for the potential of communications technology and social media as platforms through which Africans can become more politically engaged, and as tools that can be used to hold domestic and foreign actors to account. Whether social media can be used in this way, however, still depends on the availability of other channels of expression, and remains limited by the state structures in which it is embedded. Nevertheless, Kaigwa and Wu's contribution suggests that as relations between African states and China increase, so too will the arenas in which these relations are played out.

The book ends on an optimistic note with Calestous Juma's contribution. Juma speaks to lessons learned and ways forward. He argues that diplomatic relations between Africa and China present a unique opportunity for the continent to put itself squarely on the path to economic development. Doing so will require a shift in African thinking, a buildup of capabilities, and—perhaps most importantly—a realization and acceptance of the fact that, ultimately, it is up to Africa and to Africans to take responsibility for their future. Just as China pursues its own interests in its engagements with the continent, so, too, must the continent pursue its own interests in its engagements with China.

Taken together, these chapters differ in their assessment of African agency—of how and why it is expressed, the extent to which it shapes relations with China, and what this means for the future. Given that relations between China and Africa cut across disparate contexts—divergent histories, cultures, political and economic realities, and identities—this is perhaps not so surprising. What all chapters share, however, is a concerted determination to move beyond narratives of an idle continent being overrun by China, and to engage seriously with what, still, is "the other side of the story." By shedding light on a continent that is rising, slowly, to meet the challenges and opportunities of this unique engagement, the hope is to, however modestly, bring the other side of the story into the mainstream.

NOTES

1. Name changed so to preserve anonymity.
2. Howard French, *China's Second Continent: How a Million Migrants Are Building a New Empire in Africa* (New York: Alfred A. Knopf, 2014), 6.
3. Jean-Francois Bayart, "Africa in the World: A History of Extraversion," *African Affairs* 99 (2000): 217–67; *The State in Africa: The Politics of the Belly* (London: Longman Group UK Limited, 1993).
4. John Lonsdale and Bruce Berman, "Coping with the Contradictions: The Development of the Colonial State in Kenya, 1895–1914," *Journal of African History* 20, no. 4 (1979): 505.
5. These include: Angola, the Democratic Republic of Congo, Ethiopia, Ghana, Mozambique, Nigeria, Rwanda, Sierra Leone, Tanzania, Uganda, and Zambia.
6. Emile Durkheim, *Suicide: A Study in Sociology* (London: Routledge, 2002), 37.
7. Douglas Keay, "An Interview with Margaret Thatcher," *Woman's Own* (September 23, 1987).
8. Colin Wight, "They Shoot Dead Horses Don't They? Locating Agency in the Agent-Structure Problematique," *European Journal of International Relations* 5, no. 1 (1999): 114.

9. Ibid.

10. Colin Wight, "State Agency: Social Action without Human Activity?" *Review of International Studies* 30, no. 2 (2004): 275.

11. Ibid.

12. Robert Putnam, "Diplomacy and Domestic Politics: The Logic of Two-Level Games," *International Organization* 42, no. 3 (1988): 427–60.

13. Bayart, "Africa in the World: A History of Extraversion."

14. Wight, "State Agency: Social Action without Human Activity," 279.

15. Chen Zhimin and Jian Junbo, "Chinese Provinces as Foreign Policy Actors in Africa," *Occasional Paper No. 22: China in Africa Project* (South African Institute of International Affairs, 2009): 5.

16. Ibid., 12.

17. Ibid., 4.

18. Ibid.

19. Additional documents were also signed between the governments in Addis Ababa and Beijing, although the governing documentation belongs to each regional government, respectively.

20. Giles Mohan, Ben Lampert, Daphne Chang, and May Tan-Mullins, *Chinese Migrants and Africa's Development: New Imperialists or Agents of Change?* (London: Zed Books, 2014).

21. Putnam, "Diplomacy and Domestic Politics: The Logic of Two-Level Games."

I

African State Agency

Chapter One

China-Africa Trade

Causes, Consequences, and Perceptions

Joshua Eisenman

For a decade, a dynamic expansion in China-Africa trade has been underway. Many argue that the cause is political: China's desire to expand its geopolitical influence and illiberalism to a disaffected world. China's trade, we are often told, is particularly friendly to repressive African regimes; Beijing prefers similarly autocratic African trading partners, and its businesses assist in their efforts to resist calls for liberal democratic political reforms. This is part of a wider Chinese plan to "colonize" Africa—to capture it politically and economically, and make it its "second continent."[1] In the face of such political headwinds, the story goes, it is unlikely—if not outright impossible—for Africans to exercise much, if any, agency.

Meanwhile, there are long-standing economic theories—Neoclassical Trade Theory, New Trade Theory, and Structural Economics—that also promise to explain China's trade with Africa. These explanations receive more attention among economists than they do in the popular press, yet take us further in understanding China-Africa trade than much of the mainstream discourse. Unlike the Maoist era when China's trade policies served its political goals, they now aim to improve market access and find profitable investments as part of Beijing's larger domestic development strategy. China's state-run firms can channel China-Africa trade through extramarket decisions that influence flows, yet Beijing's ability to direct trade with Africa is ultimately constrained by market forces. Over the last decade, five causal factors have overwhelmingly determined China-Africa trade patterns[2]: China's comparative advantage in labor-intensive and capital-intensive production; Africa's abundant natural resource endowments; China's rapid economic growth; China's emphasis on infrastructure building at home and in Africa; and the

3

emergence of economies of scale in China's shipping and light manufacturing sectors.

China trades extensively with African democracies and autocracies alike, making it doubtful that an African country's regime type explains much about its trade with China. Rather, China's trade with African countries is deeply rooted in powerful market dynamics, the consequences of which have given rise to a wide diversity of perceptions of China among average Africans. Barry Sautman's analysis of Chinese activities in Zambia (chapter 7) points to the spread of anti-Chinese sentiments across the continent and shows how such narratives need not have coherent or predictable causes or consequences. For instance, in December 2010 soccer fans chanting "Chinese go home" rioted and attacked Chinese businesses in Lubumbashi, Democratic Republic of Congo (DRC) after their team lost to Inter Milan. Congolese fans mistook the Japanese referee as Chinese, and were angered by some of his decisions during the match.[3] Nine months later in Zambia, anti-Chinese rhetoric helped populist Michael Sata win the presidency after three previously unsuccessful campaigns.[4] Incidents like these suggest that simmering anti-Chinese sentiment at the grassroots level is an increasingly powerful force that can be activated by either spontaneous, unforeseen events or by ambitious politicians for their own purposes. At the same time, some Africans view China favorably: they see China's economic expansion as a net positive for their country's economic growth and development. Differing perceptions of China within local communities shape expressions of African agency.

This chapter seeks to reconcile these sometimes conflicting accounts to better answer three related questions about China's trade with African countries: (1) What causal arguments help explain the patterns of China-Africa trade? (2) What are the economic and political consequences of the patterns of trade between China and Africa? (3) How do these consequences shape African opinions and behaviors vis-à-vis the Chinese presence on the continent? In addressing the first query, this chapter diverges from others in this volume: while others speak of African agency alone, this chapter pays particular attention to the consequences of China's policies. By understanding the causal mechanisms and consequences of China-Africa trade we can better explain African states' and nonstate actors' reactions.

CAUSES OF CHINA-AFRICA TRADE PATTERNS

Amid the last decade or more of unprecedented growth (see figure 1.1), the question of what factors determine China-Africa trade patterns, and what those patterns are or *should* be, has elicited a myriad of hypotheses. In 2005, a report for the United Kingdom's Department for International Develop-

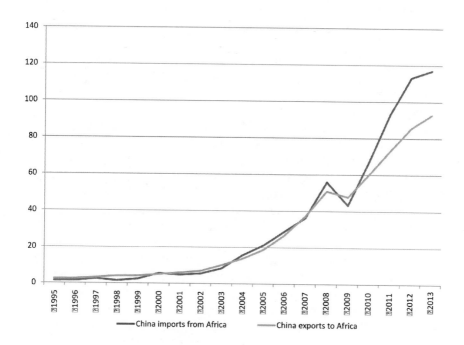

Figure 1.1.   China-Africa Trade 2000-2013 (Source: Based on a study of Global Trade Atlas data conducted by the Trade Law Centre for Southern Africa (TRA-LAC), Stellenbsoch, South Africa)

ment by Chris Edwards and Rhys Jenkins predicted a change in the structure of African exports, and identified "unexploited export opportunities which should be explored." The report argued that rising per capita incomes in China would "lead to a growing demand for food, particularly those with high income elasticity of demand such as meat products, fish, fruit and beverages." The authors also identified "new opportunities for other agricultural exports from Africa such as coffee and sugar." They were optimistic that "in the future for some [African] countries there may be opportunities for exporting labour intensive agricultural products such as fruit or coffee which could create more income or employment opportunities for poorer sections of society."[5]

By 2007, a World Bank report acknowledged that expected trade patterns had not emerged. Economist Harry Broadman was particularly puzzled by the slow growth in labor-intensive exports from African countries to China, noting that only "five oil- and mineral-exporting countries account for 85 percent of Africa's exports to China."[6] The report concluded: "Whether in terms of nationality, mode of entry, scale of investment, or geographic diversification, among other factors, one would expect to observe significant differences in the patterns of the exports and imports."[7]

Economists at the Common Market for Eastern and Southern Africa (COMESA) were similarly stumped by the slow growth in dozens of labor-intensive African exports to China. In 2007 the East African regional trade bloc published a report on the effects of China's tariff-free entry program for products from its member countries. COMESA concluded that despite China's preferential tariff scheme on 454 African product lines, resource products including copper, cobalt, and marble consistently made up the bulk of member countries' tariff-free import value. Based on a comparative advantage index, the report identified dozens of products in which member countries might have expected a comparative advantage—for example, textiles, cotton, salt and sulfur, rawhides and skins, coffee and tea, and fish and crustaceans—yet could not gain a foothold in Chinese markets.[8] Data from 2013 point to a similar trend (see figure 1.2): precious stones and metals, base metals, mineral products, and the nebulous category, "unclassified goods," accounted for over 90 percent of all of China's imports from Africa.

Variation between predicted patterns of China-Africa trade and those observed in the real world has given rise to political trade arguments. Naazeen Barma, Ely Ratner, and Steven Weber, for example, argue that the expansion of trade between China and Africa is "in excess of what standard economic models of trade would predict. This means that these patterns cannot be explained away by blistering economic growth."[9] Politics, they argue, must be at play.

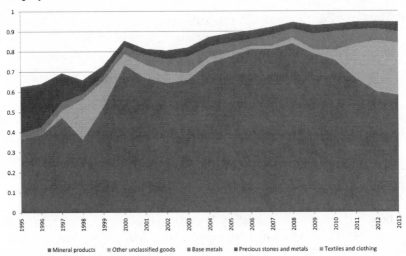

Figure 1.2. Chinese Imports from Africa (Source: Based on a study of Global Trade Atlas data conducted by the Trade Law Centre for Southern Africa (TRALAC), Stellenbosch, South Africa)

POLITICAL EXPLANATIONS

Political explanations are an amalgam of generally accepted views that some American, European, and African observers regularly use to help explain close economic ties between two liberal countries and two autocracies. President Bill Clinton broadly summarized the concept in his 1994 State of the Union address when he said: "Democracies don't attack each other, they make better trading partners and partners in diplomacy."

This linkage between shared levels of liberalism and increased bilateral trade emerged during the Cold War, when political loyalties in a bipolar world substantially determined a country's trade partners. In their landmark article "Democratic Trading Partners: The Liberal Connection, 1962–1989," Harry Bliss and Bruce Russett found that democracy is significantly and positively related to trade volume. "Trade between pairs of states with democratic polities," they conclude, "is greater than that between states not sharing such a polity type."[10] Bliss and Russett suggested that for democratic states the causal mechanism is rooted in a state's security concerns:

> States attempt to control trading patterns on behalf of private interests, and on behalf of perceived state and national interests. They promote trade with states deemed stable and reliable sources, and discourage, by various barriers, with adversaries and potential enemies. A democratic trading state will feel its security less threatened by another democratic state than by many autocracies. Democratic statesmen need to be less concerned that a democratic trading partner will use gains from trade to endanger their security than when their country trades with a nondemocracy. Their countries can enter into relationships of economic interdependence for absolute gains, without worrying as much about the hazard of relative gains as they might with nondemocratic partners.[11]

Edward Mansfield et al. affirmed Bliss and Russett's results that two liberal countries will tend to trade more than a mixed pair. They concluded: "Holding constant various economic and political factors, democratic dyads tend to trade more freely than dyads composed of a democracy and an autocracy."[12] Mansfield et al.'s research suggests: "On average, a democracy and an autocracy engage in roughly 15% to 20% less commerce than a dyad composed of two democracies."[13] However, their model does not yield determinate predictions about whether trade between autocratic pairs is more likely than between mixed pairs.[14]

Barma and Ratner used China as a qualitative case study to determine whether trade was more likely between autocratic pairs or between an autocracy and a democracy. They conclude that China advocates "illiberal capitalism . . . where markets are free but politics are not."[15] They argue that

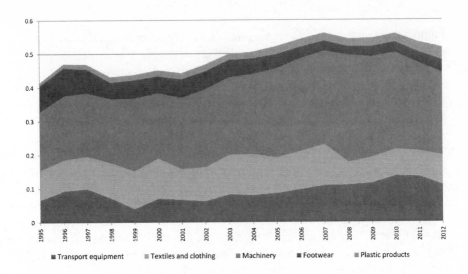

Figure 1.3. Chinese Exports to Africa (Source: Based on a study of Global Trade Atlas data conducted by the Trade Law Centre for Southern Africa (TRA-LAC), Stellenbosch, South Africa)

"through a wide array of bilateral and multilateral arrangements, the Chinese government has begun to build an alternative international structure anchored by illiberal norms."[16] "Chinese illiberalism presents the real long-term geopolitical challenge: It is easily exportable, and it is dangerously appealing to a disaffected world."[17] Furthermore, Barma and Ratner link China's political illiberalism with its economic relations by arguing that Beijing leverages its "mercantilist strength in the international system" to attain its national interests and argue that "nowhere is this trend more evident than in Africa."[18]

In the "Illiberal Regimes" section of his 2007 book, *China in Africa*, Chris Alden explains why he believes that China's demand for resource commodities instinctively increases the tendency to do business with autocracies:

> From the Chinese perspective, these economies are generally closely tied to African elites' interests, and there are fewer obstacles to rapid investment in the resource sector than they might experience in a state with stronger institutions and commitment to constitutional law.[19]

More hawkish critics, such as Peter Brookes and Ji Hye Shin, depict China's commercial competition as part of a zero-sum game that presents an inevitable threat to both liberalism and Western predominance. They contend that Chinese support for political and economic repression counters the liberalizing influences of traditional Western trading partners.[20] Others argue that as China expands economic relations with Africa its influence can actually encourage them to become more illiberal. This concern was echoed in a Council on Foreign Relations report issued in June 2008:

> The way China does business—particularly its willingness to pay bribes, as documented by Transparency International—undermines local efforts to increase good governance and international efforts at macroeconomic reform by institutions like the World Bank and the International Monetary Fund.[21]

Ian Taylor also suggests that illiberalism drives China's economic relations with Africa but remains unsure whether to attribute this to China's indifference or its design. "What is different in comparison to other countries' foreign policies is that Beijing legitimizes human rights abuses and undemocratic practices under the guise of state sovereignty," Taylor writes. "China has no civil society worth talking about."[22] Practices pursued by Chinese businesses in Africa reflect the realities of contemporary China: human rights considerations are sidestepped and civil society concerns are ignored. Writing in this volume, Taylor expands on this notion using Nigeria as a case study. He argues that existing domestic power relations within African states also constrain the trade patterns that external actors like China are able to craft, and that the local African context limits China's ability to use trade to pursue political objectives. Although China's decisions to pursue trade relations with autocratic states may be borne out of political affinity and ideological interests, the extent to which these preferred patterns are actualized is, in the end, limited by broader market forces and local power dynamics.

Those who elevate politics as a leading explanatory variable for Sino-African trade patterns are, for the most part, unsatisfied with traditional economic explanations. These researchers generally agree that economic theories of trade have failed to adequately predict the actual patterns of China-Africa trade; none, however, has developed a model that can predict the role that political variables play, not only in determining the quantities of trade, but also in explaining which types of goods are traded and which are not. Yet it is often the *types* of goods traded (raw materials vs. manufactured consumer products and capital equipment) that are the source of the social and political tensions that are emerging among China and African countries.[23] Moreover, for reasons discussed below, the tendency to emphasize either political or economic explanations at the expense of the other is overly parsimonious. China's political considerations do influence China-Africa trade patterns, but Beijing's will is bounded by existing market forces and the perceptions of local African actors.

ECONOMIC EXPLANATIONS

This section examines leading trade theories' assumptions, elements, and relevant amendments in an effort to identify the determinants of China-Africa trade patterns—including the role of politics.

Neoclassical Trade Theory (Relative Factor Abundance)

Neoclassical Trade Theory (also known as Relative Factor Abundance Theory), privileged by most trade economists, holds that differing national endowments of resources, labor, and capital should explain the composition of China's trade with Africa. The Heckscher–Ohlin (H-O) model, rooted in David Ricardo's theory of comparative advantage, is the economists' traditional explanation for bilateral trade flows between countries. H-O predicts that the relative abundance or scarcity of a country's fixed factor endowments (resources, labor, and capital) compared with those of its trade partner determines what it will sell and what it will buy. A country will export goods produced with its abundant endowments and import goods produced with inputs that are locally scarce. According to H-O, once trade barriers are removed, fixed relative factor endowments will determine trade patterns.

Supporters of Relative Factor Abundance Theory, including economist Jian-Ye Wang, speculate that China-Africa trade patterns "will be shaped by shifts in comparative advantage and changes in global supply chains."[24] Jeffry Herbst and Greg Mills agree that in Africa "the market, not grand strategy, is the Chinese motivation."[25] They suggest that Relative Factor Abundance theories have proven particularly valuable in explaining China-Africa trade because China's relatively scarce natural resource endowments mean it must "lock up as many raw materials as possible."[26] Indeed, in those African countries where relatively abundant factor endowments are natural resources, they do tend to dominate those countries' exports to China. Wang's International Monetary Fund (IMF) working paper described the resulting China-Africa trade pattern:

> Strong growth of the Chinese and African economies, together with the complementary trade pattern—China imports fuel and other commodities, Africa purchases investment and manufactured products from China—largely explains their surging trade in recent years.[27]

Theories of relative factor abundance have come to dominate contemporary thinking on the patterns of international trade between countries. But researchers have also begun to recognize differences between traditional economic theories' predicted patterns of China's trade with Africa and those observed in the real world. To account for this, researchers regularly relax one or another of the H-O theory's six basic assumptions.[28] When studying

China, the most relevant amendments are increasing returns to scale and differences in technology and transportation costs. As discussed below, these modifications to H-O assumptions help explain China-Africa trade patterns and identify the role political factors play.

New Trade Theory (Increasing Returns to Scale)

Bertil Olin first conceived the concept of increasing returns to scale. Overlooked for decades, it resurfaced in the early 1990s as a modification to Relative Factor Abundance Theory.[29] Paul Krugman describes this contribution, which came to be known as the New Trade Theory:

> In the new trade theory, the basic point was that increasing returns are a motive for specialization and trade over and above conventional comparative advantage, and can indeed cause trade even where comparative advantage is of negligible importance among industrial countries with similar resources and technology.[30]

Increasing returns to scale, according to Helena Marques, proved an important amendment to H-O and helped explain why we see both inter-industry trade still governed by the factor endowment differences and intra-industry trade where developed countries produce different varieties of the same good and trade them.[31] New Trade Theory has proven most helpful in explaining trade between two developed countries with similar technological and factor endowments—conditions not found between China and Africa. Yet the concept of increasing returns to scale is also very important for China since it has spent massive sums on government devised and funded industrial polices.

Perhaps the most well known of Beijing's initiatives to take advantage of increasing returns to scale was the selection of a handful of Special Economic Zones (SEZ) in southern China in the 1980s. Cheap labor, tax breaks, and other government-approved SEZ-specific incentives attracted foreign investment, promoted Chinese exports, and in a decade transformed the small fishing village of Shenzhen into a bustling metropolis of over eight million people. Yet it is important to remember that the comparative advantage conveyed to Chinese producers via the SEZs' economies of scale was not the result of an efficient market mechanism, but rather of bargaining among political elites in Beijing. Shanghai, for instance, was not included among the SEZ for political reasons—the personal power of party elder Chen Yun—and thus its development initially lagged behind those cities that were selected. The SEZs' success (and that of China's economic reforms more generally) was only ensured after Deng Xiaoping's 1992 "Southern Journey," which silenced powerful political critics that sought to roll back his efforts to open China to foreign trade and investment.

Over the last decade, China's government-subsidized boomtowns special-izing in only one or two consumer products have helped confer upon its producers huge trade advantages over their African competitors—who face towering barriers to entry into China's markets. In 2011, Datong, Zhejiang, produced over nine billion pairs of socks; Shenzhou, Zhejiang, was the world's necktie capital; and the province also boasts a Sweater City, Kids Clothing City, and an Underwear City.[32] Government-backed economies of scale can also be found in various consumer products in other Chinese cities and provinces—like sneakers in Quanzhou, Fujian. Jinfei Wang, the chair-man of the Jiangsu Diao Garment Factory in Nantong, believes that econo-mies of scale helped his firm gain trade advantage over African producers. He concluded: "I've been to factories all over the world and we can compete with any of them. Without restrictions, certainly China is going to be No. 1." As early as 2004 the *New York Times* described the power of China's "en-clave" approach to consumer goods production:

> This remarkable specialization, one city for each drawer in your bureau, re-flects the economies of scale and intense concentration that have helped turn China into a garment behemoth. Now, China is banking on its immense size and efficient operators to grab an even larger share of the world's clothing orders. China is not just becoming the leader of the pack. In many ways, it hopes to run away with as much of the market as possible.[33]

In 2006, China's government announced that it would support the estab-lishment of as many as fifty global SEZs. Of the nineteen zones approved so far, eight are in Africa, two in Ethiopia, two in Nigeria, and one each in Mauritius, Zambia, Egypt, and Algeria. Like those in China, SEZs in Africa are intended to create economies of scale for overseas investment. As the cost of land, labor, and water rises in China, African SEZs allow some sectors and less experienced small-and-medium-sized Chinese enterprises to go abroad in search of higher returns. By giving them a dedicated space and clear and consistent rules, the expectation, Deborah Bräutigam noted, is that companies within a value chain will cluster together in a planned zone to increase their competitiveness.[34]

The Guangdong-based shoemaker, Huajian Group, for example, which in 2012 produced twenty million pairs of footwear from operations that resem-ble small towns, is investing in the Ethio-China Light Manufacturing Indus-trial Special Economic Zone on the fringes of Addis Ababa, Ethiopia. The zone is becoming a "Shoe City," with the entire processing supply chain—over one hundred thousand workers—located there. The goal is to produce $4 billion worth of shoes and clothes annually for export by 2022.[35] Similar-ly, in 2015, Sudan inked a deal with China ExIm Bank for "interest-free loans and grants" valued at four hundred million yuan ($64 million) for the construction of projects, including "a City for the manufacturing and exporting of leather."[36] For Chinese manufacturers seeking to increase returns to scale via overseas investments, African SEZs are part of a longer-term strategy to relocate low-tech industries abroad while continuing to profit from them at home.

Structural Economics (Technology and Transport Costs)

The introduction of technology and transport costs into Relative Factor Endowment Theory (a component that H-O theory considers to be either zero or prohibitive) has been another innovation relevant to the study of China-Africa trade patterns. Structural economists suggest that differences in technology and industrial upgrading play a critical role in countries' economic development. Large differences in technology and infrastructure between China and most African countries are important deviations from neoclassical trade theory's basic assumptions of costless domestic factor mobility and equal technology. "Comparative advantage in the modern world is created not endowed," notes Thomas I. Palley, "[It] is driven by technology, and technology can be importantly influenced by human action and policy." Palley, a structural economist, believes that "differences in technology can confer an absolute advantage on one country."[37]

Although their focus has typically been on understanding the conditions favorable to economic growth in Africa rather than trade flows, structural economists' insights suggest political influences on China-Africa trade. A 2009 report issued by the World Bank's senior vice president and chief economist Justin Yifu Lin outlined the central tenants of structural economics and its relationship to neoclassical theories of trade. Lin explained: "Structural economics applies the neoclassical approach to study the mechanism of economic development," except it

> suggests a different, larger conception of endowments, including the factor endowment and hard and soft infrastructure endowment. Both factor endowment and infrastructure endowment are given at any given time and changeable over time. Based on the factor endowment, the individual firms make their choices of industries and technologies as well as production decisions. The infrastructure endowment will affect individual firms' transaction costs and rate of return to their investments.[38]

In their recognition of the disconnect between predicted and actual China-Africa trade patterns, both the aforementioned World Bank and COMESA reports acknowledge that Relative Factor Abundance Theory alone is insufficient to explain China's trade patterns with African countries. This is because Beijing exerts significant control over corporations, and national interest is factored into the country's industrial and state-owned business strategies.[39] China's domestic industrial policies have long pushed its production down the cost curve, allowing it to poach demand from other developing countries and become the low-cost producer at their expense. Beijing's trade and industrial policies can weaken the explanatory power of Relative Factor Abundance Theory if they "re-root corporations by realigning profit with the national interest," thus redistributing the gains of trade and, in turn, substantially determining its patterns.[40]

A country's infrastructure and large-scale technology investments kickstart a self-reinforcing and self-sustaining process of economic development, Lin notes. This idea is powerful in China where the government has channeled massive investment into highways, train systems, and shipping ports. In 2009, for instance, China invested $102.7 billion in its railways, with high-speed rail lines accounting for almost 60 percent of that total.[41] In 2011 and 2012, China invested an additional $75 billion and $65 billion, respectively, to maintain and expand its 91,000 kilometers of railroads.[42] (According to World Bank data, these expenditures alone are greater than all but six African countries' GDP in 2013—Nigeria, South Africa, Egypt, Algeria, Angola, Morocco, respectively.)[43] In 2011, China had the world's largest high-speed rail network with 8,358 kilometers of track, which by 2013 was expanded to 10,000 kilometers—more than all European countries combined. The network links more than one hundred Chinese cities and carries almost two million people daily.[44] By 2020, Beijing aims to have completed 25,000 kilometers of high-speed track connecting all of China's major cities.[45]

Chinese firms are also building extensive rail networks throughout Africa, linking resource-processing zones in places like the DRC and Zambia to shipping hubs in Dar es Salaam, Tanzania, Luanda, Angola, and Lagos, Nigeria. The East African Railway, agreed upon in May 2014 between China and leaders from Kenya, Uganda, South Sudan, and Rwanda, will link port Mombasa to markets and producers in neighboring states. Meanwhile, in West Africa, in 2014 the China Railway Construction Corporation signed a $12 billion contract to build a 1,402-kilometer coastal railway that will link Lagos with Calabar in the east.[46] Such infrastructure projects contribute to trade by connecting African natural resource suppliers with Chinese markets and Chinese goods manufacturers with their African customers. China's proficiency in road building has also spread to Africa where its state-run firms have won bids to construct highways in Algeria, Angola, Ethiopia, and Zambia, among other countries.

China has invested heavily in its shipping sector and overtook South Korea to become the world's top shipbuilder in the first half of 2010. This success, however, came with ample political assistance. For instance, with the approval of the powerful National Development and Reform Commission in 2009, the Tianjin Shipbuilding Industry Fund was established. Deputy mayor of Tianjin, Cui Jindu, announced that China's two major state-owned shipbuilders, China CSSC Holdings and the China Shipbuilding Industry Corporation, donated to the fund, which by 2010 had already financed forty-five new ship orders for domestic shipbuilders and had invested fifteen billion yuan in shipbuilding projects. Revealing the close relationship between shipbuilders and the state, one website reported: "Tianjin has the ear of the central government with regard to providing the right tax incentives for ship financing packages and is spearheading developments in this direction."[47] China has worked to improve the African ports of Lamu, Kenya, Luanda, Angola, Dar es Salaam, Tanzania, Abidjan, Côte d'Ivoire, and Port Djibouti, among others. In Somaliland, even a lack of official diplomatic relations with Beijing did not stop Chinese firms from agreeing in 2011 to transform Berbera port into a regional hub for Chinese traders and a disembarkation port for East African oil shipments to China.[48]

Economists acknowledge that economies of scale, infrastructure investment, and technology are born of a political process, yet they generally do not investigate the mechanisms that generate the preferential trade and industrial policies that governments use to pick winners. Instead, they argue that a country's efforts to efficiently exploit its relative factor endowments will determine its industrial policies in accordance with efficient market outcomes. In short, while "new trade" and structuralist critiques of Factor Endowment Theory have succeeded in identifying *where* political considerations might influence trade patterns (e.g., in the development of economies of scale, technology, and reducing transport costs), they continue to shy away from explaining *how* and *why* they do.

CONSEQUENCES OF CHINA-AFRICA TRADE PATTERNS

Relative factor endowments of labor, capital, and resources substantially determine China-Africa trade patterns. When aggregated, China's trade with all fifty-four African states is generally balanced, but important differences emerge when the data is disaggregated by country. Overall, on a country-by-country basis, the balance of trade between China and resource exporters tends to favor the African country. Meanwhile, China's exports dominate its commerce with nonresource–exporting African trade partners. Figure 1.4 reveals the stark split in China's balance of trade between nonresource- and resource-exporting African countries. Nigeria, largely due to its ravenous demand for Chinese products, has been the exception. Although 87 percent of Nigerian exports to China are petroleum products, and total exports to China more than doubled between 2001 and 2010, they have not kept pace with the growth of imports from China. China exports a diverse range of mostly machinery, equipment, and manufactured goods to Nigeria.[49]

Comparing China's trade with Egypt to its trade with Angola, both tightly controlled autocracies, helps to illustrate the leading role factor endowments play in determining China-Africa trade patterns while holding regime type constant. In both cases, China's comparative advantage in consumer goods and capital equipment drives steep growth in its exports. Yet the presence of an export commodity (oil) in Angola results in a large Angolan trade surplus, while resource-scarce Egypt has a severely imbalanced trade relationship in China's favor.

African countries with few resources usually endure large trade deficits with China (e.g., Egypt, Ghana, Algeria, and Morocco) while resource exporters enjoy surpluses (e.g., Equatorial Guinea, Democratic Republic of Congo, Angola, Sudan, and South Africa). This pattern reflects the dichotomous nature of China-Africa trade: China's exports are diversified by both country and product type, while African exports to China are dominated by a handful of countries and remain specialized in a narrow band of finite resource products.

Between 2001 and 2009, China's top three import categories from sub-Saharan Africa—mineral products, base metals (including oil), and precious stones and metals—gradually went from about 80 percent of total imports to 90 percent. By 2013, however, about 70 percent of China's exports from Africa were from these three categories. Between 2009 to 2013 the vaguely

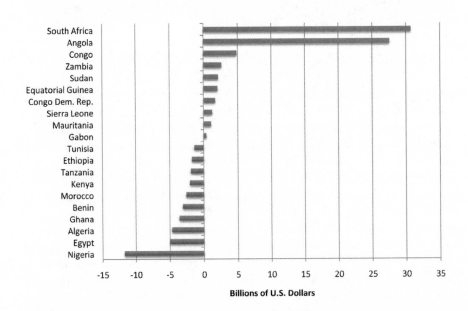

Billions of U.S. Dollars

Figure 1.4.   African countries' balance of trade with China (2012): 10 leading surpluses and 10 leading deficits (Source: IMF Direction of Trade Statistics)

named category "other unclassified goods" rose prodigiously from a consistent 2 percent between 2003 to 2009 to about a quarter of total Chinese imports in 2013. Further research is required to determine whether China's prodigious expansion of "unclassified goods" consumption amid a rapid fall in recorded finite natural resource purchases are the result of the reclassification of resource products or an actual change in the types of products that the Chinese are buying from Africa (see figure 1.2).[50] Further complicating efforts to measure the *actual* amounts (as opposed to dollar value) of traded goods were the sharp decline of oil and mineral prices on world markets in 2014.

China imports large quantities of raw materials to supply its domestic industries. Under such conditions, some African countries risk falling victim to, or further entrenching, the so-called Dutch Disease whereby the economy becomes dominated by a single export commodity enriching a small group of elites who control natural resources at the expense of the larger work force (see Corkin, in this volume). By contrast, nonresource exporters risk accumulating large and sustained trade deficits with China that may have destabilizing political consequences over time.

Although Beijing and its African counterparts regularly claim that Chinese investors do not receive preferential treatment in African SEZs, Chinese companies are the largest investors. Optimists argue that the construction of SEZs in Africa's nonresource-exporting economies will help reduce trade deficits. Pessimists counter that in the absence of significant investment from African firms, the zones will facilitate well-financed Chinese firms' displacement of Africa's nascent labor-intensive industries. Indeed, a study of ninety-seven Ethiopian footwear producers found that Chinese competition had forced 28 percent of them into bankruptcy and 32 percent lost market share.[51] The networked structure of China's African SEZs, argue Lorenzo Rotunno and Pierre-Louis Vezina, facilitates illicit avenues of trade. Consumer goods such as clothes and electronics are often brought into African countries alongside construction materials without paying duties. Meanwhile, labor-intensive African producers outside the zones pay hefty taxes and fees to political authorities for access to basic services and materials.[52]

African consumer goods markets remain dominated by Chinese manufacturers. In 2009, South Africa's textile sector lost twenty-six thousand jobs due to fierce price competition from China's clothing importers. Other labor-intensive sectors such as footwear, furniture, spinning, and weaving were also negatively affected. A 2013 study conducted by Edwards and Jenkins for the University of Cape Town estimates that during the 2000s the displacement of South African production due to increased Chinese import penetration cost the country R30 billion ($2.6 billion).[53] In 2005, Edwards and Jenkins had predicted that these trade patterns would eventually have a destabilizing effect on China's relations with some African countries:

Poverty reduction also depends on the type of growth generated by exports. There is a real danger that further expansion of mineral and petroleum exports to Asia will only reinforce an exclusionary model which will do little to reduce poverty and may exacerbate conflict and give rise to negative environmental impacts. Local producers may be displaced by competition from cheap imports from China and India and where these are in industries which employ significant numbers of unskilled workers, they may lose their jobs and be pushed into poverty.[54]

In general, China's manufacturing capacity and economies of scale supply a steady stream of affordable Chinese consumer goods for the domestic market and for export to African (and other international) markets.[55] Together, China's high demand for raw materials and its ability to produce affordable consumer and capital goods have become the dual engines for the growth of Sino-African trade. This looks set to continue as African consumers snap up Chinese consumer products, Chinese infrastructure firms win African contracts, and African governments prey upon, rather than support, domestic manufacturers. Although a boon for Chinese manufacturers and some African traders, the current patterns of China-Africa trade also inhibit African economies from getting a foothold in labor-intensive manufacturing.

AFRICAN PERCEPTIONS OF CHINA-AFRICA TRADE PATTERNS

Existing China-Africa trade patterns have given rise to mixed perceptions of China among Africans, and have sometimes yielded negative social and political externalities. Tensions have erupted in urban protests in a number of African countries. Zambia and Zimbabwe, for instance, have seen riots against Chinese merchants and products, and the exclusion of Chinese populations from business and other communities (see Sautman, chapter 7). In January 2015 in Kinshasa, DRC, local protesters attacked and looted about fifty Chinese-owned shops in working-class neighborhoods. Demonstrators shattered windows, broke down doors, and picked shelves clean. "Nothing was touched besides the Chinese stores," said one Congolese who owns dozens of businesses in the area. Thousands of Chinese laborers in DRC work on Chinese-financed infrastructure projects or run businesses that serve their compatriots. "They sell everything, (and) we're no longer doing any business because of them," complained one local telephone card vendor, who said he hoped the looting would be a "lesson" to his Chinese rivals.[56]

If China-Africa trade continues in accordance with existing patterns, China's interests will be increasingly pitted against emerging African resistance narratives at both the grassroots and elite levels. Generally, positive perceptions of China as an African development partner seem to turn negative when large numbers of Chinese enter African communities, usually as traders in the local market. In Kampala, Uganda, for instance, local merchants held a two-day strike in 2011 against the "influx of Chinese traders associated with Chinese investments." Issa Sekito of the Kampala City Traders Association explained: "Over the years, we have been complaining to government over the aliens doing petty trade, especially the Chinese—who come in as investors."[57] Similarly, in 2014, Tanzania's labor unions publically criticized the government for letting in small Chinese traders.[58]

At the elite level, the bluntest criticisms of Chinese business practices likened them to European colonialism. "The potential danger, in terms of the relationship that could be constructed between China and the African continent, would indeed be a replication of that colonial relationship," former South African president Thabo Mbeki said in 2006. "It is possible to build an unequal relationship, the kind of relationship that has developed between African countries as colonies. The African continent exports raw material and imports manufactured goods, condemning (it) to underdevelopment."[59] In 2013, Nigeria's Central Bank governor, Lamido Sanusi, also observed: "China takes our primary goods and sells us manufactured ones. This was also the essence of colonialism. The British went to Africa and India to secure raw materials and markets. Africa is now willingly opening itself up to a new form of imperialism."[60]

Not all evidence points to African dissatisfaction, however. A July 2014 Pew survey conducted through face-to-face interviews with 7,062 individuals in Tanzania, Kenya, Senegal, Nigeria, Uganda, Ghana, and South Africa found that in all countries (except South Africa) over half of those surveyed hold favorable views of China, perceive China's economic growth as beneficial for their country's economy, and believe that the Chinese government respects personal freedoms.[61] Economically, many Africans welcome the benefits of newly constructed roads, schools, communication towers, factories—as well as rising energy and commodity prices driven by China's growing demand. It remains to be seen whether a fall in oil and other commodity prices in 2014 and China's diversification of petroleum imports toward non-African suppliers will alter these positive perceptions.[62]

"China inadvertently follows the same pattern of other preceding great powers, spreading the seeds of discontent in a continent with diversified ethnicities and cultures," Eric Kiss and Kate Zhou observe.[63] China's indifference to, or active aid of, autocratic regimes in some well-covered countries such as Zimbabwe, Equatorial Guinea, Guinea, Sudan, and Ethiopia is perceived as partnering with repressive political elites against local people. By selling African governments weapons, censorship technology, and monitoring equipment to maintain social order, Chinese firms are unwittingly tapping into a reservoir of historic antiforeign resistance narratives that remain widespread among some communities. Grassroots anti-Chinese critiques frequently veer into charges against African governments; many

Africans are aware that their political leaders sanction or turn a blind eye toward adverse Chinese business practices. In a 2010 article titled "Autocracy: China's Unsolicited Export," Ephrem Madebo, an Ethiopian commentator, accused "China of mixing tyranny with its material exports to Africa." The article, which appeared in the *Addis Voice*, suggested that Ethiopia's economic relationship with China was actively supporting its repressive political system. Madebo observed:

> The push of China into Ethiopia is driven by China's desperate need for raw materials and future market opportunities. China is wrecking the efforts of building democracy in Ethiopia by bankrolling the corrupt and repressive regime in Addis Ababa. We love your export of technology, investment, and pharmaceuticals, but please keep your unsolicited export of autocracy within China. The Ethiopian people do welcome mutually beneficial Chinese investment in Ethiopia, and the Chinese are encouraged to build dams in Ethiopia, but they should better build dams that contain water, not the flow of information.[64]

At the heart of such criticism is an argument that has become increasingly common among African civil society: China's predilection for autocratic regimes determines its choice of African trade partners and is thus exploitive.[65] To examine how widely held this perception is, in 2014 the Ethics Institute of South Africa conducted an online survey of 1,056 Africans from fifteen countries.[66] The study found that African perceptions of Chinese businesses are indeed overwhelmingly negative. Africans are skeptical about the quality of Chinese goods, Chinese enterprises' environmental and economic practices, and Chinese businesses' employment policies toward their African workers. "There is a perception that Chinese companies do not treat their African staff with respect, do not provide decent working conditions, have little regard for health and safety conditions of their employees and have little regard for basic workers' rights," the study noted.[67] It seems likely that the study's small sample size and reliance on an online questionnaire (rather than face-to-face interviews like the Pew survey) may have led to a selection bias toward urban, educated respondents.

African resistance to Chinese firms takes on many forms, but it is often organized via social media and led by an emergent African civil society that demands more opportunities for locals, ethical business practices, and worker-friendly policies. In Zimbabwe, the result has been a government crackdown on Chinese business activity and a wave of popular anti-Chinese journalism. In Kenya and Uganda there is increasing resistance among some communities to the construction of the East African Railway. Citizens have started to raise questions over the bidding process and demand better jobs for locals. Soon after construction began, protestors in Voi, Kenya, blocked highway traffic, burned tires, and accused the project contractor, China Road and Bridge Construction Company, of denying them jobs in favor of Chinese expatriates. In chapter 8, Mark Kaigwa and Yu-Shan Wu explain the role that social media played in organizing the protests. They argue that as the number of communication platforms in Africa expands, so too do outlets for anti-Chinese sentiment. The railway also came under fire in Uganda amid allegations of cost inflation and design flaws. "Contracts for the projects are shrouded in secrecy, this cannot be good for us as well as future generations," said parliamentarian Geoffrey Ekanya. "The Chinese are giving us cheap loans, but this should also translate into good jobs for our people."[68] Similarly, in January 2015 Ugandan president Yoweri Museveni blocked a Chinese telecom project citing a lack of transparency and cost overruns.[69]

CONCLUSION

The ability of policymakers in Beijing to determine China-Africa trade patterns remains tightly constrained by their country's comparative advantage in labor-intensive and capital-intensive production; Africa's natural resource endowments; the growth of the Chinese economy; infrastructure expansion in both China and Africa; and the emergence of government-supported economies of scale in China's shipping and manufacturing sectors. Shared forms of autocratic governance are unlikely to determine China's trade partners or patterns in Africa, but will continue to influence Beijing's choice of political collaborators. China's policymakers and state-run firms undoubtedly use extra-market decisions to influence trade flows; its economies of scale, infrastructure investments, and technological development are the product of a centrally administered national industrial policy born of a political process rather than an efficient market mechanism. China's construction of SEZs, rail, and road networks both at home and in Africa, trade barriers and subsidies to manufacturers for power, fuel, garbage collection, and other materials and social services have all helped catalyze its "Go Global" strategy. Ultimately, however, Beijing's ability to direct trade is constrained by market demand and the location of African resources and customers.

Given relative factor endowments of resources, labor, and capital, there is little that can be done to reduce some African countries' overwhelming dependence on oil and mineral exports to China, or African consumers' preference for low-cost, Chinese consumer goods. For African countries without resources, or those seeking to diversify their exports, the persistent inability of their labor-intensive industries to compete with China at home—let alone in Chinese markets—remains a source of frustration that will continue to generate political and social challenges.

Africans are growing increasingly impatient with China's subsidies to manufacturers, trade barriers against foreign goods, and material support for autocratic regimes. If unchanged, existing patterns of China-Africa trade will continue to produce unwelcome negative perceptions of Chinese involvement among disaffected African communities and civil society. The social and political externalities that spring from these perceptions will, in turn, make it difficult for existing trade patterns to continue without engendering further African dissatisfaction and rising levels of violence toward Chinese in some African cities. Although African SEZs may someday help ameliorate these tensions, so far this has not been the case. Instead, SEZs like the Ethio-China Light Manufacturing zone are extending Chinese firms' competitive advantage into Africa by bringing its manufacturers closer to their material inputs and customers.

Many Africans are growing increasingly disillusioned with their governments' seeming inability to manage China-Africa trade and relations in ways that are broadly beneficial. Although China's trade patterns are rooted in powerful market dynamics only partially created by Beijing's policies, they have generated mixed and often politically charged reactions among many Africans that reflect the expansion of nascent anti-Chinese resistance narratives. To avoid the further erosion of African sentiments toward China, both Chinese and African political and business leaders must expand the existing conception of "win-win" economic cooperation to include a broader swath of the local population. Meanwhile, new forums for online expression enhance the possibility for intra-community and cross-national collective action and provide a venue for Africa's bourgeoning civil society and opportunistic politicians to tap into anti-Chinese sentiment and amplify their voices. If existing trends continue, China will face mounting blowback by leaders and organizations promising to give local communities a say in determining future China-Africa trade patterns.

NOTES

This chapter is derived in part from an article published in the *Journal of Contemporary China* on May 23, 2012,http://wwww.tandfonline.com/.

1. Howard French, *China's Second Continent: How a Million Migrants Are Building a New Empire in Africa* (New York: Knopf, 2014).

2. The term *trade patterns* refers to both the quantity of trade flows as well as the composition of goods traded.

3. "Unrest in DR Congo after TP Mazembe Lose to Inter Milan," *BBC*, December 18, 2010, http://www.bbc.co.uk/news/world-africa-12030051.

4. Howard French, "In Africa, an Election Reveals Skepticism of Chinese Involvement," *The Atlantic*, September 29, 2011,http://www.theatlantic.com/international/archive/2011/09/in-africa-an-election-reveals-skepticism-of-chinese-involvement/245832/.

5. Rhys Jenkins and Chris Edwards, "The Effect of China and India's Growth and Trade Liberalisation on Poverty in Africa," *DCP 70 Department for International Development of the United Kingdom*, May 2005, 18.

6. Harry G. Broadman, *Africa's Silk Road: China and India's New Economic Frontier* (Washington, DC: The World Bank, 2007), 10.

7. Broadman, *Africa's Silk Road*, 296.

8. Themba Munalula, "China's Special Preferential Tariff Africa," *Statistical Brief Issue No. 3*, Statistics Unit, Regional Integration Support Programme, Division of Trade, Customs and Monetary Affairs COMESA Secretariat, July 2007.

9. Naazneen Barma, Ely Ratner, and Steven Weber, "A World without the West," *The National Interest* 90 (July/August 2007): 25.

10. Harry Bliss, and Bruce Russett, "Democratic Trading Partners: The Liberal Connection, 1962–1989," *The Journal of Politics* 60, no. 4 (November 1998): 1127.

11. Ibid., 1128.

12. Edward D. Mansfield, Helen V. Milner, and B. Peter Rosendorff, "Free to Trade: Democracies, Autocracies, and International Trade," *American Political Science Review* 94, no. 2 (2000): 306.

13. Mansfield et al., "Free to Trade," 314. In 2002 and again in 2005, Mansfield et al. reaffirmed their earlier work and concluded that two democracies are more than double as likely to sign a trade agreement as are a mixed pair. Edward D. Mansfield, Helen V. Milner, and B. Peter Rosendorff, "Why Democracies Cooperate More: Electoral Control and International Trade Agreements," *International Organization* 56, no. 3 (Summer 2002): 505. B. Peter Rosendorff, "Do Democracies Trade More Freely?" Unpublished manuscript dated September 29, 2005.

14. Mansfield et al., "Free to Trade," 314. Not everyone agrees, however. According to Penubarti and Ward, "results are both biased and inconsistent [and] produce not only inefficient, but also biased estimates of the parameters," thus causing "the linkages virtually all other studies have uncovered between 'joint democracy' and trade to evaporate." They are also critical of using only a "loose fitting gravity model" to determine bilateral trade flows and include economic variables (i.e., factor endowments, scale economies, and trade barriers) as well. These variables and falling trade barriers, not liberal politics, they conclude, are an increasingly important determinant of bilateral trade flows. Mohan Penubarti and Michael D. Ward, "Commerce and Democracy," conference paper presented at "The Development and Application of Spatial Analysis for Political Methodology" at the University of Colorado, Boulder, March 10–12, 2000.

15. Naazneen Barma and Ely Ratner, "China's Illiberal Challenge," *Democracy: A Journal of Ideas* 2 (Fall 2006): 57.

16. Ibid., 64.

17. Ibid., 61.

18. Ibid., 61 and 64.

19. Chris Alden, *China in Africa* (New York: Zed Books, 2007), 70.

20. Peter Brookes, and Ji Hye Shin, "China's Influence in Africa: Implications for the United States," *Backgrounder #1916: The Heritage Foundation*, February 22, 2006,http://www.heritage.org/research/asiaandthepacific/bg1916.cfm.

21. Stephanie Hanson, "China, Africa, and Oil," *Backgrounder: Council on Foreign Relations*, June 6, 2008,http://www.cfr.org/publication/9557/.

22. Ian Taylor, " The 'All Weather Friend'? Sino-African Interaction in the 21st Century," in Ian Taylor and Paul Williams, eds., *Africa in International Politics: External Involvement on the Continent* (New York: Routledge, 2004), 99.

23. The early roots of this argument can be traced back to dependency theory, see Patrick J. McGowan, "Economic Dependence and Economic Performance in Black Africa," *Journal of Modern African Studies* 14, no. 1 (March 1976), and Michael B. Dolan and Brian W. Tomlin, "First World–Third World Linkages: External Relations and Economic Development," *International Organization* 34, no. 1 (Winter 1980). See also James A. Caporaso, "Dependence, Dependency, and Power in the Global System: A Structural and Behavioral Analysis," *International Organization* 32, no. 1 (1978).

24. Jian-Ye Wang, "What Drives China's Growing Role in Africa?" *Working Paper No. 07/211: International Monetary Fund*, August 2007, 22.

25. Jeffrey Herbst, and Greg Mills, "Commodities, Africa and China," *S. Rajaratnam School of International Studies (RSIS) Commentaries* (Singapore: Nanyang Technological Uni-

versity), January 9, 2009,http://www.rsis.edu.sg/rsis-publication/rsis/1161-commodities-africa-and-china/ -.VUPNqq1VhBc.

26. Herbst and Mills, "Commodities, Africa and China."

27. Wang, "What Drives China's Growing Role in Africa?" 20.

28. The H-O model is based on a half-dozen assumptions, they are: *Dimensionality*: The number of goods is equal to the number of productive factors. *Factor Immobility*: (a) The factors of production move freely among industries within a country but are completely immobile among countries; (b) goods move internationally with no transport costs and there are no other impediments to trade. *Competition*: Both goods and factor markets clear competitively; all agents act as if they could buy or sell unlimited quantities at the prevailing market price. *Technology*: The same technological knowledge about the production of goods is available without cost to all countries. *Factor Endowment Similarity*: The variability of factor endowments ratios among countries is less than the variability of factor input intensities across industries. *Demand Similarity*: Individuals consume as if each were maximizing an identical utility function. Edward E. Leamer, *Sources of International Comparative Advantage: Theory and Evidence* (Cambridge: Massachusetts Institute of Technology, 1984), 2.

29. Paul Krugman, "Was It All in Ohlin?" Massachusetts Institute of Technology, October 1999, http://web.mit.edu/krugman/www/ohlin.html.

30. Ibid.

31. Helena, Marques, "The 'New' Economic Theories," *FEP Working Papers 104: Universidade do Porto, Faculdade de Economia do Porto*, 8.

32. Tania Branigan, "Sock City's Decline May Reveal an Unraveling in China's Economy," *The Guardian*, September 8, 2012.

33. David Barboza, "In Roaring China, Sweaters Are West of Socks City," New York Times, December 24, 2004, http://www.nytimes.com/2004/12/24/business/worldbusiness/24china.html?pagewanted=print&position=.

34. Deborah Bräutigam, and Tang Xiaoyang, "African Shenzhen: China's Special Economic Zones in Africa," *Journal of Modern African Studies* 49, no. 1 (2011): 27–54.

35. William Davison, "Africa Rising: China Steps up Production in Ethiopia with Drill Instructors, Investors," *Christian Science Monitor*, April 3, 2012.

36. "Sudan Heading towards Using Chinese Currency in Trade Exchanges," Sudan Vision (official), January 31, 2015.

37. Thomas I. Palley, "Institutionalism and New Trade Theory: Rethinking Comparative Advantage and Trade Policy," *Journal of Economic Issues* 42, no. 1 (March 2008): 199.

38. Justin Yifu Lin, "New Structural Economics: A Framework for Rethinking Development and Policy," *Policy Research Working Paper: The World Bank*, February 2010, 28.

39. Palley, "Institutionalism and New Trade Theory," 204.

40. Palley, "Institutionalism and New Trade Theory," 202.

41. "High-Speed Railway Accounts for Over Half of China's Railway Investment," *The People's Daily*, April 27, 2010, http://english.peopledaily.com.cn/90001/90778/90860/6965110.html.

42. "China Blames 54 Officials for Bullet Train Crash," *USA Today*, December 28, 2011, http://usatoday30.usatoday.com/news/world/story/2011-12-28/china-train-crash-blame/52249874/1.

43. World Bank World Databank, "Gross Domestic Product 2013," December 16, 2014, http://databank.worldbank.org/data/download/GDP.pdf.

44. "High-Speed Railways: Faster Than a Speeding Bullet," *The Economist*, November 9, 2013.

45. Sarwant Singh, "China High-Speed Rail Juggernaut, While Most of US Stands By and Waves—But Not Elon Musk (Part I)," *Forbes*, July 17, 2014.

46. "China Railway Construction Wins $12 Billion Nigeria Deal: Xinhua," *Reuters*, November 20, 2014.

47. Mary Swire, "China's Shipping Sector Develops in Tianjin," *Tax-News.com* (Hong Kong), August 5, 2010, http://www.tax-news.com/news/Chinas_Shipping_Sector_Develops_In_Tianjin____44636.html.

48. Mark T. Jones, "Somaliland President Stops Over in Addis Ababa Enroute China," *Somaliland Press*, August 9, 2011,http://www.weedhsan.com/index.php/20-english-news/323-somaliland-president-stops-over-in-addis-ababa-enroute-china.

49. Margaret Egbula, and Qi Zheng, "China and Nigeria: A Powerful South-South Alliance." *Sahel and West Africa Club Secretariat (OECD)*, no 5 (November 2011),http://www.oecd.org/china/49814032.pdf.

50. Data from 1995 to 2013 is available from the Trade and Law Centre for Southern Africa (TRALAC) in Stellenbosch, South Africa.

51. Tegegne Gebre-Egziabher, "Impacts of Chinese Imports and Coping Strategies of Local Producers: The Case of Small-Scale Footwear Enterprises in Ethiopia," *Journal of Modern African Studies* 45, no. 4 (2007): 647–79.

52. Lorenzo Rotunno, and Pierre-Louis Vezina, "Chinese Networks and Tariff Evasion," Graduate Institute of International and Development Studies, University of Geneva, Working Paper no 20/2010,http://www.eiit.org/WorkingPapers/Papers/TradePatterns/FREIT239.pdf.

53. Lawrence Edwards, and Rhys Jenkins, "The Impact of Chinese Import Penetration on the South African Manufacturing Sector," Southern Africa Labour and Development Research Unit, University of Cape Town, Working Paper No. 102, 22–23,http://www.opensaldru.uct.ac.za/bitstream/handle/11090/618/2013_102.pdf?sequence=1.

54. Rhys Jenkins, and Chris Edwards, *The Effect of China and India's Growth and Trade Liberalisation on Poverty in Africa*, DCP 70 (Department for International Development of the United Kingdom, May, 2005), 18 and 39.

55. Although it is outside the scope of this publication, African countries' inability to compete with China in third-country markets like the United States and the EU is another troubling trend.

56. Marthe Bosuandole, "Chinese Become Targets in DR Congo Riots," *Agence France Presse*, January 26, 2015.

57. "Uganda Traders Close Shops in Protest," *BBC*, July 6, 2011.

58. "China in Africa: One among Many," *The Economist*, January 17, 2015,http://www.economist.com/news/middle-east-and-africa/21639554-china-has-become-big-africa-now-backlash-one-among-many.

59. Victor Mallet, "The Chinese in Africa: Beijing Offers a New Deal," *The Financial Times*, January 23, 2007.

60. Lamido Sanusi, "Africa Must Get Real about Chinese Ties," *Financial Times*, March 11, 2013.

61. Pew Research Center, "Global Opposition to U.S. Surveillance and Drones, but Limited Harm to America's Image," July 2014, 26–25,http://www.pewglobal.org/2014/07/14/chapter-2-chinas-image/.

62. "China's October Pipeline Gas Imports Rise 9% on Year to 2.75 Bcm," *Platts*, November 24, 2014.

63. Eric Kiss, and Kate Zhou, "China's New Burden in Africa," in *Dancing with the Dragon: China's Emergence in the Developing World*, edited by Dennis Hickey and Baogang Guo (Lanham, MD: Rowman & Littlefield Publishers, Inc., 2010), 156.

64. Ephrem Madebo, " Autocracy: China's Unsolicited Export," *Addis Voice*, August 12, 2010, http://addisvoice.com/2010/08/autocracy-chinas-unsolicited-export/.

65. For additional African commentaries that reflect this emerging anti-Chinese narrative see: Catherine Sasman, "Chinese in Gobabis," *The Namibian* (Windhoek), January 12, 2012, http://www.namibian.com.na/indexx.php?archive_id=90247&page_type=archive_story_detail&page=1330. Also see: Bisong Etabohen, "Cameroon Looks to Fix Chinese Employment Blues," *Africa Review* (Nairobi), January 15, 2012, http://www.africareview.com/Special+Reports/Cameroon+looks+to+fix+Chinese+employment+blues/-/979182/1305980/-/view/printVersion/-/69xk9i/-/index.html.

66. Angola, Benin, Cameroon, Democratic Republic of Congo, Ethiopia, Ghana, Kenya, Mozambique, Nigeria, South Africa, South Sudan, Sudan, Tanzania, Zambia, Zimbabwe.

67. Ethics Institute of South Africa, "Africans' Perceptions of Chinese Business in Africa: A Survey," February 2014, 34.

68. Nicholas Bariyo, "East African Rail Expansion Meets Growing Opposition," *Wall Street Journal Frontiers blog*, November 14, 2014,http://blogs.wsj.com/frontiers/2014/11/14/east-african-rail-expansion-meets-growing-opposition/.

69. Eriasa Mukiibi Sserunjogi, "Museveni Stops Shs300b Inflated Telecom Project," *The Daily Monitor*, January 4, 2015,http://www.lightwaveonline.com/news/2015/01/09/museveni-stops-shs300b-inflated-telecom-project.html.

Chapter Two

The Good, the Bad, and the Ugly

Agency-as-Corruption and the Sino-Nigerian Relationship

Ian Taylor

When discussing Nigerian agency and the environment encountered by Chinese actors in the country, the political economy of Nigeria must be reviewed, as it is in this sphere that Nigerian agency is most vividly displayed. Indeed, any analysis of Nigeria must be placed squarely within the context of ongoing dominant modalities of governance and the prevailing political and societal culture that this engenders. It is this milieu that fosters both the structure and agency of actors and informs how intersubjective relationships are shaped and how they play out. This chapter examines the overriding features of Nigeria's sociopolitical environment, arguing that the neopatrimonial modes of governance that characterize the country ensure a type of politics and economics—termed agency-as-corruption—that is challenging for most external players, including the Chinese. Such a background provides local actors with a set of behavioral norms that may not be readily understood by foreigners, and also makes available a diverse social space in which the agency of connected Nigerians may be expressed.

Currently, a great deal of interest is directed toward Nigeria and elsewhere in West Africa, with the focus predominantly on energy in what has been dubbed a "second Scramble for Africa."[1] The past decade or so has witnessed marked changes in the volume and composition of financial flows to the region and the continent. In the first decade of the twenty-first century, the level of foreign direct investment (FDI), portfolio investment, and official development assistance surged from $27 billion in 2000 to about $126 billion in 2010. "Since 2005, Africa has received more FDI than official development assistance. According to Ernst & Young's 2012 Attractiveness Survey on Africa entitled 'Building Bridges,' the number of FDI projects rose by 27 per cent in 2011, with a total of 857 projects, a steep increase from 421 in 2007."[2] Many have dubbed the continent as the next "big destination" for global investment; record amounts are being raised to invest in businesses there.[3]

Yet unlike the nineteenth-century scramble for Africa, which "was driven and dictated by European colonial interests,"[4] African agency is far more present in this contemporary rush for African oil, with important implications for the nature of the relationships unfolding. Indeed, "African leaders [today] act in the role of decision-makers"[5] ; Nigeria and its leadership is no exception.

Of course, many African states are rich in oil but lack the capital needed to exploit these resources in a way that would create formative conditions whereby African elites might be seen as dependent upon external actors to facilitate exploitation.[6] Still, the ability of governments to negotiate favorable contracts should not be discounted. In fact, many oil-rich African states are quite skillful in playing the oil game—albeit for the benefit of the incumbent elites rather than the broad masses.[7]

The purpose of this chapter is to firmly situate relations between China and Nigeria within the framework of existing power relations in Nigeria, which inevitably influence the types of relationships that external actors are able to craft. Understanding this is the first step to understanding how Nigerian agency is exercised in this, and other, foreign relations. It is argued that Nigerian agency, operating at different levels, makes doing business in the country unpredictable, even hazardous in certain circumstances. Navigating these hazards and working out the why and wherefores is not easy, as the Chinese presence in Nigeria clearly demonstrates.

THE QUESTION OF AGENCY

As a concept, agency implies that individuals ("agents") are capable of directing their structurally formed capabilities in ways that are imaginative and inventive, for personal or communal advancement. It is axiomatic that this does not take place in a vacuum: as Marx's aphorism reminds us, "Men make their own history, but they do not make it just as they please; they do not make it under circumstances chosen by themselves, but under circumstances directly encountered, given and transmitted from the past."[8] Agency exists within constraints, but it is free within those constraints. The agency of individuals is constrained beyond a certain boundary, but is free (or devolving upon the individual) within such limitations. The factors that are held to influence behavior are known as structures. In this sense, "structures must not be conceptualized as simply placing constraints on human agency, but as enabling."[9]

In discussing agency and structure, it is critical to avoid the two extremes in approaching the duality identified by Marx. The first extreme, as reflected by Emile Durkheim and his intellectual descendants, practically dismisses human agency; human thought and action are seen as regulated by social structures. Durkheim famously asserted in this regard that "the individual is dominated by a moral reality greater than himself: namely, collective reality."[10] This determinism was then later applied by Louis Althusser in his discussion of ideology,[11] and by Michel Foucault in his discussion of power.[12] For Foucault, individuals are passive "subjects" and the mediums or sites of power, knowledge claims, and discourses. "Power is everywhere" and "comes from everywhere."[13] Individualism expressed through agency as a materialization of rationality, autonomy, and reflexivity ultimately disappears. Marx and Engels were critical of such determinism, and commented that "history does nothing, it does not possess immense riches, it does not fight battles! It is real living men who do all this . . . History is nothing but the activity of men in pursuit of their ends."[14]

The other extreme inclines to exaggerate the individual and to minimize or even discount the importance of structures; this view, too, is in error. The abstraction of the individual was intrinsic to Ludwig Feuerbach's humanism, which Marx and Engels so trenchantly critiqued as unhistorical.[15] Similarly, only the "rational" substance of Georg Hegel's dialectics was developed by Marx, leaving it unencumbered from agential idealism.[16] Following on, bourgeois political economists like David Ricardo and Adam Smith were scorned in the *Grundrisse* as "Robinsonades" (after Robinson Crusoe), for they assumed rational isolated individuals, detached from all social ties and histories.[17] Remarkably, such ontological individualism currently dominates mainstream economics, despite its obvious failings.

In short, the dialectic between structure and agency has to be seen as the decisive factor for behavior and outcomes. In this, agency exercised by different persons is not—cannot—be uniform, differing immensely in both type and degree. This room for maneuverability and the exercising of agency and in what direction(s) varies dramatically from one social world to another, contingent on the sort of precise structures that help form those social worlds. As William Sewell notes, "Structures, in short, empower agents differentially, which also implies that they embody the desires, intentions, and knowledge of agents differentially as well. Structures, and the human agencies they endow, are laden with differences in power."[18]

The above set of dynamics is important to remember when discussing the exercising of agency in the Sino-Nigerian context. Precisely because different Nigerian actors exercise their agency in different manifestations, which has a profound effect on Chinese engagement with the country, the question of Nigerian agency needs to be foregrounded. When doing so, normative judgments need to be set aside, as the exercising of much extant agency is, through the prism of liberal understandings of state-society relations, deviant, even predatory. Such assessments, however, do not really help in the study of what is going on. Rather, understanding such processes throws light on how and where agency is exercised and how this affects the relationships being crafted between China and Nigeria. This is particularly important given the fact that Nigeria is rapidly becoming one of China's largest African trading partners.

THE NIGERIAN CONTEXT

With its economic rebasing in 2013, Nigeria was revealed to have a gross domestic product (GDP) of nearly $510 billion, easily making it Africa's largest economy. The revenue from oil and gas accounts for about 90 percent of total export earnings and 80 percent of government revenue. Nigeria has proven crude oil reserves of thirty-seven billion barrels, making it the continent's leading oil producer.[19] The country also has an estimated 159 trillion cubic feet of proven natural gas reserves, giving it one of the top ten natural gas endowments in the world.[20] Undeniably, Nigeria is famed for its spectacular natural wealth. Yet it is also a country where grotesque inequalities exist. As Geoffrey York of the *Globe and Mail* put it in a June 2014 report:

> The economic inequality in Nigeria is among the most extreme in the world—and growing worse. Despite its rising oil wealth, the percentage of Nigerians living in absolute poverty (earning less than a dollar a day) has increased to 61 per cent over the past decade, compared with 55 per cent in 2004. Yet at the same time, Nigeria has nearly 16,000 millionaires, and that number has jumped by 44 per cent over the past six years.[21]

The World Bank has estimated that as a result of corruption, 80 percent of Nigeria's energy revenues benefit only one percent of the population.[22] This 1 percent is not afraid to flaunt its wealth: some accounts rank Nigerians as the third highest non-EU consumer spenders in London.[23] Although the Niger Delta region produces 90 percent of Nigeria's oil and over 75 percent of the country's export earnings, very little of the wealth has been seen by Delta residents.[24] Inequality in Nigeria is also significant and on the increase. Indeed, Nigeria has consistently experienced a sharp deterioration in income distribution: in 1970 the top 2 percent and the bottom 17 percent of the Nigerian population earned the same total amount of income, but by 2000, the top 2 percent had the same income as the bottom 55 percent.[25] Since independence, too, there has only ever been one Nigerian head of state with origins in any of the country's oil-producing states—the current president,

Goodluck Jonathan of Bayelsa State. In fact, "the northern predominantly Hausa region has benefited in a disproportionate manner from oil resources, contributing to grievances by the rest of the country and ongoing instability."[26]

Regrettably, Nigeria is a byword for corruption and malgovernance.[27] Well-connected political insiders exercise agency by embezzling approximately over one hundred thousand barrels of oil per day, worth circa $1.46 billion a year.[28] At the same time, government budgets are routinely estimated on projected incomes that themselves are based on assumptions that are wildly below the actual revenues collected.[29] Despite "improvements in fiscal management [in recent years], budgets [are] not implemented as stated, funds [are] impounded by the President, and extra-budgetary spending continue[s]."[30] It is anyone's guess as to where the surplus finances from oil sales go—certainly not into government coffers or to the broad mass of Nigeria's citizens. Indeed:

> Some Western diplomats estimate that Nigeria lost a minimum average of $4 billion to $8 billion per year to corruption over the eight years of the Obasanjo administration. That figure would equal between 4.25% and 9.5% of Nigeria's total GDP in 2006. To put those numbers in perspective, a loss of 9.5% of the United States' GDP to corruption in 2006 would have translated into $1.25 trillion in stolen funds or $222 billion (GBP 108.6 billion) in the case of the United Kingdom's economy.[31]

The conspicuous discrepancy between Nigeria's abundant natural resources and the actual welfare of its citizens is an embodiment of the perennial crises confronting the country under the neopatrimonial modalities of governance that dominate Nigerian society. In patrimonial political systems, "an individual rules by dint of personal prestige and power; ordinary folk are treated as extensions of the 'big man's' household, with no rights or privileges other than those bestowed by the ruler. Authority is entirely personalized, shaped by the ruler's preferences rather than any codified system of laws." The ruler, moreover, "ensures the political stability of the regime and personal political survival by providing a zone of security in an uncertain environment and by selectively distributing favors and material benefits to loyal followers who are not citizens of the polity so much as the ruler's clients."[32] In Nigeria, this diversion of public funds for private purposes by connected elites has frequently led to violence and disorder.[33]

Those who control Nigeria's institutions are corrupt, self-serving, and uninterested in promoting broad-based development.[34] What exists in the country is thus a longstanding form of "pirate capitalism," brought about by the dialectics between the structures that oil and the extant polity have crafted interacting with the agential power of Nigeria's elites.[35] Where the state is the major source of wealth and fortune, agency for self-advancement is necessarily focused on capturing power within the state, whereby rent from oil can be appropriated.[36] Agency-as-corruption and its exercise thereof therefore means that "Nigeria's elite is hardly known for its vision and foresight nor for its willingness to accept the sacrifices needed to build a diversified economy that is not dependent on oil for 95 per cent of foreign exchange earnings and three-quarters of government revenues."[37] This exercising of agency by one segment of the population (an infinitesimal minority) then generates counterreactions from those who are marginalized by such structures.

What agency the elites do exercise is directed toward self-accumulation and gaming the system to their own benefit, rather than any notional national public good. Consequently, Nigeria's population "has assumed a pyramidal shape, with a tiny but fabulously rich elite at the apex, a 'disappearing' middle class in the center, and a huge and ever expanding impoverished mass at the base."[38] Ethnic tension has long been rife, through which excluded actors seek to exercise their own agendas through the manipulation of identities.[39] In Nigeria, as Richard Joseph famously noted, prebendalism dominates.[40] Prebendalism is a clerical term, signifying the medieval right of a member of a chapter to a share in the revenues of a cathedral where he is employed. Prebendalism then reflects intersubjective expectations about the arrogation of state offices and the resources that accrue to them. This *appropriation* is, within the neopatrimonial system, accepted as normal and by right.

Nigeria is thus a country where there is a well-understood dictum that there is "nothing seriously wrong with stealing state funds, especially if they [are] used to benefit not only the individual but also members of his community. Those who [have] the opportunity to be in government [are] expected to use the power and resources at their disposal to advance private and communal needs."[41] Agency-as-corruption (from the Weberian perspective), then, is absolutely central to Nigerian public life.[42] Opposition to corruption, with few exceptions, is "condemned only in so far as it benefits someone else rather than oneself."[43]

In his seminal work, Peter Ekeh argues that one of the most important legacies of colonialism was the development of two public realms: the primordial and the civic public realms, which interrelate differently with the private realm vis-à-vis morality. The civic public realm refers to the armed forces, police, public service, and the executive, legislative, and judicial arms of government. The primordial public refers to village and rural communities and traditional African groups and associations. Only rights and benefits are claimed from the state by its citizens, who owe responsibilities and duties to a native sector. The former then forms the basis of an "amoral civic public realm" and the latter a "moral primordial public realm."[44] The civic public realm was associated with the colonial state, which, being an external transposition onto the native sector was deemed illegitimate, with no moral linkages to the private realm. Cheating the system then was considered a duty.[45] The result has been that in the postindependence era, Nigerian actors maneuver in and between the two realms, with the state used by the primordial public for accumulation. According to Ekeh:

> A good citizen of the primordial public gives out and asks for nothing in return; a lucky citizen of the civic public gains from the civic but enjoys escaping giving anything in return whenever he can. But such a lucky man would not be a good man were he to channel all his lucky gains to his private purse. He will only continue to be a good man if he channels part of the largesse from the civic public to the primordial public. That is the logic of the dialectics. The unwritten law of the dialectics is that it is legitimate to rob in order to strengthen the primordial public.[46]

In other words, those who possess the chance to be in government are expected to exercise agency in exploiting the prebends that they control; occupants of public office at all levels feel that their positions entitle them to unchecked access to the resources of the civic public realm. Agency-as-corruption is expressed through power and resources found at an actor's disposal and are used to press forward individual and collective needs.[47] As one Nigerian commentary put it when discussing the behavior of Nigerian officialdom:

> If you look at it from the point of view of specific officials—(presidents), governors, managers, civil servants, or administrators—graft is us. If you look at offices—ministries, legislatures, foreign missions, law enforcement, and industry—graft is us. If you look at programmes—budgets, agriculture, Millennium Development Goals, banks, or roads—graft is us.[48]

Clientelism, patronage, and corruption are absolutely central to the whole political economy of the country and the vehicles through which agency is effected.[49] It is the "acme of the dialectic," according to Ekeh, where corruption takes on two dimensions: the embezzlement of public funds from the state, and the routine giving and taking of bribes for services provided by the civic public.[50] However, we should make a distinction between patronage and prebendalism—even if both go hand in hand and certainly exist at every level in Nigeria. Patronage is the practice of using resources from the civic realm to deliver employment and services for clients. Prebendalism, on the other hand, is the distribution of public office(s) in order for clients to access state resources.[51] In Nigeria, prebendalism has dominated as the multiethnic and confessional nature of the country necessitates intraelite accommodation, which is facilitated by making available access to civic resources via public offices—prebends.

The structures in which agency in Nigeria is employed, and which foreign actors like the Chinese must maneuver, are thus found in the nature of the Nigerian state itself:

> Unlike in the West, the state in Nigeria is not perceived or seen in the Weberian sense of an impartial and impersonal entity. Due to its colonial historical trajectory, the state is conceptualized as an alien institution whose powers are used to further the interests of those who wield them. As a result of the interplay between formal and informal spheres, political reciprocity between patrons and clients influences the operation of political institutions and makes them susceptible to private capture and personalization. [52]

This, however, leads to counterreactions by those not able to benefit from such matrices.

COUNTERAGENCY

Michel Foucault suggests that "there are no relations of power without resistances; the latter are all the more real and effective because they are formed right at the point where relations of power are exercised . . . [resistance] exists all the more by being in the same place as power; hence, like power, resistance is multiple."[53] The deeply embedded practices outlined above are ambiguous or even contradictory from the perspective of the marginalized (the majority of) Nigerians. The rationalization of cheating the civic public only works for a few, and an uneasy relationship develops with those outside the patronage loops. The uncertainties and frustrations generated by such dynamics opens up the possibilities for alternative forms of action—for counteragency—to be developed. Nigeria's citizens are not patiently waiting for the crumbs from the table of the wealthy to fall down. They actively respond to policies and practices and engage—sometimes violently—with the state and its representatives, who are seen to have failed them in the wider distribution of the benefits that should come their way, *by right*, through the dialectic. This is what Ilufoye Sarafa Ogundiya was referring to when he asserted:

> In Nigeria today, the success of an ethnic group or a politician is synonymous with the level of access of such group to state resources, defined in terms of the number of political appointments such group is able to secure in the political arrangement. This to a large extent also, in the common erroneous thinking in Nigeria, determines the group percentage share of the national cake. Therefore, to steal from the common wealth is an acceptable norm. It was a misconception that this is used to fatten the primordial public. Contrarily, it has only been used to further fatten the purse of the politico-bureaucratic elite at the peril of the primordial public. [54]

If it is accepted that it is legitimate to steal in order to strengthen the primordial public (the kernel of agency-as-corruption), when the primordial public (or huge segments of it) are not beneficiaries of this, problems develop and counteragency strategies become necessary. This then introduces a highly destabilizing dynamic into the relationship(s) between the civic public and the primordial realms. The scope for outcomes is mediated through the agency of the actors involved.

Due to serious inequalities, those outside the loop increasingly exercise their agency through the deployment of violence, which is often seen as a righteous response to an inequitable and intolerable situation. In Nigeria, violence has become an agential norm in the absence of other possibilities for self-advancement. The Boko Haram insurgency in the north of the country is one example of such expressions. Widespread crime, of course, exists in most urban areas, and the Chinese community in Nigeria has not been immune. However, within the context of Sino-Nigerian relations, activities in the oil-rich Niger Delta have been more significant with regard to the manifestation of certain forms of counteragency.

Militants from the Movement for the Emancipation of the Niger Delta (MEND) have been targeting the oil industry since the mid-2000s, manifested in kidnappings, assassinations, and car bombings.[55] In early 2006, MEND militias began attacking oil installations and kidnapping foreign oil workers, leading to a 20 percent reduction in Nigeria's oil production. MEND was a more efficient organization than the armed gangs that have sought to extort money from oil companies in the Delta region, although it similarly engaged in the theft of oil. In an interview with the BBC, a MEND leader stated that his organization was fighting for "total control" of the Niger Delta's oil wealth, stating that local people had not gained from the riches under the ground and the region's creeks and swamps. He noted that the Delta had been exploited for the benefit of other parts of Nigeria and foreign companies, and ordered all oil companies and Nigerians whose roots lie elsewhere to leave the region.[56] Thus as an agential expression of resistance to the ongoing milieu, MEND can be seen as an articulation of long-held grievances.

Similarly, the recent rise of Boko Haram is another expression of counteragency. Boko Haram is an Islamic militant sect that believes that politics in northern Nigeria have been captured by corrupt elites—false Muslims who have marginalized the poor and who live in luxury while the faithful suffer. The group's aim is to create a "pure" Islamic state ruled by sharia law *throughout Nigeria*. Since August 2011, Boko Haram has planted bombs and engaged in gun attacks on an almost weekly basis, targeting government officials, schools, churches, and anyone perceived to fall below the standards set by their Wahabbist-influenced theology.[57] The country's northeast has been hardest hit, although attacks have also targeted the federal capital, Abuja. This exercising of counteragency against the dominant political culture has implications for China. Indeed, in May 2014 a Chinese national was killed and ten others were kidnapped after an attack in northern Cameroon by Boko Haram militants from Nigeria.[58] Although the hostages were later released, the emergence of Boko Haram and its seeming ability to strike at will makes doing business in northern Nigeria extremely dangerous. Indeed, the activities of the jihadist group has meant that in whole swathes of the north of the country, exploration won't be possible without a significant change in the security situation.[59] To date, this has not occurred.

NIGERIA'S OIL AND CHINA

Nigeria is one of Africa's leading oil producers; some 80 percent of Abuja's revenues come from oil. Nigerian crude oil is of high quality and has a light, low sulphur grade known as "sweet," which is highly valued thanks to its high gasoline content and relatively cheap processing outlay. Nigeria exports about two million barrels per day (in October 2014 it was 1.83 million barrels per day). Despite its attractiveness, however, finding buyers for Nigeria's oil is increasingly a problem due to the dumping of the nation's crude by the United States owing to the discovery of alternative energy supplies (shale gas and light tight oil); the United States stopped importing oil from Nigeria in October 2014.[60] Other countries, notably Brazil and India, have since been sought out as replacement export destinations.

In earlier times, China was altogether absent from Nigeria's oil industry, which has historically been dominated by Western oil companies. However, this changed in the early 2000s through a mix of canny diplomacy, sweetener deals (often unrelated to the actual oil industry), and a close relationship between China and the then president of Nigeria, Olusegun Obasanjo. According to Obasanjo's biographer, John Iliffe, Obasanjo had "long been exasperated by the international oil companies that were eager to exploit Nigeria's oil and gas but refused to invest in enterprises such as oil-refining or in infrastructural development that were not essential to their own core businesses." In 2004, therefore, as dramatic economic growth in Asia stimulated the so-called new scramble for Africa, Obasanjo "offer[ed] Asian national oil companies 'rights of first refusal' to explore and develop oil blocks in return for undertakings to invest capital and technology in Nigerian infrastructure."[61]

In October 2004 the Nigerian government announced that the country needed an annual investment of $10 billion to reach the target of forty billion barrels of reserve by 2010. Consequently, China National Offshore Oil Corporation (CNOOC) signed an agreement with the Nigerian government to locate upstream oil and gas assets that might be incorporated into downstream projects. In December 2004 the state-owned Chinese oil company Sinopec and the Nigerian National Petroleum Corporation (NNPC) signed an agreement to develop Oil Mining Lease (OML) 64 and 66 in the Niger Delta. Within OML 64 five exploration wells have been drilled, with one well coming across hydrocarbon resources. OML 66 has been far more successful, with eighteen exploration wells drilled but with twelve wells meeting hydrocarbon resources.[62] Sinopec also has a contract with the Nigerian Petroleum Development Company (NPDC) and Italy's Eni to develop the Okono and Okpoho fields, which have combined reserves of five hundred million barrels. CNOOC and NNPC later in July 2005 signed an $800 million contract that guaranteed thirty thousand barrels per day to China over a five-year period, to be reviewed every year.[63]

Building on such developments, in April 2006 the Nigerian government offered China four oil exploration licenses in exchange for $4 billion worth of infrastructure investment. The two countries then signed seven development agreements granting Abuja export credit worth $500 million.[64] China agreed to repair the Kaduna Refining and Petrochemicals Company, while undertaking other investment projects, such as building a hydropower plant in the Mambilla, Plateau State. All of this was in return for exercising the "right of first refusal" on oil blocs. Previous operators of Production Sharing Contracts that had run through 1993 to 1998 relinquished several oil blocs. The NNPC also approved the acquisition by CNOOC of a working interest in a deep-water area of the Niger Delta. The deal included the lucrative Akpo oil field, discovered in 2000 and with production commencing in 2009. The Akpo field is said to hold seven hundred million barrels of crude oil reserves, and gas reserves of about 2.5 trillion cubic feet.[65]

CNOOC also took over the commitments of a contractor of the deep-water block, Oil Prospecting Lease (OPL) 246,[66] which had earlier been assigned to South Atlantic Petroleum Limited, a company owned by former Nigerian defense minister Theophilus Danjuma. Illustrating that politics, patronage, and oil are inextricably linked in Nigeria, as elsewhere, Danjuma immediately took steps in the courts to negate the deal, claiming that his company's acreage had been revoked for political reasons linked to his non-support for Obasanjo's attempt, in late 2006, to change the Nigerian constitution and run for a presidential third term. The Federal High Court in Lagos later, on October 4, 2006, delivered judgment in favor of the Obasanjo government. Consequently, CNOOC bought a 45 percent working interest in OPL 246, paying $2.3 billion plus an adjustment of $424 million for other expenses. The $2.3 billion will finance the NNPC's 50 percent equity stake in OPL 246 and, in return, CNOOC will have a share in the 70 percent profit oil from the field, while the NNPC takes the remaining 30 percent, as well as in the 80 percent cost of oil. As part of the deal, CNOOC agreed to refund the

$600 million already spent by French oil and gas company Total in developing the field.[67]

The Chinese company CNPC in 2006 also purchased claims in Nigeria, buying rights to blocks OPL 298, 471, 721, and 732 from the Nigerian government. This purchase was followed by a 2012 purchase of the rights to blocks OML 64 and OML 66.[68] Moreover, "[t]he Chinese oil giant Sinopec also has made inroads in Nigeria, [in 2014] finalizing a deal with [France's] Total to pay $2.5 billion for a 20% share in block OML 138. This purchase from Total comes on top of the 90,000 barrels per day that are currently being produced for Sinopec by their client company Addax."[69] Moreover, while CNOOC's much-publicized 2013 purchase of Canada's Nexen largely focused on the Chinese company's acquisition of Canadian oil sands, the purchase also included significant offshore oil reserves in Nigeria.[70] As almost all investments by Chinese companies are in "buying shares in blocks, not sole control [. . .] the Chinese often rely on their [international oil company] partners to do most of the actual production work for them."[71] Yet in an environment like Nigeria's, the acquisition of contracts and the signing of deals often fall to the side when elites clash. These contentions may be seen as expressions of what we might refer to as counteragency.

ELITE COUNTERAGENCY

Just as counteragency is articulated when outsiders feel that they are not benefitting from the dialectic identified by Ekeh, so, too, may elites similarly articulate such tendencies when they believe that arrangements made by previous incumbents disadvantage them and the gains from robbing the civil public realm are not theirs to capture. This can then lead to situations in which external actors are caught between contending politicoeconomic struggles by elites. In these circumstances, the upshot of intraelite rivalry—which must be seen as part of the exercise of agency within the logics of Nigeria's political economy and modes of governance—may be highly unpredictable, but usually end up with winners and losers. This alternative dynamic of agency-as-corruption is quite clearly evident in developments following Obasanjo's departure from office in 2007.

In March 2007 it was announced that the Nigerian government was considering reviewing its plans to hand over management of the Kaduna refinery to CNOOC as Chinese promises to invest in the refinery had not materialized. Previously, China had been awarded four oil-drilling licenses in exchange for it buying a controlling stake in the 110,000-barrel-a-day Kaduna oil refinery. Nigeria offered first right of refusal to the Chinese company for four exploration blocks during a licensing round in mid-2006. Yet in early 2007, the director general of Nigeria's Bureau of Public Enterprises, Irene

Chigbue, stated that the plan to get CNOOC to manage the 110,000-barrels-per-day Kaduna refinery "had run into hitches as the CNOC have not been forthcoming with the takeover plans."[72]

Indeed, the Chinese had initially agreed to manage the Kaduna refinery as a precondition to winning oil blocks for which Chinese companies were bidding. However, "the arrangement which was tied to oil block allocation as a result of the peculiar nature of the refinery, which requires heavy investment, was being considered for review, as the Chinese firm had not shown appreciable interest."[73] "No appreciable progress had been made since the allocation took place," and the Chinese had not fulfilled their part of the deal, said the director general.[74] Such a situation of nonimplementation was particularly important for Nigeria, as Abuja is desperate to offload its former public enterprises to competent management.[75] That China was seen as a potential help in this regard seems to have—already—run foul. This is very much tied up with the personalized nature of Nigeria's neopatrimonial system of governance, where contracts can mean very little. In the run-up to Obasanjo finally retiring (after his aborted attempt at changing the constitution), much of the apparently "robust" Sino-Nigerian ties, as showcased by high-profile launches of various plans and agreements, started to unravel:

> When Obasanjo left office . . . nothing of [the plethora of] plans was yet visible on the ground, but the difficulties were increasingly obvious. The viability of the projects . . . was often uncertain. The agreements had no binding provisions regulating the relative timing of the oilfield and infrastructure developments . . . The infrastructural estimates were often inflated and the financial details opaque, disputed and burdensome to Nigeria. Suspicions proliferated of kickbacks to finance Obasanjo's political schemes and line his agents' pockets. The Asian firms realised that they had plunged into a political and business environment they did not understand.[76]

Although the NNPC and China State Construction Engineering Corporation (CSCEC) in May 2010 signed a $23 billion deal to jointly seek financing and credits from Chinese authorities and banks to build three refineries and a fuel complex in Nigeria, this announcement was met by suspicion that it was business as usual, no doubt informed by previous events under Obasanjo:

> The recent $23 billion loan for building three new refineries should concern most Nigerians. To build these refineries, Nigeria will create almost as much debt as the $30 billion that was eliminated during President Obasanjo's tenure in office . . . One thing we tend to be poor at is capacity building. Who will run four massive new plants? Us or the Chinese? If it is the Chinese, as is likely, how will technology transfer take place? . . . Many feel that the rush by politicians to sign these agreements and large loans was driven less by thoughtful consideration of Nigeria's needs than by their desire for the large commissions and bribes that are rumoured to have to accompanied them. In

the end, this arrangement could be hugely ruinous for Nigeria . . . Vast loans
are being taken out with abandon by reckless, greedy politicians who have
learned little from the past.[77]

The vagaries of Nigerian politics being as they are, property rights and
contracts may be annulled if political actors become involved and feel that
there are possibilities for accumulation or capture means that the security of
investments can be quite shaky. This is particularly so for new actors in the
country such as the Chinese, who do not enjoy the long-standing relationships that many Western actors possess in Nigeria. The Chinese government's clout in protecting Chinese interests in the country is also less ham-
pered both by a lack of expertise and experience, as well as a lingering desire
not to be seen to "interfere" in domestic matters.

CONCLUSION

Nigeria's politics have long been an open scramble for power in which elites
compete for control of the state in order to capture the mega benefits associated with the country's enormous oil revenues. This is the environment in
which foreign actors like China must navigate their Nigerian relations. But as
other actors have found, this environment is inherently unstable and dangerous, where long-term guarantees mean little. Massive profits may be accrued
quickly, but violence in the Niger Delta and the perpetual crisis within Nigeria's polity mean that the engagements China is pursuing in Nigeria will
always be highly vulnerable.

Any understanding of how Chinese interests play out in a country like
Nigeria has to begin from the perspective of Nigerian agency and an appreciation of the forces that act at any one time and in any given context. Indeed,
the main challenge for Chinese actors in Nigeria is in negotiating and confronting the various manifestations of agency and counteragency that develop out of the reality of Nigeria's political economy. This is something that no
amount of high-sounding rhetoric from Beijing about fraternal ties and mutual benefits can hide or escape.

At the same time, any benefits that Nigeria might generate from Chinese
investment depend on what Nigerians do for themselves far more than what
Beijing might do for Abuja. As noted by a 2009 report of the Economic
Commission for Africa:

> Nigeria's elite officials have made China's engagement a priority, but the
> strongest leadership has been observed on the Chinese side. African leaders
> have dictated to the Chinese which development projects they would like to
> undertake, but the absence of true leaders who are willing to stand up and
> articulate a long-term development strategy that adequately addresses the

needs of the majority of Nigerian citizens remains a key challenge. Nigeria's rampant corruption has also proven to be a serious cultural obstacle that must be overcome if Nigeria is to successfully leverage its demands vis-à-vis China.[78]

This quote captures the dynamics of agency and counteragency and the dialectic between the civil public realm and the private primordial. On the one hand, agency-as-corruption is accepted practice for those with connections to loot the state and craft profitable relationships under the rubric of prebendal public offices. This is manifested as corruption-as-agency in the distribution of such diverted resources through intricate clientelistic networks. Indeed, as Linus Marvelos Nnatuanya aptly notes, "It can be argued that most of the politicians currently holding various offices in Nigerian [*sic*] were not motivated by true patriotism to serve the nation rather they were driven by greed and the pathological urge to loot in order to enhance their parochial interests."[79] This one dialect is accepted by those within the system and is aspired to by those without; in Nigeria this constitutes recycled elites waiting in the wings for their turn. However, these relationships are exclusive and, as Wole Soyinka put it, discount the electorate.[80] Those discounted then construct strategies that express their own counteragency. In the context of Nigeria, where democratic space is foreclosed and nonviolent options are few and far between, this is then articulated through bodies such as MEND and Boko Haram. Hijacking the public sphere and treating one's illegal exploitation of the civic public as a right then results in the impoverishment of the bulk of the people by the few.

This situation outlined above creates a dialectic that engenders various expressions of agency, which Chinese actors must encounter. Though graft may be acceptable in order to strengthen the primordial public, if and when the primordial public is not the recipient of any largesse from such processes, counteragency strategies become essential. An intensely dislocating set of dynamics then develops into civic public-primordial encounters. The possibility for satisfactory results for those actors involved is then arbitrated by the exchange of expressions of agency between them. Those caught in the middle, as the case study of China in Nigeria demonstrates, find themselves in an uncomfortable and opaque terrain where outcomes may remain perennially undecided. This permanent crisis is, after all, the leitmotif of postindependence Nigeria.

NOTES

1. Jedrzej Frynas and Manuel Paulo , "A New Scramble for African Oil? Historical, Political, and Business Perspectives," *African Affairs* 106, no. 423 (2007).

2. Nkwelle Ekaney, "Scramble for Africa," *The Diplomat*, September 2012, 6.

3. "A Sub-Saharan Scramble," *The Economist*, January 24, 2015.

4. Frynas and Paulo, "A New Scramble for African Oil?" 235.

5. Ibid.

6. Ran Goel, "A Bargain Born of Paradox: The Oil Industry's Role in American Domestic and Foreign Policy," *New Political Economy* 9, no. 4 (2004): 482.

7. See Lucy Corkin's chapter in this volume.

8. Karl Marx, *The 18th Brumaire of Louis Bonaparte* (Moscow: Progress Publishers, 1976).

9. Anthony Giddens, *New Rules of Sociological Method: A Positive Critique of Interpretive Sociologies* (London: Hutchinson, 1976).

10. Emile Durkheim, *Suicide: A Study in Sociology* (London: Routledge, 2002), 37.

11. Louis Althusser, *Lenin and Philosophy and Other Essays* (New York: Monthly Review Press, 1971).

12. Michel Foucault, *Michel Foucault: The Essential Works, Power, Volume 3*, edited by Colin Gordon (London: Penguin, 2002).

13. Michel Foucault, *The History of Sexuality: The Will to Knowledge* (London: Penguin, 2008), 63.

14. Karl Marx and Frederick Engels, *The Holy Family or Critique of Critical Criticism* (London: Lawrence and Wishart, 1956), 125.

15. See Frederick Engels, *Ludwig Feuerbach and the End of Classical German Philosophy* (Honolulu, HI: University Press of the Pacific, 2005).

16. See Karl Marx, "Critique of Hegel's Philosophy in General," in *Economic and Philosophical Manuscripts of 1844* (Moscow: Progress Publishers, 1959).

17. Karl Marx, *Grundrisse: Foundations of the Critique of Political Economy* (London: Penguin, 1993).

18. William Sewell, "A Theory of Structure: Duality, Agency, and Transformation," *American Journal of Sociology* 98, no. 1 (1992).

19. "OPEC—Oil Reserve Remains Stagnant at 37 Billion Barrels," *Daily Trust* (Lagos), November 13, 2013.

20. Nigerian National Petroleum Corporation, " Development of Nigeria's Oil Industry," http://www.nnpcgroup.com.

21. Geoffrey York, "Boko Haram Insurgency Exposes Nigeria's Extreme Economic Inequality," *Globe and Mail* (Toronto), June 15, 2014.

22. Gbadebo Olusegun Odularu, "Crude Oil and the Nigerian Economic Performance," unpublished paper, 2008, 3.

23. *The Wealth Report* (London: Knight Frank, 2014), 54.

24. Austin Avuru, *Politics, Economics and the Nigerian Petroleum Industry* (Lagos: Festac Books, 2005).

25. Xavier Sala-i-Martin and Arvind Subramanian, "Addressing the Natural Resource Curse: An Illustration from Nigeria," *IMF Working Paper WP/03/159*, 2003.

26. Gregory White and Scott Taylor, "Well-Oiled Regimes: Oil and Uncertain Transitions in Algeria and Nigeria," *Review of African Political Economy* 28, no. 89 (2001), 333.

27. Peter Lewis, "From Prebendalism to Predation: The Political Economy of Decline in Nigeria," *Journal of Modern African Studies* 34, no. 1 (1996): 79–103; Karl Maier, *This House Has Fallen: Nigeria in Crisis* (London: Penguin, 2000).

28. Peter Cunliffe-Jones, *My Nigeria: Five Decades of Independence* (New York: Palgrave, 2010).

29. Agwuncha Nwankwo, *Nigeria: The Stolen Billions* (Enugu, Nigeria: Fourth Dimension, 2002).

30. Alexandra Gillies, "Obasanjo, the Donor Community and Reform Implementation in Nigeria," *Round Table* 96, no. 392 (2007): 576.

31. Ibrahim Muhammed, "The Double Yoke of Corruption and Ignorance," *Daily Trust* (Abuja), December 14, 2007.

32. Michael Bratton and Nichola van de Walle, *Democratic Experiments in Africa* (Cambridge: Cambridge University Press, 1997), 65.

33. Ayokunle Omobowale, "Disorder and Democratic Development: The Political Instrumentalization of Patronage and Violence in Nigeria," *African Journal of Political Science and International Relations* 5, no. 6 (2011).

34. See Michael Peel, *A Swamp Full of Dollars: Pipelines and Paramilitaries at Nigeria's Oil Frontier* (London: IB Tauris, 2009).

35. Sayre Schatz, "Pirate Capitalism and the Inert Economy of Nigeria," *Journal of Modern African Studies* 22 (1984).

36. Ibid.

37. Ibrahim Gambari, "From Balewa to Obasanjo: The Theory and Practice of Nigeria's Foreign Policy," in *Gulliver's Troubles: Nigeria's Foreign Policy After the Cold War*, edited by Adekeye Adebajo and Abdul Mustapha (Scottsville: University of KwaZulu-Natal Press, 2008), 61.

38. Ibid.

39. Okwudiba Nnoli, *Ethnic Politics in Nigeria* (Enugu: Fourth Dimension, 1980).

40. Richard A. Joseph, *Democracy and Prebendal Politics in Nigeria: The Rise and Fall of the Second Republic* (New York: Cambridge University Press, 1987).

41. Eghosa Osaghae, *Crippled Giant: Nigeria Since Independence* (London: Hurst and Company, 1998), 21.

42. Max Weber's rational-legal bureaucratic model defines corruption as the abuse (or misuse) of public power for private (or personal) benefit—see Max Weber, *Economy and Society* (Berkeley, CA: University of California Press, 1978). Jean-Pierre Olivier de Sardan's discussion of corruption in Africa is a valuable corrective to an uncritical assumption of essentially Western ideal types. See Jean-Pierre Olivier de Sardan, "A Moral Economy of Corruption in Africa?" *Journal of Modern African Studies* vol. 37, no. 1 (1999).

43. Christopher Clapham, *Third World Politics: An Introduction* (London: Croom Helm, 1985), 49.

44. Peter Ekeh, "Colonialism and the Two Publics in Africa: A Theoretical Statement," *Comparative Studies in Society and History* 17, no. 1 (1975): 91–112.

45. E. A. Ifidon, "Citizenship, Statehood and the Problem of Democratization in Nigeria," *Africa Development* 21, no. 4 (1996): 102.

46. Ekeh, "Colonialism and the Two Publics in Africa," 108.

47. These collective needs are (usually) communally based and serve to exacerbate societal fractures.

48. "Graft Fatigue," *The Guardian* (Lagos), October 6, 2009.

49. Daniel Smith, *A Culture of Corruption: Everyday Deception and Popular Discontent in Nigeria* (Princeton, NJ: Princeton University Press, 2007).

50. Ekeh, "Colonialism and the Two Publics in Africa," 110.

51. Nicolas Van de Walle, "Meet the New Boss: Same as the Old Boss?: The Evolution of Political Clientelism in Africa," in *Patrons, Clients and Policies: Patterns of Democratic Accountability and Political Competition*, edited byHerbert Kitschelt and Steven Wilkinson (Cambridge: Cambridge University Press, 2007).

52. Osumah Oarhe and Iro Aghedo, "The Open Sore of a Nation: Corruption Complex and Internal Security in Nigeria," *African Security* 3, no. 3 (2010): 130–31.

53. Michel Foucault, "Body/Power" and "Truth and Power" in *Michel Foucault: Power/Knowledge*, edited by C. Gordon (London: Harvester, 1980), 142.

54. Ilufoye Sarafa Ogundiya, "Political Corruption in Nigeria: Theoretical Perspectives and Some Explanations," *Anthropologist* 11, no. 4 (2009): 284.

55. See Ike Okonta, *When Citizens Revolt: Nigerian Elites, Big Oil and the Ogoni Struggle for Self-Determination* (Trenton, NJ: Africa World Press, 2008).

56. "Nigeria's Shadowy Oil Rebels," BBC News Online (London), April 20, 2006.

57. See Abimbola Adesoji, "The Boko Haram Uprising and Islamic Revivalism in Nigeria," *Africa Spectrum* 45, no. 2 (2010).

58. "Suspected Boko Haram Rebels Attack Chinese Plant in Cameroon," *Agence France-Presse* (Paris), May 29, 2014.

59. Patrick Renz, "Nigeria's Northern Territories: Untapped Oil and Gas Potential?" *Africa Monitor*, October 20, 2014.

60. Sulaimon Salau, "Nigeria's Oil Export Slides to 1.83 Million Barrels Per Day," *The Guardian* (Lagos), September 2, 2014.

61. John Iliffe, *Obasanjo: Nigeria and the World* (Oxford: James Currey, 2011), 275.

62. "China, Nigeria Sign Oil Development Agreement," *China Daily* (Beijing), December 9, 2004.

63. Michelle Chan-Fishel, "Environmental Impact: More of the Same?" *Pambazuka News*, December 14, 2006.

64. "Beijing-Abuja Export Credit Worth $500 Million," *The Vanguard*, April 27, 2006.

65. Mike Oduniyi, "Chinese Investors Offer $2bn for Nigerian Oil Field," *This Day*, January 9, 2006.

66. An OPL has a life span of five to ten years, while an OML covers twenty years and may be renewed at expiration. An OPL is converted to an OML if the operator has discovered or proved oil in commercial quantities, and is able to demonstrate that the OPL is capable of producing a minimum of ten thousand barrels per day of oil.

67. "NNPC Approves CNOOC's $ 2.3 bn Stake in Block OPL 246," *This Day* (Abuja), April 21, 2006.

68. Sam Quigley, "Chinese Oil Acquisitions in Nigeria and Angola," *Khamasin*, June 1, 2014.

69. Ibid.

70. Ibid.

71. Ibid.

72. "FG to Review Sale of Kaduna Refinery," *This Day* (Abuja), March 6, 2007.

73. Ibid.

74. Ibid.

75. This is because between 1975 and 1988 Nigeria spent billions in establishing and maintaining about 590 parastatals, of which 160 were involved in production and services. Yet the profit generated by these concerns was on average 0.5 percent, with 420,000 employees, many in basically corrupt sinecures. This milieu soaked up over half of Nigeria's oil revenues in the 1970s and accounted for over half of its international debt (ibid.).

76. Iliffe, *Obasanjo*, 276.

77. "The Usual Story," *Nigerian Inquirer* (Lagos), May 18, 2010.

78. Djeri-Wake Nabine, *The Impact of Chinese Investment and Trade on Nigeria's Economic Growth* (Addis Ababa: Economic Commission for Africa, 2009), 22.

79. Linus Marvelos Nnatuanya, *The Frozen Democracy: Godfatherism and Elite Corruption in Nigeria* (Enugu: Triumphant Creations, 2006), 60.

80. Wole Soyinka, "Discounting the Electorate," *West Africa Review* 5, 2004.

Chapter Three

China and the Shaping of African Information Societies

Iginio Gagliardone

On November 8, 2006, Chinese telecommunications giant ZTE Corporation and the Ethiopian Telecommunication Corporation signed the largest agreement in the history of African telecommunications. Backed by China Development Bank, ZTE offered a loan of $1.5 billion (to which ZTE added $0.4 billion for engineering) to overhaul and expand Ethiopia's telecommunication system. The loan, to be repaid in thirteen years, was disbursed in three phases. The first phase had a particularly symbolic value. Branded as the "Millennium Plan," it was expected to produce its results—the laying down of more than two thousands kilometers of fiber optic cable connecting Ethiopia's thirteen largest cities—by September 11, 2007, the day marking the beginning of the new millennium in the Ethiopian calendar. The second and third phases similarly focused on infrastructure development, expanding coverage to rural areas, and building the capacity of the system to support twenty million mobile users (from the initial 1.2 million), and more than a million Internet broadband users.

A little more than five years later, on January 12, 2012, the Chinese government launched CCTV Africa, the largest non-African TV initiative on the continent. Counting more than one hundred journalists, mostly African, spread across its headquarters in Nairobi and various reporting locations across the continent, CCTV Africa immediately became the only international television initiative to guarantee one hour of original reporting from Africa each day, with African and global audiences as its target. One year later, the network increased its reporting time to one-and-a-half hours, split into two tranches and featured globally on CCTV News.

These two initiatives are indicative of China's increasing, albeit uneven, significance for Africa's media and telecommunication sector. China has a long history of engagement with the continent, and since the 1950s it has sought different avenues of communication with African audiences: via radio broadcasts aimed at supporting socialist revolutions or the opening outposts of its news agency, Xinhua, to serve diplomatic functions in the absence of Chinese embassies.[1] More recently, in 2006, the Third Forum on China-Africa Cooperation (FOCAC) marked a new phase in China-Africa media relations. For the first time, media featured prominently in the Forum's Action Plan; packages of the kind that allowed Ethiopia to dramatically expand its telecommunications infrastructure have since then come to inform a new pillar of China-Africa cooperation, and China has become an increasingly important partner in the shaping of African information societies. The Chinese government and Chinese companies are engaged both in lying down the infrastructures on which these societies are built and in the production of their content and meaning.

Based on fieldwork conducted in Ethiopia, Kenya, and Ghana between 2010 and 2013, this chapter examines both components of this new relationship—their connections and contradictions. In each country, semistructured interviews were conducted with ministers and cadres in ministries of communication and/or information technology; civil society organizations (local and international NGOs promoting freedom of expression and media development); and the private sector (employees of major telecommunication companies). In Kenya and Ethiopia, representatives of Chinese telecommunication and IT companies, as well as Chinese journalists working for Xinhua News Agency, China's Central Television (CCTV), and the *People's Daily Africa* edition were also interviewed. For countries other than Ghana, Kenya, and Ethiopia, secondary data was collected to build a continental perspective of China's role in the media and telecommunication sector, and how this role is leveraged by various African governments to advance their respective social and political agendas.

WHOSE AGENCY MATTERS IN BUILDING AFRICA'S INFORMATION SOCIETIES?

The increasingly abundant literature on China-Africa cooperation has started to reveal some key features that characterize China as a development actor: from disbursing resources outside the channels of officially recognized aid, to its emphasis, still, on a "no-strings attached" approach.[2] Initiatives in the media and telecommunications sector are no exception to these observed norms, but rather build upon them; China's engagement in the African media and telecommunications sectors runs parallel to other areas of Chinese cooperation. Yet the ways in which China's government has disciplined its own domestic media and constrained the domestic freedom of expression has raised new questions about the consequences of China's growing role in African communication, and about whether and how China may export some aspects of its own media system to the continent.

Critics have suggested that China may be "reshap[ing] much of the world's media in its own image" and "promoting an anti-Western media model."[3] Others have alleged that Chinese telecommunications giants Huawei—which is a private company, but whose founder served as an engineer in China's People's Liberation Army (PLA)—and ZTE—which is partially state owned—may be hiding "backdoors" in their equipment that allow Beijing to spy on users, including African citizens, or to shield its own spying efforts elsewhere.[4] Recent leaks from former US National Security Agency (NSA) contractor Edward Snowden add an interesting twist to such accusations: they reveal that the NSA itself has tried to install backdoors in Huawei's networks. As Thomas Rid notes, "There is now more publicly available evidence that the [United States'] NSA exploited Huawei than there is public evidence that shows the PLA or other Chinese agencies did so."[5] The commonly accepted global practice of singling China out to denounce problematic practices that are shared by a wider variety of actors[6] may prove particularly risky in the communication sector, and may obfuscate the actual repercussions of China's engagement for African information societies.

Rather than taking sides in this ongoing debate, this chapter explains how China's presence in the media and telecommunication sector in Africa displays characteristics of the "flexigemony" described by Pádraig Carmody and Ian Taylor in their analysis of Chinese engagement in Sudan and Zambia. "Chinese actors adapt their strategies to suit the particular histories and geographies of the African states with which they engage," argue Carmody and Taylor. "[They] must negotiate resource access through cooperation with African state elites."[7] This chapter's comparison between Chinese support for information infrastructure construction in Ethiopia and Kenya shows that China has indeed adapted to the policy environments and the power dynamics distinctive of each state—sometimes to its own (immediate) disadvantage.

Acknowledging this flexibility, however, should not distract from an appreciation of how China concurrently seeks to acquire influence in the continent, possibly in subtler, but no less effective, ways. While the survey of Chinese interventions in Africa's media and telecommunication sector is necessarily incomplete as the interactions are still nascent, it nevertheless points to two important tendencies. First, while China employs a variety of financial resources to support projects in African media and telecommunications sectors,[8] the largest share of resources tends to go to initiatives developed by government actors reflecting China's interest in developing strong institutional ties with its African counterparts. Chinese aid of African state projects offers greater space for African state agency to find expression in ways that are less constrained by conditionalities and template approaches. At the same time, this support and its potential consequences should be understood in relation to the mechanisms that lead to the creation of functioning information societies, which emerge from the negotiation between governments and a variety of other actors in the private sector, the civil society, and the media. While other donors have in most cases taken this plurality into account and have promoted issue-based agendas (e.g., better governance), China's preference for government actors may risk skewing the balance of power in the long run.

Second, while the Chinese government has repeatedly declared there is no such thing as a "China model" and has denied any intentions of exporting the strategies that it adopted to develop its own domestic sector, this has not prevented some of these strategies from gaining traction in Africa. As the Ethiopian case indicates, governments that struggle to maintain control of their information spaces while at the same time expanding access look with interest at the measures adopted by the Chinese state. While China may purport to be inactive in promoting any one development strategy over any other, African governments are active in picking and choosing those that suit their own political and economic ends. The next two sections offer concrete examples of these two tendencies and elaborate on some of their possible consequences.

THE BUILDING OF AFRICA'S INFORMATION INFRASTRUCTURE

The largest share of Chinese resources in the media and telecommunication sector has been channeled toward supporting Africa's information infrastructures. Similar to what has been the case with roads and railways, in many African countries China has emerged as one of the most important actors in ensuring connectivity—also in the digital realm. The significance of its contribution to the development of African terrestrial and mobile information infrastructures, however, varies widely from country to country. So far, China has displayed an impressive ability to fit in and adapt to preexisting markets and regulatory environments.

To date, Ethiopia is the African country that has benefited the most from a partnership with China in the telecommunications sector. The 2006 ZTE deal is indeed the largest agreement in African telecommunications history. Most of its resources were channeled to expand telecommunication infrastructure; to expand coverage to rural areas; and to build up the capacity of the system to support twenty million mobile users and more than a million Internet broadband users.[9] Some of the funding also went toward the upgrade of

WoredaNet and Schoolnet, two large-scale systems that have been instrumental in the Ethiopian government's realization of its state- and nation-building project. WoredaNet, which stands for a "network of district (woreda) administrations," uses the same protocol upon which the Internet is based, but rather than allowing individuals to independently seek information and express their opinion, it enables ministers and cadres in Addis Ababa to videoconference with regional and woreda offices and instruct them on what they should be doing and how. Schoolnet uses a similar architecture to broadcast prerecorded classes in a variety of subjects, ranging from mathematics to civics, to all secondary schools in the country. Schoolnet also provides "political education" to schoolteachers throughout the country, and to other government officials outside of Addis.

WoredaNet and Schoolnet are unique as far as government outreach programs go: they represent a concrete instantiation of the concept of "revolutionary democracy" discussed by Aleksandra Gadzala in this volume. As the guiding ideology of the Ethiopian government and the leading Ethiopian People's Revolutionary Democratic Front (EPRDF), revolutionary democracy rejects the emphasis on individual rights and liberties characteristic of liberal democracies, choosing instead to emphasize group rights and consensus. Revolutionary democracy favors a populist discourse, believing that only through such a discourse can there be a direct connection between the leadership and the masses; it bypasses notions of negotiations with other elites who advance competing ideas of the nation-state and the role assumed by differing groups within it.[10] Both WoredaNet and Schoolnet have as their aims improved service delivery and improved standards of living, especially in Ethiopia's rural communities. Yet by opening new communication channels between the vanguard and the grassroots, they also quite obviously play to government efforts to increase its presence on the ground.

On a practical level, WoredaNet is intended to build the capacity of the peripheral nodes of the state by training and instructing individuals—"messengers"—some of whom have little formal education, to enable them to provide better services. This is intended to benefit the whole of Ethiopian society, but at the same time clearly emphasizes the commitment of the government to Ethiopia's rural populations. Local officials are expected to reflect the principles of the EPRDF's state-building project through their actions, and to become the disseminators of government strategy. As one woreda official explained: "This time it is possible that even the people at the grassroots level can receive the same information, they can receive the very voice of the Prime Minister. We have been using the system mostly for videoconferencing. It helps a lot to understand what the line of the government is, but also to learn new practices."[11] Conveying a unified message is intended to unite the entire country around similar principles—Ethiopia's ethnic diversity notwithstanding. Through WoredaNet, EPRDF leaders at the center can reach the grassroots in a mediated way by turning the members of the state apparatus in the peripheries into messengers of ideas and policies formulated in the capital.

As a complement to WoredaNet, Schoolnet is designed to reach targets in the peripheries in a more direct way. Its main objective is to enable students living in Ethiopia's remote countryside to have access to the same quality of education as those in major towns and cities. The goal is for students in remote areas to no longer have to rely on poorly trained teachers for their education, as has often been the case. Schoolnet is a powerful symbol of the EPRDF's commitment to guarantee every citizen equal opportunities; it is furthermore crucial in addressing the urban-rural education divide. At the same time, it is advantageous for the government to have all students exposed to the same programming. It facilitates their training in the founding principles of the state and of the ideals of "revolutionary democracy," which all Ethiopian citizens are to uphold. Perhaps not surprisingly, civic and ethical education was among the first subjects to be included in the Schoolnet program.

While both systems were designed and operational before Chinese government support found its way to the country, both nevertheless benefited from the 2006 ZTE agreement. Many nodes of WoredaNet, for example, have started to rely on fiber optic laid down by ZTE rather than on more expensive and less reliable satellite communication on which it had been previously reliant.

Beyond WoredaNet and Schoolnet, China's support of the Ethiopian media and telecommunications sectors have allowed the Ethiopian government to achieve goals that no other African country has so far been able to achieve, dramatically expanding access in a regime of monopoly. Elsewhere in Africa, market liberalization has been the key driver behind the expansion of telecommunications coverage and declining costs. Countries that have opted for a system tightly controlled by the state, such as neighboring Eritrea, have severely lagged behind in the development of information infrastructure and services.[12] By providing capital, equipment, and expertise, ZTE—and more recently other Chinese telecommunications firms—has not only brought the Ethiopian government out of the cul-de-sac in which it had put itself by stubbornly defending its monopoly, but has also—either unknowingly or indifferently—helped it to realize its vision of a tightly controlled but developmentally oriented national information society.

As Amare Anslau, CEO of the Ethiopian Telecommunication Corporation at the time the ZTE project took shape, remarked in a June 2008 interview: "Holding telecommunications is not just about security. We need this instrument for development. We need it for the people. Ethiopia is not like any other African country. Those countries just think that they can become rich, the individual can become rich. But what we want is instead building in the mind of people the attachment to their land and to their country. Once you have technology you become addicted to it. So, if you allow the private they can certainly make money. But what about the society? The society will not benefit from it. So the government is the one that has to make sure that things are done in the interest of the people [. . .] You have to hold all keys in your hands otherwise change, real change, will be impossible."[13]

Five years later, on June 7, 2011, the now rebranded Ethio-Telecom issued a tender to further boost the capacity of Ethiopia's mobile phone network to fifty million subscribers by 2015, and to introduce 4G connectivity—a mobile broadband technology that allows browsing speeds of up to 100 Mbit per second. Like the 2006 agreement, the tender was similarly based on a vendor-financing scheme. Yet unlike the 2006 agreement, the tender was public with various companies competing. The EPRDF had come under heavy scrutiny for its mishandling of the 2006 agreement: critics suggested that its commitment to purchasing all equipment from a single supplier exposed Ethio-Telecom (then ETC) to the risk of overpaying for what it was getting.[14] Reports like that in the *Wall Street Journal* similarly warned that the poor service could ultimately harm the ability of Ethio-Telecom to generate revenues and repay its debts.[15] By 2011, too, the EPRDF was looking for the best deal that would allow it to continue its project of expanded telecommunication services under tight government control. As the *Wall Street Journal* stated, however, "again, financing won the day, with the two [ZTE and Huawei] pledging a total of $1.6 billion. Western equipment suppliers, such as Ericsson and Alcatel Lucent SA, couldn't match the Chinese offer."[16] With the signing of two separate contracts of $800 million each with Huawei and ZTE, competition between ZTE and Huawei was introduced in the Ethiopian market. The two companies have for many years been contending for shares of the Chinese market; domestic Chinese competition seems to have been transported overseas. A representative of Huawei in Ethiopia suggests, "It is normal that Huawei and ZTE compete for resources. ZTE in Ethiopia did not do a good job. It did not have enough incentives. So the government asked Huawei to come, because we have a better reputation in Africa."[17]

Contrary to popular perceptions of a unified Chinese front in Africa, Chinese companies are often competitors more than they are partners in their African ventures. Often, like in Ethiopia, governments spur this competition: pitting Chinese competitors against one another has proven to be a successful strategy for African leaders to advance their own objectives.

Taken together, China's 2006 and 2011 Ethiopian telecommunications deals surpass $3 billion. Both are indicative of the different approaches taken by the Chinese government and Chinese telecoms to enter the increasingly crowded African ICT markets, and to acquire greater influence. China is aggressive when providing financial resources to governments that are struggling to expand ICT infrastructure and services, and it relies on state-owned banks (China Development Bank and the Export-Import Bank of China) to offer export credit to Chinese companies willing to expand their operations abroad. Despite this increasingly outward exposure, however, the Chinese government continues to avoid public assertions of its willingness to export its own development strategies overseas, or to suggest that these strategies are in some way superior to those advanced by Western donors or partners. The lack of proactivity on the side of China, however, has not prevented these strategies from gaining appeal among African partners. A Wikileaks cable documenting a meeting between Sebhat Nega, a founder of the Tigray People's Liberation Front—the leading faction within the EPRDF coalition—and among the most influential ideologues within the Ethiopian government, and the US ambassador Donald Yamamoto, documents Sebhat openly declaring his admiration for China, and stressed that Ethiopia "needs the China model to inform the Ethiopian people."

In neighboring Kenya, where the market is more liberalized and competitive, China has played a different role while still maintaining some similarities with the approach it has adopted in Ethiopia. As in Ethiopia, China has been deeply involved in the extension of Internet connectivity. Huawei and ZTE, together with the French company Sagem, have been participants in Kenya's first National Optic Fibre Backbone Infrastructure (NOFBI) expansion, bringing fiber optic infrastructure to the main urban centers and allowing a first series of e-government projects to be delivered regionally.[18] Under the terms of the project, the country was divided into three sections, each handled by a different company: Sagem laid out cables in the coast and northeastern areas, Huawei in Nairobi and the central area, and ZTE in western Kenya. A second round of NOFBI (known as NOFBI II) was directly funded with Chinese resources: in 2012, China's ExIm Bank provided a $71 million loan to support further extension to thirty-six administrative district centers across the country, with the objective of allowing people in remote areas to access faster Internet. A key condition on the loan was that Huawei had to be the implementing company. At the time of writing, Huawei is in charge of the project's realization.[19]

As in Ethiopia, the Chinese government and Chinese companies in Kenya support the expansion of government-led initiatives that aim to extend Internet connectivity and improve e-government services. In the Kenyan case, however, Chinese support fits into a context characterized by competition among a plurality of actors that seek to offer better services at lower prices. For example, soon after signing the agreement for NOFBI II, Kenya's leading telecom operator, Safaricom, decided to invest an additional $95 million to build 2,400 more kilometers of fiber optic cable to support its growing customer base. Interestingly, a large share of the contract has been assigned on a commercial basis to Huawei, which had already worked in collaboration with Safaricom to roll out the 4G network at a cost of $143 million. A remaining share of Safaricom's expansion project was assigned to Ericsson.[20] As Bitange Ndemo, permanent secretary of Kenya's Ministry of Information and Communication during Kibaki's second term, remarked: "China is not bringing an ideology, but with its support it is winning hearts and minds. But we are a free market economy and that won't change. The Chinese understood and have adapted to it."[21]

Beyond Ethiopia and Kenya, China has been instrumental in supporting numerous other projects in the African telecommunications sector, helping either state or private operators to develop infrastructure and provide value-added services. In Guinea, ExIm Bank loans have supported the state-owned Societé des Telecoms de Guinée (SOTELGUI) expand its fiber optic infrastructure.[22] In Nigeria, ExIm Bank offered Nigeria a $100 million loan for the development of its Galaxy Backbone ICT network, to boost "the sophistication and effectiveness of the government's efforts to tackle security challenges."[23] In 2010, ExIm Bank supported e-government projects in Ghana with two concessionary loans, worth $30 million and $150 million, respectively.[24] In Tanzania, Chinese concessionary loans have funded the construction of the National ICT Broad Infrastructure Project.[25]

China is not unique in its support of African ICT infrastructure. What is unique, however, is that its ability to act as a very large lender has progressively set it apart from other development actors. China today has become an essential partner in the development of telecommunications connectivity across significant portions of the continent. The implications of its role are still difficult to assess at these early stages, but some tendencies have begun to emerge.

CONTENT CREATION OR PUBLIC DIPLOMACY?

Another important area where China has made inroads into Africa is in the expansion of its own media, including CCTV, Xinhua, and China Radio International. Initiatives like these are usually comprised under the rubric of "public diplomacy" that suggests a government's efforts to communicate with, and possibly influence, foreign audiences. Chinese journalists and diplomats, however, have often sought to advance a different narrative, suggesting that China is opening media outposts in Africa to help the continent tell a more positive story of its history and development, and to produce content that more closely represents African interests.

At a seminar on China-Africa media cooperation in 2013, China's ambassador to Kenya, Liu Guangyuan, for example, lamented that it had become "unacceptable to continue to portray Africa as a continent overtaken by poverty, war and turmoil. It is also unethical to force a bad image on China-

Africa relations. Indeed, China and Africa should flatly refuse to be part of this insincere scheme. [. . .] [M]ore and more Chinese media groups are setting camp in Africa. They have gradually changed the rules of the game and created a regime in which Africa is positively presented to the world. I call this 'the Chinese perspective.' [. . .] [O]ur media should report China-Africa friendship positively. [. . .] It is normal for others to both admire and be suspicious about the current China-Africa relations. But this must not be in the case among the Chinese and African media players."[26]

When CCTV Africa—the news production center created in Nairobi by state-owned international broadcaster China Central Television (CCTV)—launched on January 12, 2012, it became the largest non-African TV initiative in Africa. In being the largest, however, it was not the first; CCTV Africa is another in a long line of Chinese media initiatives on the continent. In Kenya, China Radio International (CRI) had launched its own local FM stations in three East African cities, broadcasting in English, Mandarin, and Swahili; it additionally has AM channel coverage across the country.[27] Chinese state news agency Xinhua, whose presence in Africa dates back to the 1950s, also significantly expanded its scope and reach in Africa in the 2000s and 2010s, and its news stories have begun to appear regularly in national newspapers.[28] In 2012, the same year that CCTV Africa started operating, the state-controlled English-language newspaper *China Daily* launched its *Africa Weekly* edition, the "first English language newspaper published in Africa by a Chinese media enterprise."[29]

Agencies like Xinhua tend to be seen as closer to the Chinese state interest,[30] while CCTV Africa is generally more innovative.[31] Nevertheless, some common traits are apparent across most Chinese outlets. Chinese media actors insist on a conception of the media that positions them at the center of a country's efforts to build the state and the nation, and to guarantee better development prospects. This idea has also been expressed by African journalists working in the Chinese media. As Douglas Okwatch, an experienced Kenyan producer working for CCTV Africa, explained: "A lot of debate has been going on in this country about watchdog journalism. In the 1980s and 1990s during the transition period we required a more aggressive style of journalism, we required watchdog media and we were working to produce change. This change came more slowly than we expected but it eventually came. The media freedom is there now. And now the question is different. Now the question is about the use that we can make of the space that we created. Now it is not the time for fighting as much as before. Now we have to play a better role in promoting growth in our countries, in promoting development."[32]

In principle, CCTV Africa is not only creating a new platform for more African journalists to speak to African and global audiences, but is also offering the opportunity to articulate and experiment with a conception of journalism that is distinctive from what has been advanced by mainstream international networks, including CNN and BBC. In practice, however, this conception seems to have struggled to find a concrete application in everyday reporting. As the few analyses of the content broadcast by CCTV Africa—mostly through Okwatch's news program *Africa Live*—indicate, the Chinese channel does not dramatically distinguish itself from other international broadcasters in terms of reporting conflicts and crises.[33] CCTV may offer a different spin on certain news, be more critical of Western initiatives and interests, but it still struggles to find a narrative that is at the same time appealing and different from the aggressive styles of journalism championed by channels such as Al Jazeera, which have become increasingly popular among African audiences.[34]

CONCLUSION

The analysis of Chinese support to media and telecommunications in Africa indicates that China has largely adapted to the requests of its local partners, rather than supporting template approaches, offering greater space for maneuver to state actors trying to fend off Western conditionalities, and to put forward their own agenda. African state agency, rather than the exportation of a difficult-to-identify Chinese model, seems to be the driver behind most initiatives, especially when it comes to building national information infrastructures.

The tendency to privilege relationships with incumbent governments across its various lines of support, however, poses questions as to whose agency China is supporting in Africa. Functioning media systems are built through the contribution of a variety of actors, including the private sector, grassroots organizations, and the state. By reinforcing the ability of the latter rather than the former to shape the evolution of national information societies, China is indirectly supporting a vision that is skewed toward the state. While the interest in building functioning and capable states is not exclusive to China, this tendency can potentially lead to harmful consequences. China's support to incumbents, for example, and to a vision in which the state is seen as the prime mover, may lead to deepening divisions between "Western powers" and civil society organizations on one side—no doubt framed by various African governments as advancing foreign agendas that may harm a country's sovereignty—and government actors supported by China in their path toward development on the other. While this dichotomy is of course a result of a selective reading of the national and international politics of development, it has already started to gain ground in countries like Ethiopia, as exemplified by the imprisonment of bloggers accused of using social media to incite unrest in collaboration with "foreign human right activist organizations."[35]

Another important question that emerges from this selective examination of Chinese projects in African media and telecommunication sectors is whether the insistence on a "no-strings-attached" policy may in some instances leave both China and its African partners worse off. Support for the expansion of access in a regime of monopoly in Ethiopia, as required by the Ethiopian government's revolutionary democratic ideals but against China's own experience in expanding its telecommunication system, for example, has led to the creation of a poorly functioning system and little Ethiopian government incentive to improve it.

In its own path toward development, China has demonstrated a remarkable ability to localize foreign technologies and use aid and foreign direct investment to strengthen its domestic market and industries.[36] The insistence on a no-strings-attached approach and the tendency to privilege turnkey projects, however, has created few opportunities for knowledge transfer and for some of the strategies that China has progressively developed, often through trial and error, to be transferred to its African partners. This determination goes so far that Chinese support for the expansion of access to mobile phones and Internet under monopoly in Ethiopia goes against the very experience China acquired in expanding its own telecommunications system.

China's transition from a socialist regime that emphasized monopoly to an increasingly liberalized market, under internal and external pressures to reform—the latter particularly tied to the process of accession to the World Trade Organization—could have offered important lessons for Ethiopia. China's path toward liberalization was initially marred by failed attempts to open up, and by power struggles between different ministries. Eventually, however, it led to the creation of the largest market of mobile and Internet users in the world.[37] The Chinese government began this process by first allowing limited forms of competition among companies still closely tied to central power, and then progressively opening to foreign direct investments. Rather than shaking the market with a sector reform that would have potentially led to uncontrollable transformations, smaller changes were introduced, tested, and in some cases reversed.[38] This sequence of trial and error is far from a textbook approach to liberalization, but could have offered an important base from which to develop targeted measures for opening up the Ethiopian telecommunications system, which is similarly characterized by a socialist emphasis on monopoly and resistance to the kinds of changes to which a sudden liberalization might lead. This point was even recognized by Chinese experts working in Ethiopia's telecommunication sector. As a representative of Huawei remarked: "Ethiopia should open up and allow more competition in the market if it wants to achieve its goals. Ethio-Telecom, because of its poor standing, is too afraid that if anybody comes in the market all customers will go to the new company and Ethio-Telecom will not survive . . . Working with governments that are too centralized is frustrating because they slow things down a lot, as there is not urgency in responding to their competitors."[39] Huawei has even gone so far as to publicly express its frustration over the slow pace at which the Ethiopian government makes decisions.[40] This, however, has not translated into policy advice or attempts to challenge the Ethiopian way of doing things.

The persistently poor quality of Ethiopian telecommunications has affected the reputation of Ethio-Telecom, as well as that of ZTE and Huawei. Even the tightly controlled official Ethiopian government media, including *Addis Zemen* and *The Ethiopian Herald*, have been allowed to criticize technical glitches and management incompetence.[41] The Ethiopian case diverges from the Kenyan example in which the government's liberalized market policies have led to significant advancements in media and technology. While engagement of Chinese telecommunications firms and media outlets in both countries are in many ways similar, their disparity is a product of the approaches and policies of both governments, respectively, and of China's so far demonstrated ability to work in, and adapt, to both.

NOTES

This chapter is based on a previous article that appeared in the Winter/Autumn issue of the *Global Media Journal* in 2014.

1. Emmanuel Hevi, *The Dragon's Embrace: The Chinese Communists and Africa* (London: Pall Mall Press, 1967); David H. Shinn and Joshua Eisenman, *China and Africa: A Century of Engagement* (Philadelphia: University of Pennsylvania Press, 2012).

2. Deborah Bräutigam, "Aid 'With Chinese Characteristics': Chinese Foreign Aid and Development Finance Meet the OECD-DAC Aid Regime," *Journal of International Development* 23, no. 5 (2011): 752–64; May Tan-Mullins, Giles Mohan, and Marcus Power, "Redefining 'Aid' in the China–Africa Context," *Development and Change* 41, no. 5 (2010): 857–81; Giles Mohan, "Beyond the Enclave: Towards a Critical Political Economy of China and Africa," *Development and Change* 44, no. 6 (2013): 1255–72; Howard W. French, "China and Africa," *African Affairs* 106, no. 422 (2006): 127–32.

3. Douglas Farah and Andy Mosher, "Winds From the East: How the People's Republic of China Seeks to Influence the Media in Africa, Latin America, and Southeast Asia," Center for International Media Assistance, 2010, 4.

4. Emil Protalinski, "Former Pentagon Analyst: China Has Backdoors to 80% of Telecoms," *ZDNet*, July 14, 2012, http://www.zdnet.com/former-pentagon-analyst-china-has-backdoors-to-80-of-telecoms-7000000908/.

5. Thomas Rid, "Snowden, 多谢 多谢 | Kings of War," 2014, http://kingsofwar.org.uk/2014/03/snowden-thanks-very-much/.

6. Yan Hairong and Barry Sautman, "'The Beginning of a World Empire?' Contesting the Discourse of Chinese Copper Mining in Zambia," *Modern China* 39, no. 2 (2013): 131–64.

7. Pádraig Carmody and Ian Taylor, "Flexigemony and Force in China's Resource Diplomacy in Africa: Sudan and Zambia Compared," *Geopolitics* 15, no. 3 (2010): 497.

8. Iginio Gagliardone, "Media Development with Chinese Characteristics," *Global Media Journal* 4, no. 2 (2015): 1–16.

9. See Gadzala, in this volume.

10. Tobias Hagmann and Jon Abbink, "Twenty Years of Revolutionary Democratic Ethiopia, 1991 to 2011," *Journal of Eastern African Studies* 5, no. 4 (2011): 579–95, doi:10.1080/17531055.2011.642515.

11. Interview, civil servant, Awasa, Ethiopia, April 27, 2008.

12. Iginio Gagliardone and Nicole Stremlau, *Digital Media, Conflict and Diasporas in the Horn of Africa* (Open Society Foundations, 2011), http://www.alnap.org/pool/files/sf-media-report-handbook-digital-media-conflict-and-diaspora-in-the-horn-of-africa-02-20-2012-final-web.pdf.

13. Interview: Amare Anslau, CEO, Ethiopian Telecommunication Corporation, Addis Ababa, June 27, 2008.

14. Janelle Plummer, *Diagnosing Corruption in Ethiopia: Perceptions, Realities, and the Way Forward for Key Sectors* (Washington: World Bank, 2012), http://econ.worldbank.org/external/default/main?pagePK=64165259&theSitePK=469372&piPK=64165421&menuPK=64166093&entityID=000386194_20120615035122.

15. Matthew Dalton, "Telecom Deal by China's ZTE, Huawei in Ethiopia Faces Criticism," *Wall Street Journal*, January 7, 2014, sec. World, http://online.wsj.com/news/articles/SB10001424052702303653004579212092223818288.

16. Dalton, "Telecom Deal by China's ZTE, Huawei in Ethiopia Faces Criticism."

17. Interview: Representative of Huawei in Ethiopia, Addis Ababa, May 9, 2013.

18. Okuttah Mark, "Safaricom Loosens China's Grip on Local Contracts with Sh14bn Tender," *Business Daily*, December 6, 2012, http://www.businessdailyafrica.com/Corporate-News/Safaricom-loosens-China-grip-on-local-contracts/-/539550/1638364/-/11xotu6z/-/index.html.

19. Margaret Wahito, "Kenya: China to Fund Kenya's Fibre Optic Project," *Capital FM*, June 28, 2012, http://allafrica.com/stories/201206290024.html.

20. Okuttah, "Safaricom Loosens China's Grip on Local Contracts with Sh14bn Tender."

21. Interview: Bitange Ndemo, permanent secretary of Kenya's Ministry of Information and Communication 2008–2013, Nairobi, May 2, 2013.

22. TeleGeography, "Huawei Bags Guinean Backbone Contract, Sotelgui Rescue Plans Ongoing," 2013, https://www.telegeography.com/products/commsupdate/articles/2013/01/03/huawei-bags-guinean-backbone-contract-sotelgui-rescue-plans-ongoing/.

23. Francis Ndubuisi, "FG, China Exim Bank Seal $600m Deal on Abuja Light Rail, Galaxy Backbone," *This Day Live*, September 13, 2012, http://www.thisdaylive.com/articles/ fg-china-exim-bank-seal-600m-deal-on-abuja-light-railgalaxy- backbone/124857.

24. Iginio Gagliardone, Nicole Stremlau, and Daniel Nkrumah, "Partner, Prototype or Persuader? China's Renewed Media Engagement with Ghana," *Communication, Politics & Culture* 45, no. 2 (2012), http://mams.rmit.edu.au/xbo3w37se3t8z.pdf.

25. Pius Rugonzibwa, "Tanzania: China Aid to Boost National Budget," *Tanzania Daily News*, March 27, 2013, http://allafrica.com/stories/201303270063.html.

26. Guangyuan Liu, "China out to Correct 'Distorted' Sino-Africa Perception," 2013.

27. Yu-Shan Wu, *The Rise of China's State-Led Media Dynasty in Africa* (South African Institute of International Affairs, 2012).

28. Xin Xin, "Xinhua News Agency in Africa," *Journal of African Media Studies* 1, no. 3 (2009): 363–77.

29. *China Daily*, "*China Daily* Launches Africa Weekly Edition," *China Daily*, December 14, 2012, http://www.chinadaily.com.cn/china/2012-12/14/content_16016334.htm.

30. Yuezhi Zhao, "The State, the Market, and Media Control in China," *Who Owns the Media*, 2004, 179–212.

31. Iginio Gagliardone, "China as a Persuader: CCTV Africa's First Steps in the African Mediasphere," *Ecquid Novi: African Journalism Studies* 34, no. 3 (2013).

32. Interview: Douglas Okwatch, senior producer, *Talk Africa*, CCTV Africa, September 12, 2012.

33. Vivien Marsh, "Chinese State Television's 'Going Out' Strategy—a True Global News Contraflow? A Comparison of News on CCTV's *Africa Live* and BBC World News TV's Focus on Africa," in *Conference: China's Soft Power in Africa: Emerging Media and Cultural Relations between China and Africa* (Nottingham University's Ningbo campus, China, 2014);

Xiaoling Zhang, *How Ready Is China for a China-Style World Order? China's State Media Discourse under Construction* (University of Nottingham: China Policy Institute, 2013).

34. Geoffrey York, "Why China Is Making a Big Play to Control Africa's Media," *The Globe and Mail*, September 11, 2013, http://www.theglobeandmail.com/news/world/media-agenda-china-buys-newsrooms-influence-in-africa/article14269323/; Zhang, *How Ready Is China for a China-Style World Order?*

35. Aaron Maasho, "Ethiopia Charges Nine Bloggers, Journalists with Inciting Violence," *Reuters*, April 28, 2014, http://www.reuters.com/article/2014/04/28/us-ethiopia-politics-idUS-BREA3R0YC20140428.

36. Xiaolan Fu, Carlo Pietrobelli, and Luc Soete, "The Role of Foreign Technology and Indigenous Innovation in the Emerging Economies: Technological Change and Catching-Up," *World Development* 39, no. 7 (2011): 1204–12; Xiaolan Fu, "Foreign Direct Investment, Absorptive Capacity and Regional Innovation Capabilities: Evidence from China," *Oxford Development Studies* 36, no. 1 (2008): 89–110.

37. Ping Gao and Kalle Lyytinen, "Transformation of China's Telecommunications Sector: A Macro Perspective," *Telecommunications Policy* 24, no. 8 (2000): 719–30; Milton Mueller, *China in the Information Age: Telecommunications and the Dilemmas of Reform* (New York: Greenwood Publishing Group, 1997), 169; Bing Zhang, "Understanding China's Telecommunications Policymaking and Reforms: A Tale of Transition toward Liberalization," *Telematics and Informatics* 19, no. 4 (2002): 331–49.

38. China Unicom, the first company to enter in competition with former monopolist China Telecom, was created under a strategy defined as CCF (China-China-Foreign) by which a foreign partner of a venture invested in a joint venture, which, in turn, invested in China Unicom. As Zhang remarks, "This financing mechanism aimed to bypass the prohibition of foreign investments in telecommunications services and resolve the financing problem at the same time." After this practice was allowed for five years, it was later sanctioned as "irregular" by the newly created Ministry of Information, and foreign investors had to draw back their investments" (343).

39. Interview: Representative of Huawei in Ethiopia, Addis Ababa, May 9, 2013.

40. Dalton, "Telecom Deal by China's ZTE, Huawei in Ethiopia Faces Criticism."

41. See, for example, Aregu Balleh in this undated article from *The Ethiopian Herald*: www.ethpress.gov.et/herald/index.php/herald/development/4160-a-worthwhile-move-to-comfort-rather-jaded-subscribers.

Chapter Four

Understanding Angolan Agency: The Luanda-Beijing Face-Off

Lucy Corkin

This chapter examines the origins of agency in the Angolan context, tracing its manifestation since the country's independence, and exploring the relationship between sovereignty and legitimacy. It shows how the Angolan government and its elites have manipulated the balance of power in their relations with China, both in the limiting of Chinese influence in a domestic context and leveraging the relationship with China to accrue benefits in the international, regional, and domestic spheres. As Michael Handel[1] notes, the misreading of power is at the root of politics: an assumed passivity or underestimation of Angola on the part of China has allowed the smaller country to manipulate the relatively more powerful country's strength. Unlike in many other African countries, Angola's political elite has carved out considerable policy space through its management of its relationship with China.

The proactive stance assumed by Angolan elites is visible most clearly in the way in which Luanda has limited Chinese government influence on the Angolan economy relative to the size of the extended credit lines. The credit lines have also been used to strengthen the incumbents' hold on political power. Indeed, the Angolan government has effectively adapted its strategy of extraversion to take into account shifting political geographies; it has seized upon opportunities presented by its engagement with China to strengthen and reinforce the mechanisms through which it retains power.[2] This chapter examines these strategies, and briefly traces their origins. It then discusses the ruling party's relations with China, both in terms of oil-backed credit lines and Chinese participation in Angolan oil blocs, to demonstrate the manner in which the Angolan government has used extraversion to effectively manage diplomatic and economic relations with a far more powerful counterpart.

UNPACKING ANGOLAN SOVEREIGNTY

The Angolan state is in many ways unique. Fundamentally, it diverges from classic, "Western" definitions of statehood whereby a state broadly consists of a set of institutions that possesses the means of legitimate coercion, and with the monopoly over the use of force exercised over a territory and population.[3] Christopher Clapham argues that notions of statehood in Africa[4] imply—and to a large extent rest upon—external legitimacy; that is, the recognition of a state as a legal and equal member of the international community of states. Such external legitimacy enables states to engage in international relations in an increasingly interconnected world. Clapham notes: "The power of rulers derives not only from the material resources and the ideological support of their own people, but equally from their ability to draw on the ideological and material resources provided by other states, and also non-states."[5] Dominant conceptions of statehood in the academic literature that posit the "state as might" frequently fail to pass muster when applied to African states; this is what Clapham refers to as "the gap between the myth and reality of statehood."[6] When the international community in 1975 recognized the Angolan government, led by the *Movimento Popular para Libertaçao de Angola* (MPLA), and in so doing granted Angola its statehood, for example, the country was in the midst of a civil war. The MPLA's political control at the time extended little beyond the outer reaches of the capital city of Luanda. Yet although Angola's internal legitimacy was in doubt, the country was nevertheless acknowledged as a state by virtue of its membership in the wider international state system. Through this membership, Angola's political elites were afforded certain rights and privileges that are the preserve of governments: state monopoly on economic rents, establishment of official exchange rates and import licenses, and recognition as the only legitimate wielder of force (i.e., the military), among others.[7]

This gap between external and internal legitimacy is described by Robert Jackson and Carl Rosberg as the gap between *de jure* (negative or externally derived) and *de facto* (positive or internally derived) statehood;[8] it is the former that has ensured the persistence of many African countries. States like Angola have "negative" sovereignty, in that sovereignty is ascribed to them by other states and they exist only insofar as their existence is mandated by the international community. Angola does not have "positive" sovereignty, which would derive from an effective control of the state,[9] implicit in which is the accountability to, and the approval of, the Angolan citizenry. Jackson and Rosberg therefore argue that the sovereignty regime has become a tool leveraged by weak states to protect themselves against strong states, or when statehood is internally challenged. Indeed, Angolan elites define their political existence on the back of brokered deals in the international arena; they marshal external support and resources to maintain domestic control via their monopoly on foreign relations,[10] irrespective of whether or not they are, in fact, legitimately representative of the people. In this way, the MPLA successfully leverages Angola's membership in the sovereignty regime to ensure its self-preservation. In this, China has recently proven to be a pivotal actor.

Garnered in this way, however, sovereignty as a proxy for state power is fragile, dependent as it is on the tacit acceptance of both the international community and domestic constituencies.[11] Any lack of internal legitimacy inevitably leads to an overreliance on external legitimacy. We see this in Angola, where the history of the modern state—and the MPLA's role in it— remains a point of domestic contention.

THE *ASSIMILADOS* AND THE QUESTION OF MPLA LEGITIMACY

Throughout the occupation of her African territories, colonial Portugal practiced a policy of assimilation whereby native Africans, *indígenas*, could acquire certain civil rights by proving that they were fluent in Portuguese, literate, and without a criminal record; this allowed them to become *civilizado*, or *assimilado*. Such a policy of *lusotropicalism*, whereby the power of the Portuguese culture was seen as civilizing, perpetuated a myth of multiracial utopias in the Portuguese colonies.[12] Achieving *civilizado* status, however, was often arbitrary: in Angola, the policy ultimately drove a wedge between black Angolans and mixed-raced *mulatto*, or *mestiço* Angolans, the latter of which were perceived as assimilated by virtue of blood. The policy also entrenched the divide between Angolan rural and urban communities insofar as the races were divided among the locales.

The Rise of the Angolan Political Elite

In order to understand the set of Angolan political actors who today negotiate with China, it is important to understand their historical context and their internal structures of power. Angola's current ruling party, the MPLA,[13] was formed in 1956; it largely drew its support from intellectuals; educated, urban-based Mbundu; and Afro-Portuguese.[14] *Frente Nacional de Libertação de Angola* (FNLA), which would later become its political opponent, was formed in 1962[15] by Holden Roberto to champion northern-based Bakongo political ambitions.[16] Angola's other leading opposition party, *União para a Libertação Total de Angola* (UNITA), was formed in 1966 as a FNLA breakaway by Jonas Savimbi; UNITA garnered most of its support from the predominantly southern Ovimbundu ethnic group. During the war for independence, Angola's liberation movements formed and were consolidated largely along ethnic lines, although this was by no means the overriding determinant of party affiliation. Tony Hodges argues that ethnic divisions were exploited to drum up support for the deeply divided leaderships of Angola's three liberation movements.[17] Similarly, Jakkie Cilliers notes that ethnic divisions existed only among the movements' leaders rather than among average Angolans.[18] All three movements were led by figures who increasingly centralized political control and refused to share power. Both Roberto's FNLA and Savimbi's UNITA, too, claimed that as black Africans they were better representatives of the Angolan liberation cause, deriding the privileges received by *mestiços* and educated black Angolans (most of which flocked to MPLA) under Portuguese colonialism. According to some, both leaders feared domination by the MPLA intellectuals. Whatever the case, their accusations laid bare the MPLA's vulnerability as a genuine African liberation movement, representative of Angolans.[19]

Such was the sensitivity surrounding this issue that, according to John Marcum and Fernando Guimarães, Angolan history was rewritten so to lay a stronger claim to the MPLA's leadership of the anticolonial struggle, emphasizing in particular its genuine Angolan roots.[20] In fact, however, the MPLA was hugely influenced by the Portuguese Communist Party; it was first established in Paris. In 1963, in what was a serious blow to the MPLA, the then newly formed Organisation of African Unity (OAU) recognized the FNLA and its precociously formed *Govêrno Revolucionário de Angola no Exílio*[21] (GRAE) as the only true Angolan party fighting for Angolan self-determination. Angola's nascent independence movements placed great importance on OAU recognition, as this provided access to financial resources and was in itself a foot in the door to recognition as a legitimate postindependence government. The MPLA, FNLA, and UNITA constantly challenged each other's legitimacy as representatives of the Angolan people in order to claim a monopoly on such legitimacy and, in turn, state sovereignty.

Yet by 1971, with the MPLA's skillful maneuvering and its ability to drum up African support for its cause, the MPLA came to be regarded as the dominant anticolonial force.[22] This was aided in no small part by UNITA's misguided acceptance of military assistance from apartheid South Africa, which gave the MPLA the moral high ground to defend itself against forces allied with an internationally recognized racist regime. By 1976, the OAU recognized MPLA state structures as the structures of the Angolan state. Still, the question of MPLA's legitimacy was never conclusively resolved. On the one hand, while the party came to denounce mistrust of mulattoes as racist,[23] it remained haunted by the overrepresentation of whites, *mestiços*, and *assimilados* within its leadership. On the other hand, the MPLA's early reliance on external rather than domestic support laid bare its vulnerability in terms of its legitimacy as a genuine African liberation movement, representative of all Angolans.

Extraversion in the Angolan Context

The MPLA's consistent use of relations with external actors to bolster its power has weakened its internal legitimacy; Angola is thus in many respects a weak state. Such a characterization is seemingly at odds with the existence of a government that displays considerable agency, and which has over the years consolidated its political position into what is a de facto one-party state. Yet Angola's weakness, as that of many other African states, stems from its compromised governing authority, which is different from its governing capacity. As Clapham points out, an inherent feature of postcolonial third world states is to be simultaneously "strong" (i.e., to exercise capacity) and "fragile" or weak (i.e., to lack legitimacy).[24] A state can be considered "strong" if it has the ability to penetrate society, regulate social relationships, extract resources, and appropriate them.[25] This definition rests on a comparison of the relative strength of the state apparatus and societal institutions. On these terms, Angola is undeniably a strong state—its reach is vast. Yet the state as a political space is very different from the political elites who are agents of the state but who are not the state, as such. Although Angola's centralized political elite is considerably powerful (high despotic power), the state bureaucracy is weak and inefficient (low infrastructural power),[26] with the important exception of the state-owned oil company, Sonangol.[27] This weakness is perpetuated by design in order to loosen the institutional framework that would otherwise bind elites and limit their power. Angola is what many call a "successful failed state."[28]

Since independence, the MPLA has faced constant threats to its monopoly on power: intraparty factionalism, rural resistance, and foreign intervention.[29] Throughout, its leadership has sought to counterbalance these threats by the repeated sanction of external interventions, which in circular fashion both uphold and erode its domestic legitimacy. This perpetuates a vicious cycle whereby the MPLA increasingly prizes its externally recognized sovereignty as a key to its retention of power and purposefully sustains its external dependence. Such a tactic reflects what Jean-Francois Bayart refers to as "extraversion,"[30] a strategy through which states leverage their monopoly of access to foreign resources as a tool to maintain domestic power. African political elites position themselves as a bridge between international actors and their citizens, perfectly placed to take a cut from these transactions.[31] While external powers are often portrayed as the villains in this relationship, they are in fact the mechanisms through which political elites extract economic rents from their country's internal resources and forge and maintain clientelistic relationships with the outside world.[32] There is thus a symbiotic relationship between the political elite and transnational business interests, whereby the former can extort benefits from the latter, as much as, if not more so, than the other way around. African elites exploit their "weakness" in the international system to bolster their internal position—in a legal sense, through externally derived sovereignty, and in a commercial sense, through the acquisition of internationally derived economic rents.

When the MPLA assumed control of Angola's government in 1975, for example, it quickly nationalized all land and industry.[33] This was intended to allow it to take over property left by the fleeing Portuguese, and to break the backs of the rich landowners so they would not pose a threat as a viable competing power center and an independent economic base. Nationalization also allowed the state to bring what had been the externally focused economy under indigenous control.[34] Yet the MPLA left untouched property that was owned by foreigners so long as its owners were prepared to cooperate with the party. While the MPLA was intent on eliminating domestic threats to power, it was equally intent on maintaining astute relations with foreign investors as a means of revenue collection.

Throughout the Cold War, the MPLA continued to manipulate external powers, successfully adapting them to its needs.[35] As Clapham notes, "African leaders were not always as powerless in the face of the superpowers as a crude comparison of relative capabilities would suggest."[36] Rather than imposing themselves on the various parties to African proxy war conflicts, for example, major Cold War powers such as the Soviet Union or the United States were in fact "sucked into them,"[37] and used by African governments to enact their own battles while paying lip service to the causes espoused by their patrons. This in part explains the MPLA's early reluctance to proclaim its Marxism and related alliance with the Soviet Union before the imperative to garner material support made this necessary. As Linda Heywood suggests, sharper ideological positions were formed only to garner support from external allies by conforming to Cold War polemics.[38] Early on, MPLA president Agostinho Neto and other party leading lights including Mário Pinto de Andrade and Lúcio Lara maintained a position of ideological neutrality. Yet, as John Marcum and Fernando Guimarães aptly note, the MPLA was, in fact, Marxist.[39] Yet prior to 1964 nonalignment was more advantageous insofar as it allowed the MPLA to garner broad international support, particularly from the vehemently anticommunist United States. When in the mid-1960s it became clear that identification with Marxism would guarantee greater material and financial support from the Soviet Union and its allies,[40] however, MPLA elites swiftly and openly shifted their loyalties to Moscow, proclaiming Marxism-Leninism as their guiding ideology.

Interestingly, the MPLA in 1962 experienced a schism over whether to align with Soviet Russia or Communist China. It is suspected that it ultimately turned to the former to access more advanced weapons technology than that available from the latter. The pragmatism of material benefit then out-weighed ideological concerns. From the mid-1960s, the MPLA also lever-aged Marxism-Leninism as a guiding ideology to deflect class-based criti-cisms against the Afro-Portuguese, and because, as a popular conceptual vehicle for the independence movements of the time, it reflected the era's revolutionary zeitgeist and enabled the party to amass a following.[41]

During the Angolan Civil War (1975–2002), the MPLA similarly sus-tained itself via oil revenue, leveraging external resources for internal bene-fit. As Ricardo Soares de Oliveira notes, the exploitation of oil requires that a host area have a sovereign government with which oil investors can trans-act.[42] Angolan de jure sovereignty facilitated such an exchange. Oil was exploited by Cabinda Gulf Oil Company, owned by US oil major Chevron—this, despite the fact that Washington officially supported UNITA. Indeed, throughout the conflict, American-operated rigs exploited oil in collusion with the Marxist MPLA; the rigs were guarded by Cuban troops against US-funded guerrilla groups, and the oil revenue was used by the MPLA to purchase Soviet weapons.[43] If nothing else, the MPLA was astutely skilled at manipulating external actors for its own benefit. Nicholas van de Walle and Patrick Chabal even argue that Angolan elites used the support of foreign allies to not only bolster and advance their political standing but also to actively prolong the conflict; war is a facilitative environment for the politi-cally connected to amass wealth.[44] Over the three decades of conflict, the MPLA leveraged the ongoing hostilities as an excuse for distracted govern-ance and as a cover for elites with access to oil to accrue fortunes. This resulted in the stark socioeconomic inequality found in Angola today.

By the time that structural adjustment programs (SAPs) were introduced in the 1980s, the MPLA was skilled at fashioning external circumstances to its advantage. By their nature, the fiscal austerity measures imposed on African states required the buy-in of political elites whose privileged posi-tions would be compromised by the reforms.[45] The overall failure of the structural adjustment programs was partly the result of the ability of African governments to manipulate and frustrate the "would-be interveners."[46] While Angola is among the few African states that did not succumb to a SAP, it until 2002 had an IMF staff-monitoring program. Like the structural adjust-ment programs, the program demanded heightened levels of transparency and the implementation of macroeconomic stabilization policies aimed at reducing inflation by cutting public expenditure and minimizing borrowing. Under IMF constraints, any large-scale infrastructure construction program would additionally have to be put on hold until Angola had achieved a healthy fiscal situation, as determined by the IMF. As neither condition was acceptable to the MPLA, President dos Santos in 2002 appealed instead to China. Quick off the mark in exploiting the emerging polarity between the

West and China, MPLA elites brokered alternative and less conditional financing from Beijing.

LUANDA-BEIJING RELATIONS

Certain African states have been able to play the China card well. Implicit in this has been the capacity to, first, solicit renewed interest from other, non-Chinese, foreign powers and, second, to successfully use the leverage this has afforded them to exploit China as a counterbalance to the influence of other states on their political economies. Angola has successfully managed both.

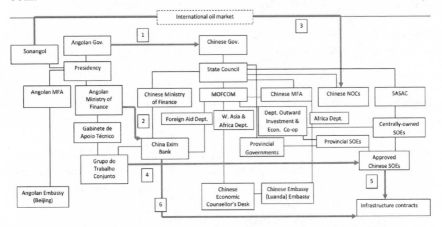

Figure 4.1.   The Angolan Government's commercial relations with China

Figure 4.1 depicts the standard procedure that governs commercial relations between Angola and China, including all the government bodies—and their interactions—purported to be involved in the transactions. In most cases, the interactive process proceeds as follows:

1. The Angolan government signs a framework agreement with the Chinese government, represented by the Angolan Ministry of Finance and the Chinese Ministry of Commerce.
2. The Angolan Ministry of Finance signs a loan agreement with the China Export-Import (ExIm) Bank.
3. Sonangol, Angola's oil and gas parastatal, sells oil offtake to China at the international spot price on the day of shipment. The monies from the sales are deposited into an account in the Angolan government's name together with China ExIm Bank.
4. The joint commission (*Grupo do Trabalho Conjunto*) formed by the *Gabinete de Apoio Técnico* (GAT)[47] and China ExIm Bank agree on a

set of projects that are then put up for tender for a preapproved list of Chinese companies.

5. The Chinese companies complete the projects and present invoices for their work to the Angolan Ministry of Finance.

6. These invoices are paid by China ExIm Bank directly to the Chinese companies, drawn down from the Angolan's government's account with China ExIm Bank.

Negotiations over the first Chinese loan agreement in Angola began in 2002 and culminated in the signing of a framework agreement on November 26, 2003, between the Chinese Ministry of Commerce and Angolan's Ministry of Finance. The agreement reportedly stipulated that loans would over time extend up to $10 billion.[48] Chinese Vice Premier Zeng Peiyan visited Angola in March 2004, at which time the first $2 billion loan was announced; the first tranche was released in December 2004. On July 19, 2007, it was extended by $500 million in supplementary funding.[49] On September 28, 2007, the loan was further extended by $2 billion.[50] Angola's Minister of Finance Carlos Alberto Lopes in July 2010 confirmed that negotiations were underway to finalize a third tranche of $6 billion to assist with Angola's reconstruction.[51] However, in December 2011, Lopes reported to the Angolan Parliament that the third tranche was only $3 billion, indicating a total pledged loan amount of $7.5 billion. Other Chinese financial institutions, including the China Industrial and Commercial Bank and China Development Bank, have signed separate loan agreements with the Angolan government, rendering a collective total of $14.5 billion. This makes China the single largest player in Angola's postwar reconstruction process.

Overall, the loan is intended to assist Angola in the rebuilding of vital infrastructure; the Angolan Ministry of Finance manages it. The loan operates like a current account held in China under the name of the Angolan government and is paid directly to Chinese companies responsible for the construction work. According to the Angolan Minister of Finance, the first loan tranche of US$2.5 billion is repayable at three-month Libor[52] + 1.5 percent over fifteen years, including a grace period of three to five years, and the second tranche of US$2 billion is repayable at Libor + 1.25 percent over eighteen years. Added to these terms is a management fee of 0.3 percent of the loan amount, and a 0.3 percent "commitment fee." The fee is not to be used by the individual projects; rather, the Angolan government must provide a down payment of 10 percent of the project value of each financed project.[53] Late payments garner an interest rate of three-month Libor + 3 percent. While the conditions of the loan suggest that it was crafted purely to the benefit of the Chinese, key Angolan political actors have greatly benefitted from this arrangement.

LEVERAGE IN NEGOTIATIONS

When discussed, the issue of African agency is almost always one of "how far [are] African states able to hold up their national interests."[54] Such a discourse implies that African political elites act in the "national interest." While many profess to do so, it is also often these very political elites who define the national interest—almost certainly to their own advantage, and often to the detriment of other domestic actors not within their sphere of influence. As Kate Macdonald and Stephen Woolcock argue, the national interest is defined by governments and serves their most powerful interests.[55] Clapham similarly notes that African elites manipulate their Chinese counterparts and negotiate terms for their own political agendas[56] as opposed to the "collective national interest"[57] as argued by Handel in his analysis of weak states in the international system. In its negotiations with China, the MPLA is self-serving.

International negotiations are, as Robert Putnam's theory of "two level games" contends,[58] an interplay of domestic and external factors. In Angola, the MPLA's reliance on external relations for its power suggests that domestic and foreign policy are inextricably intertwined.[59] Where such interplay exists, there emerge what Andrew Moravcsik terms "creative opportunities for statecraft"[60]—opportunities for states to leverage relations with foreign partners in ways that favorably shift the balance of power in domestic affairs. Such "creative opportunities," or what Peter Evans calls "dynamic interactions,"[61] are especially apparent in the MPLA's leverage of superpower agendas to serve its own interests. Luanda's need for Chinese finance is related to its domestic imperative for national reconstruction and the legitimacy that this confers on the government vis-à-vis its citizens. As Robert Jackson and Carl Rosberg note, Africa's international negotiations are often rooted in one of three things: "domestic authority, the apparatus of power, and economic circumstance."[62]

When the MPLA began negotiations with China in 2002, Angola was devastated from civil war. Eighty-five percent of road and railway infrastructure had been destroyed, the agriculture sector—as important for Angola's GDP as the petroleum sector in the 1970s—was defunct, and almost half of the country's population had fled the interior to live in slums around Luanda. Alternate sources of financing on terms satisfactory to the MPLA were few and far between. The successful negotiation of Chinese finance was therefore relatively more important for the Angolan regime than for its Chinese counterparts; China, too, devoted far less attention and resources to ensuring the success of the negotiations than Angola, reflecting what Albert Hirschman refers to as a "disparity of attention."[63] Because China came to the negotiating table with a clear upper hand, Angola's negotiating team "devote[d] its attention with single-minded concentration to this uncomfortable situation."[64] Effective negotiation with China was at the time the foremost priority for Angola's elites. On the other hand, Angola was not yet a top priority for China's commercial relations. China, too, then saw Angola as one among many African states—taking what Jackson calls a "world view"[65] approach—rather than as a strategic stand-alone partner. Chinese analysts still tend to succumb to this folly: many African states are considered too small, given terms of trade, to be handled individually. This approach has facilitated a considerable underestimation of Angolan actors by the Chinese.

In Angola's negotiations with China, the strategic nature of oil is key: Angola has successfully manipulated China's growing desperation for sustainable petroleum sources to its own advantage. In 2003, the Chinese leadership faced a pronounced energy crisis[66] as coal supplies were failing to meet domestic energy demand; demand increased by 9 percent in 2003 and a further 17 percent in 2004.[67] When Hu Jintao became president in 2003, he made the internationalization and diversification of China's oil supplies a priority[68]—central to which was a shift toward African, and Angolan, sources. The gradual importance assumed by Angola in China's foreign policy started to tilt the "disparity of attention." Substantial increases in Angolan petroleum exports to China have made Angola one of China's largest sources of oil imports: 15 to 20 percent of China's total imports come from Angola, and China is today considerably more dependent on Angola for petroleum that it was ten years ago. Contrary to classic foreign dependency theories that suggest the economic reliance of small countries on larger countries, primarily in terms of trade (the importance of the foreign exchange relative to the size of the economy)[69] here, Chinese dependence on oil and Angola's role as a leading supplier have made it such that the larger country is the significantly more dependent party in the relations.

A la Carte Diplomacy

Of course, China is neither Angola's only financier nor its only provider of oil-backed loans. Nevertheless, credit lines advanced by China's ExIm Bank continue to receive immense media scrutiny. It is often suggested that the loans are advanced as a means of securing access to oil equity and winning political favor and preferential status as Angola's trade and investment partner. Yet since the end of the civil war, the Angolan government has continued to successfully strengthen relations with alternative partners.

A flurry of international credit lines from the United States and various European partners followed in the wake of China ExIm Bank's loans to Angola, with many signed between 2004 and 2006. By 2007, arrangements were made for the Angolan government to normalize its Paris Club debt; the bulk of the $2.3 billion owed had been paid in December 2007, and plans were then made to service the $1.8 billion outstanding in interest accrued during the civil war.[70] In 2009, with the advance of Angola's relations with other, non-Chinese, financiers, the IMF made provisions for a standby loan agreement of SDR 858.9 million,[71] equivalent to $1.4 billion (2009 USD), over twenty-seven months. This amounted to 300 percent of Angola's allocated borrowing quota. Implicit in this arrangement was the requirement that a $2 billion ceiling would be placed on the Angolan government's nonconcessional borrowing.[72] The World Bank, too, has been mollified by the Angolan government's policy of debt normalization, and has seemingly ceased to regard Angola as a pariah state.

Angola's government has made concerted efforts to repair relations with numerous creditors to ensure that access to credit from a diversified portfolio of lender countries will mitigate against the need to lean too heavily on China. Angola in this regard diverges from Africa's other oil states: rather than fostering anti-Western sentiment, it encourages Western business in the country. On one hand, this is out of necessity: Angola's extroverted economy requires that its elites collaborate with Western interests to maintain access to the oil wealth that fuels their patronage networks.[73] On the other hand, engagement with the West serves as a countervailing force to mounting Chinese influence. The emergence of multiple alternative financing sources has shifted the power balance decisively in Angola's favor, as China no longer holds the advantage as its primary funding source. The loss of such an advantage has spurred increasing amounts of financing from Beijing in a last-ditch effort to regain it. In March 2011, the then Chinese ambassador to Angola, Zhang Bolun, confirmed that Chinese institutions had facilitated financing totaling $14.5 billion.[74] China Development Bank (CDB) and the Industrial and Commercial Bank of China (ICBC) have similarly come forward with funding. CDB has invested $1.5 billion in Angola's agriculture sector,[75] while the ICBC has so far provided $2.5 billion in general finance.[76] The inaugural provision of Chinese funds seems to have in a circular way acted as a kind of catalyst for other flows of (non-Chinese) financing, which have in turn spurred the additional provisioning of Chinese funds.[77] Most recently, China Development Bank in December 2014 announced a $2 billion loan to Sonangol.

The Angolan government has been astute in perpetuating this funding circle and at playing funding sources off one another to preserve Angola's domestic status quo. Under the $2 billion ceiling implicit in the IMF standby agreement, for example, any increase in borrowing from China ExIm Bank, whose loans are not considered concessional by the IMF, is in violation of the agreement. Nevertheless, the very month that the letter of intent was sent to the IMF, the Angolan government signed an additional loan facility totaling $6 billion with China ExIm. It turns out that the IMF both implemented and waived this stipulation within the self-same document, likely in an attempt to maintain relations with the Angolan government,[78] while at the same time ensuring that it did not veer too far in the direction of China. Article 10 of the Memorandum of Economic and Financial Policies notes:

> However, we are of the view that this borrowing ceiling could be reviewed in the context of SBA program reviews in the event that concessional loans to Angola fall short of our expectations to avoid jeopardizing our vital infrastructure reconstruction process. As concessional resources increase, the level of non-concessional borrowing decreases in the same amount. The government is also working with the World Bank and the Africa Development Bank to reduce implementation costs of infrastructure projects by strengthening the project appraisal framework and improving the procurement system. [79]

In this way, the Angolan government is able to override the nonconcessional borrowing ceiling; it is unlikely that it would have entered into the agreement in good faith without the inclusion of such a clause. According to Christine Messiant, Article 10 gives the Angolan government the tools necessary to ignore its own prescriptions with impunity; [80] Messiant sees the international community as complicit in the Angolan government's abuse of political power. [81] William Reno similarly notes that some within international financial institutions tend to value the internal political stability of states above overly zealous attempts to dismantle patronage networks, indicating a train of thought that Angola should not be pushed too hard to reform. [82] Angola, for its part, holds to the IMF as a countermeasure against the influence of actors like China over its economic sovereignty. Angola is unlikely to become a client state of any country anytime soon, and will instead continue to engage with all international actors in ways tailored to its advantage. Angola's is a "multi-vector" foreign policy that manages "to keep a balance of interests regarding foreign intervention in its domestic markets," [83] effectively keeping everyone on their toes.

An Oily Mirage: China's Access to Angolan Petroleum Bloc Equity

Examples from Angola's oil sector suggest that the Angolan government has in recent years managed to manipulate commercial relations such that the greatest financial benefit indeed goes to it, rather than to China or any other foreign player. Chinese interests first entered the Angolan oil sector in 2004 when China Petroleum and Chemical Corporation (Sinopec) formed a joint venture with the Angolan state-owned oil company, Sonangol. Sonangol is also the oil industry concessionaire and is mandated to at minimum hold a minority stake in all Angolan oil blocks. The joint-venture vehicle that was formed, Sinopec-Sonangol International (SSI), saw Sinopec taking a 55 percent share. [84] In 2004, SSI bought a 50 percent stake of Block 18, touted to be one of Angola's most promising oil exploration sites, for the reported sum of $725 million. [85] Through its shareholder position in SSI, Sinopec has additionally acquired equity in several other Angola oil blocks, with SSI initially attaining 27.5 percent, 40 percent, and 20 percent in the offshore blocks 17, 18, and 15, respectively. The signature bonuses of $1.1 billion of the concessions in blocks 17 and 18 are the highest ever offered in the history of Angola's oil industry.[86] In 2004, Sinopec was also in negotiations with the Angolan government to develop a two-hundred-thousand-barrel-per-day oil refinery, Sonaref, at Lobito. While China ExIm's loans were central to these early Sinopec successes, their strategic importance has waned with time. Despite a promising start, too, Sinopec has now largely retreated.

The proposed refinery deal was called off in March 2007, reportedly due to a lack of consensus over the intended destination of the refined product; it is unclear as to which side imposed the deal breaker. Similarly, in October 2008, Sinopec and China National Overseas Oil Company (CNOOC) negotiated with Marathon the purchase of a 20 percent stake in Block 32 for $1.8 billion.[87] By October 2009, however, Sonangol, as an equity holder, had exercised its right of first refusal, blocking the Chinese purchase by announcing its own intention to buy it.[88] The sale was finalized in February 2010. It was subsequently awarded to China Sonangol. Blocks 31 and 32 are now reflected as being owned by entities called "SSI 31" and "SSI 32" of unknown shareholding (see table 4.1). This is presumed to have been a negotiation brokered between China Sonangol and SSI, from which China Sonangol is likely to have profited handsomely.

China Sonangol was also considerably more successful in Angola's 2011 presalt exploration round. On the one hand, this may have been for practical reasons: Chinese state-owned companies do not possess the technology needed to exploit Angola's deep and ultradeep blocks in the Gulf of Guinea, and have been increasingly sidelined since 2006.[89] On the other hand, it is likely that in this case the Angolan government, through Sonangol, was intent on sending a clear message to China that it does not, in fact, have the political upper hand. Since 2006, there is increasingly little evidence of the preferential treatment of Chinese state-owned oil companies. In fact, Chinese national oil companies are now junior partners in the Angolan oil industry. Firms in which Angolan partners have a larger stake dominate.

Since 2011, for example, China Sonangol has been overall more successful in the acquisition of Angolan oil blocks than Sinopec (via SSI). China Sonangol was formed in 2005. It is jointly owned by Sonangol (30 percent) and the private Chinese company, New Bright International Development Ltd. (70 percent). Sonangol owns a far greater percentage of China Sonangol than it does of SSI. Sonangol has access to 4.05 percent of SSI through its 30 percent shareholder position in China Sonangol, which in turn is a 13.5 percent shareholder position in SSI.[90] Yet Sonangol owns 30 percent of China Sonangol, with the result that it stands to benefit far more from increased oil equity in China Sonangol rather than SSI. Since 2005, China

Sonangol has effectively become *the* broker for Angolan oil sales to China, acting as a very profitable intermediary.[91]

The success of China Sonangol represents the triumph of Angolan state and private interests over Chinese government access to Angolan oil bloc equity. It also illustrates a shift in power from Beijing to Luanda. While in the early years of Angola's relations with China the Angolan government's weaker position made it more likely to agree to Chinese acquisition of oil blocks, its ability to successfully manoeuvre multiple financiers has since ceded it more control and negotiating power. Luanda no longer has to award oil blocks to Chinese state companies. In fact, China's eagerness to acquire oil equity works in Angola's favor at the negotiating table.

CREDIT LINES AND CAMPAIGN PROMISES

On the back of Chinese credit lines, the Angolan government has over the years been able to initiate various prestige projects that have proven important in galvanizing its image domestically and abroad. Since the end of the civil war, the MPLA has upheld national reconstruction as a key government priority. This is designed to consolidate dos Santos's role as the nation's "peacemaker" and to bolster the MPLA's internal legitimacy, particularly during critical election cycles.

With an eye on the 2008 national polls, for example, the Angolan government sanctioned the Chinese construction of stadiums for the August 2007 African basketball championships (Afrobasket); ahead of the 2012 elections, the regime again approved construction of additional stadiums for the 2010 African Cup of Nations (COCAN). Additional political pressure was placed on the construction schedules of several large-scale road and railway projects and a number of housing schemes so that they would be completed before the elections. In theory at least, Angolans benefit from such projects insofar as they provide desperately needed infrastructure; Chinese firms also build roads and railways, often much faster than other foreign financiers. Yet in most cases the projects are leveraged by MPLA elites to reap the political dividends of public infrastructure investment. Many of the works constructed ahead of the 2008 and 2012 polls, respectively, were, for instance, presented as distinct achievements of the MPLA and as exemplars of its commitment to its development agenda. Such posturing was particularly important in rural areas where infrastructure was not only sorely needed but where the MPLA's image was in need of some brushing up. The MPLA has traditionally been an urban-based party with its stronghold in Luanda.

In the 2008 polls, the MPLA secured 87 percent of parliamentary seats in an election that international observers largely decried as "free and fair."[92] Lara Pawson argues that in this election, specifically, the MPLA used its

Table 4.1 Angolan Oil Block Concessions, 2004–2011

Shareholder	Year Acquired	Oil Block	Stake (%)	Other Shareholders	Operator
SSI	2004	Block 18	50		BP (50%)
China Sonangol	2005	Block 3/05	25	AJOCO (20%); ENI (12%); Somoil (10%); INA (4%); Naftagas (4%)	Sonangol (25%)
China Sonangol	2005	Block 3/05A	25	AJOCO (20%); ENI (12%); Somoil (10%); INA (4%); Naftagas (4%)	Sonangol (25%)
SSI	2006	Block 15/06	25	Sonangol (35%); Falcon Oil (5%)	ENI (35%)
SSI	2006	Block 17/06	27.5	Sonangol (20%); Somoil (10%); Falcon Oil (5%); ACREP (5%); Partex (2.5%)	Total (30%)
SSI	2006	Block 18/06	40	Sonangol (20%); Falcon Oil (5%); Geminas (5%)	Petrobras (30%)
SSI 13	2010	Block 31	15	Sonangol (45%); Statoil (13.33%)	BP (26.67%)

SSI 32	2010	Block 32	20	Sonangol (35%); Esso (15%)	Total (30%)
China Sonangol	2011	Block 6/06	20	Sonangol (20%); Falcon Oil (10%); Initial Oil & Gas (10%)	Petrobras (40%)
China Sonangol	2011	Block 19/ 11	10	Sonangol (40%)	BP (50%)
China Sonangol	2011	Cabinda Northern	11	Teikoku (17%); Soco (17%); ACREP (15%); ENI (10%); Petrobras (10%)	Sonangol (20%)

political dominance to subvert the electoral process to gain international sanction for the consolidation of its hold on power[93] —what Messiant has elsewhere referred to as the MPLA's "consolidation of hegemonic power."[94] Indeed, the victory imbued the regime with much-needed domestic legitimacy and facilitated the further consolidation of its power, not least through the passage of a new constitution that now allows the ruling party president to automatically assume the position of "head of state" absent presidential elections. Like in 1975, the international community's acceptance of this outcome affirmed the MPLA's continued legitimacy. By leveraging Chinese resources to boost its domestic appeal, the MPLA was able to secure a majority in the polls. This, in turn, elicited international approval and has perpetuated the regime's domestic legitimacy—at least for now.

Extraversion in the Era of Discontent

Despite claims made by the Angolan government that national reconstruction was fundamentally "for the people," the Angolan population is in fact largely removed from the process. This is perhaps not so surprising. As Abdul Mustapha argues, Bayart's concept of extraversion is reductionist and deprives "the people" of political agency, reducing them to a "passive mass."[95] According to Rafael Marques de Morais, Chinese credit lines are but a new avenue for elite enrichment under the guise of national reconstruction:

> Such economic arrangements have insulated the dos Santos regime from the will of the Angolan people, who remain economically and politically irrelevant. China's new prominence is part of an effort by the ruling elite to keep them that way by excluding society at large from the task of national reconstruction.[96]

The regime sees reconstruction as a patrimonial provision of services by a paternalistic government with the aim of reinforcing the state as the source of all public goods. Where it should be an interactive process that solidifies reciprocal ties between the rulers and the ruled, Angola's national reconstruction instead entails the delivery of turnkey products. It is also an increasingly paid-for service, outsourced to foreigners with little to no provision for Angolans to maintain, or even organically expand upon, what external contractors provide Rafael. Marques de Morais argues that China's role in the Angolan reconstruction process has "enabled a string of political measures aimed at perpetuating the power of the president's inner circle, while setting back internal dialogue on national reconstruction even within the ruling party itself." The Chinese presence has also "spawned a mass fantasy about national goals that bears no resemblance to what can really be accomplished—the sheer weight of which, along with threats of repression, often silences critics of the dos Santos regime."[97] This reflects a conscious strategy on the part of the MPLA to prevent economic growth outside of its purview, in this way blocking the emergence of any alternative bases of power that could contest its legitimacy.

For many years this did not pose an epistemological problem. Periodic political purges coupled with the fatigue of several decades of war ensured that there were no concerted popular uprisings against the government. Since early 2011, however, the party's continued monopoly of Angolan political life has started to backfire. Defunct government policies over the years have given rise to a generation of jobless and disaffected youth with no memory of the civil war or Soviet-style purges. Inspired by the 2011 Arab Spring that toppled dictators like Hosni Mubarak and Muammar Gaddafi, sporadic political protests have started to break out in Luanda. Between March and December 2011, six antigovernment rallies calling for dos Santos's resignation were organized through social media. "Progovernment" rallies organized in retaliation in contrast received waning popular support.[98] The occurrence of such actions—still limited albeit nevertheless unthinkable only a few years ago—underlines the MPLA's chronic vulnerability to weak internal legitimacy and the fine line it must tow to maintain hold of its political power. Going forward, the regime will likely engage more directly in survival politics and strategies of extraversion. In this, China will remain key. Indeed, China may well be merely the next in a long line of foreign actors to be channelled by Angolan elites for their own political agendas.

CONCLUSIONS

Since 2003, the Angolan political elite has successfully leveraged its relationship with China to advance both foreign and domestic policy objectives. Internationally, Chinese loans have proven politically expedient. At a time when Angola was experiencing difficulties securing other sources of capital—and on MPLA-friendly terms—Chinese finance provided a quick and ready alternative. Chinese finance also opened the door to additional sources of funding[99] —an opportunity that was rapidly seized and capitalized upon by Angola's political elites. The MPLA has diversified its financing base such that no one power holds any more sway over the country's economy than does any other. Domestically, too, Chinese loans have provided the MPLA with the means to undertake national reconstruction. Aside from its practical necessity, however, the MPLA has used Chinese finance to kickstart a state-building process that has been crafted in a way that ultimately facilitates the consolidation of state power—what Hodges refers to as "manufactured legitimacy."[100] MPLA control of Chinese credit lines ensures the regime's monopoly over both the process through which they are allocated and disbursed and the economic rents that they imply. Despite a rash of policies and public overtures concerning economic diversification and local participation, the structural contradictions of the Angolan economy remain unaddressed.

So far, the Angolan government has been able to navigate its internal weaknesses. Whether it will continue to do so in the longer-term is unclear, as are the implications for its relations with China. If history is any indicator, however, innovations in Angolan governance will continue to implicate China for some time to come. Inasmuch as China needs Angola, Angola, it seems, needs China too.

NOTES

This chapter is adapted from the author's book, *Uncovering African Agency: Angola's Management of China's Credit Lines* (New York: Ashgate, 2013).

1. Michael Handel, *Weak States in the International System* (London: Frank Cass, 1981), 130.

2. This research is based on almost two hundred in-depth interviews conducted in both Angola and China between July 2009 and February 2011. Extensive use was also made of Portuguese and Chinese language sources where available to supplement the research.

3. Max Weber, *The Theory of Social and Economic Organization*, edited by Talcott Parsons (New York: Free Press, 156).

4. The discourse on African statehood is broad. For additional views in this regard, see: Jean-François Bayart, *The State in Africa: The Politics of the Belly* (London: Longman Group UK Limited, 1993); Jean-François Bayart et al. "From Kleptocracy to the Felonious State?" in *The Criminalisation of the State in Africa*, edited by Jean-François Bayart et al. (Oxford: James Curry, 1999), 1–31; Patrick Chabal, "E Pluribus Unum: Transitions in Angola," in *Angola: The Weight of History* (London: Hurst Publishers Ltd., 2007); Christopher Clapham, *Third World Politics: An Introduction* (London: Croom and Helm, 1985); Christopher Clapham, *Africa and the International System: The Politics of Survival* (Cambridge: Cambridge University Press, 1996); Christopher Clapham, "Sovereignty and the Third World State," *Political Studies* XLVII (1999): 522–37.

5. Clapham, *Africa and the International System*, 11.

6. Clapham, *Africa and the International System*, 12.

7. Clapham, "Sovereignty and the Third World State," 527.

8. Robert H. Jackson and Carl G. Rosberg, "Why Africa's Weak States Persist: The Empirical and the Juridical in Statehood," *World Politics* 35, no. 1 (October 1982): 1–24. Elsewhere, Robert Jackson also refers to this as "quasi-statehood"; that is, states that are recognized as sovereign independent entities by other states within the international system, but are not able to exercise the demands and duties of a state as they relate to the effective exercise of power over territory.

9. Clapham, *Africa and the International System*, 12.

10. Clapham, *Africa and the International System*, 62.

11. Clapham, "Sovereignty and the Third World State," 530.

12. According to Fernando Guimarães, less than 5 percent of the local Angolan population ever achieved *civilizado* status. See Fernando Guimarães, *The Origins of the Angolan Civil War: Foreign Intervention and Domestic Political Conflict, 1961–1970* (New York: Pagrave Macmillan, 2001).

13. According to David Sogge, the MPLA has discarded the name Popular Movement for the Liberation of Angola but retains the acronym as a name. See David Sogge, "Angola: Reinventing Pasts and Futures," *Review of African Political Economy* 38, no. 127 (2011): 85–92.

14. *Afro-Portuguese* is the term given to mixed-race descendants of Portuguese settlers who retained Portuguese cultural, language, and identity.

15. FNLA was a united front formed by three political parties but dominated by the leadership of Holden Roberto, the leader of the largest party in the alliance, *União dos Povos de Angola* (UPA).

16. Holden Roberto, the leader of FNLA, was in fact a kinsman of Mobutu Sese Seko by marriage and received support from Zaire throughout Angola's civil war.

17. Tony Hodges, *Angola: Anatomy of an Oil State* (London: James Curry, 2004).

18. Jakkie Cilliers, "Resource Wars—A New Type of Insurgency," in *Angola's War Economy: The Role of Oil and Diamonds*, edited by Jakkie Cilliers and Christian Dietrich, 1–15 (Pretoria: Institute for Security Studies, 2000).

19. Marcum (29) and Guimarães (45) both point to inconsistencies in the stories of how the MPLA was established, and both suggest that history was rewritten in order to lay a stronger claim of legitimate leadership of the anticolonial struggle with genuine Angolan roots; respectively commenting on the omission of the influence of the Portuguese Communist Party and the fact that the movement was first established in Paris. See: John Marcum, *The Angolan Revolution*, 2 vols. (Cambridge, MA: 1978 [1969]); Fernando Guimarães, *The Origins of the Angolan Civil War: Foreign Intervention and Domestic Political Conflict, 1961–1970* (New York: Palgrave McMillan, 2011).

20. Marcum, *The Angolan Revolution*, 29.

21. Revolutionary Government in Exile.

22. Guimarães, *The Origins of the Angolan Civil War*, 72.

23. Marcum, *The Angolan Revolution*, 161.

24. Clapham, *Third World Politics*, 39.

25. Joel S. Migdal, *Strong Societies and Weak States* (Princeton: Princeton University Press, 1988).

26. In describing state power, Mann (1985:113) distinguishes despotic and infrastructural power, the former referring to "the range of actions that the elite is empowered to undertake without routine" and the latter the ability to execute them.

27. Ricardo Soares de Oliveira explores in detail the rise of Sonangol as a relatively efficient state in the midst of the weakness and chaos of the rest of the Angolan state institutions. See: Ricardo Soares de Oliveira, "Business Success, Angola-Style: Postcolonial Politics and the Rise and Rise of Sonangol," *Journal of Modern African Studies* 45, no. 4 (2007): 595–619.

28. See, for example: de Oliveira, "Business Success, Angola-Style"; David Sogge, "Angola: 'Failed' yet 'Successful,'" *Fundación par alas Relaciones Internacionales y el Diálogo Exterior (FRIDE)*, Working Paper 81, April 2009, 1–28.

29. Lucy Corkin, *Uncovering African Agency: Angola's Management of China's Credit Lines* (Farnham: Ashgate, 2013), 21.

30. Bayart, *The State in Africa: The Politics of the Belly*, 74.

31. Clapham, *Africa and the International System*, 26.

32. Clapham, *Third World Politics: An Introduction*.

33. Manuel Ennes Ferreira, "Nacionalização e confisco do capital português na indústria transformadora de Angola (1975–1990)," *Análise Social* 37, no. 162 (Spring 2002): 47–90.

34. Clapham, *Third World Politics: An Introduction*, 105.

35. Clapham, *Third World Politics: An Introduction*, 5.

36. Clapham, *Africa and the International System*, 135.

37. Clapham, *Africa and the International System*, 139.

38. Linda Heywood, *Contested Power in Angola, 1840s to Present* (Rochester, NY: University of Rochester Press, 2000), 183.

39. See, for example: John Marcum, *The Angolan Revolution*, 254, and Guimarães, *The Origins of the Angolan Civil War*, 61.

40. Christine Messiant, "The Mutation of Hegemonic Domination," in *Angola: The Weight of History*, edited by Patrick Chabal and Nuno Vidal, 93–123. (London: Hurst and Company, 2007).

41. Guimarães, *The Origins of the Angolan Civil War*, 170.

42. Ricardo Soares de Oliveira, *Oil and Politics in the Gulf of Guinea* (London: Hurst and Company, 2007).

43. Nicholas Shaxson, *Poisoned Wells: The Dirty Politics of African Oil* (New York: Palgrave Macmillan, 2007), 49.

44. See Chabal, "E Pluribus Unum" and Nicolas van de Walle, *African Economies and the Politics of Permanent Crisis* (Cambridge: Cambridge University Press, 2001).

45. Miles Kahler, "Bargaining with the IMF: Two-Level Strategies and Developing Countries," in *Double-Edged Diplomacy: International Bargaining and Domestic Politics*, edited by Peter Evans et al. (Berkeley: University of California Press, 1993), 363–94.

46. Clapham, "Sovereignty and the Third World State," 535.

47. Technical Support Office, Angolan Ministry of Finance

48. See: Executive Research Associates (ERA), "China in Africa: A Strategic Overview," report prepared for the Institute of Developing Economies, Japan External Trade Organisation (IDE-JETRO), October. http://www.ide.go.jp/English/Data/Africa_file/Manualreport/cia.html. Interestingly, the US ambassador to Angola, Dan Mozena, reported on January 27, 2009, in a confidential diplomatic cable leaked by Wikileaks that the Chinese ambassador, Zhang Bolun, confirmed that lending to Angola would be capped at US$10 billion. (See:http://angola-luanda-pitigrili.com/archives/8740). The Chinese vice president, on his visit to Angola in November 2009, confirmed that Chinese lending to Angola had reached US$10 billion (*Angola Press* , "'Angola e China Rubricam Acordos de Cooperação,'" November 19, 2010).

49. Gabinete de Apoio Técnico (GAT), "Linha de Crédito com o Eximbank da China: Relatório das actividades desenvolvidas II trimestre de 2008," June 2008, 2. http://www.minfin.gv.ao/fsys/China-Relatorio_do_II_trim_2008SitedoMINFIN2.pdf.

50. Gabinete de Apoio Técnico (GAT), "Linha de Crédito com o Eximbank da China."

51. Angolan Minister of Finance, Carlos Alberto Lopes, broadcast on Radio Nacional de Angola, 4 p.m., July 9, 2010.

52. Interest rate is quoted according to the Angolan Ministry of Finance. Libor, according to the British Banker's Association, is the most widely used benchmark or reference rate for short-term interest rates.

53. Nancy Dubosse, "Trade, Investment, and Legal Cooperation between China and Africa," in *Chinese and African Perspectives on China in Africa*, edited by Axel Harneit-Sievers, Stephen Marks, Sanusha Naidu (Cape Town: Pambazuka Press, 2010), 70–81. Dubosse does not elaborate on what the significance of this is. According to Dubosse (75), an "assembly commission" of 1 percent applies if the loan is syndicated. In the case of China ExIm Bank, this does not apply as the loan was not arranged to be syndicated. Dubosse (75) also states that the interest rate is three-month Libor + 3 percent, although this contradicts other sources. See, for example Ana Cristina Alves, "The Oil Factor in Sino-Angolan Relations at the Start of the 21st Century," *South African Institute for International Affairs*, Occasional Paper No. 55, February Interview, Angolan Ministry of Finance, Luanda, July 6, 2010.

54. Alistair Fraser, Philomathia Fellow and College Lecturer in Politics, University of Cambridge, Chatham House conference, "Emerging Agents of Change: African and International Negotiations," London, February 2, 2011.

55. Kate Macdonald and Stephen Woolcock, "State Actors in Economic Diplomacy," in *The New Economic Diplomacy: Decision-Making and Negotiation in International Economic Relations*, edited by Nicholas Bayne and Stephen Woolcock (Farnham: Ashgate, 2007), 66.

56. Christoper Clapham, "Fitting China In," in *China Returns to Africa: A Rising Power and a Continent Embrace*, edited by Chris Alden, Daniel Large, and Ricardo Soares de Oliveira (London: Hurst and Company, 2008), 361–70, 366.

57. Handel, *Weak States in the International System*, 44.

58. Robert Putnam, "Diplomacy and Domestic Politics: The Logic of Two-Level Games," *International Organization* 42, no. 3 (1988): 427–60.

59. Clapham, *Third World Politics: An Introduction*, 113.

60. Andreew Moravcsik, "Introduction: Integrating International and Domestic Theories of International Bargaining," in *Double-Edged Diplomacy: International Bargaining and Domestic Politics*, edited by Peter Evans et al. (Berkeley: University of California Press, 1993), 3–42.

61. Peter Evans, "Building an Integrative Approach to International and Domestic Politics: Reflections and Projections," in *Double-Edged Diplomacy: International Bargaining and Domestic Politics*, edited by Peter Evans et al. (Berkeley: University of California Press, 1993), 397–430.

62. Jackson and Rosberg, "Why Africa's Weak States Persist," 7.

63. Albert Hirschman, "Beyond Asymmetry: Critical Notes on Myself as a Young Man and on Some Other Old Friends," *International Organization* 32, no. 1 (1978): 45–50.

64. Hirschman, "Beyond Asymmetry," 47.

65. Steven F. Jackson, "China's Third World Foreign Policy: The Case of Angola and Mozambique, 1961–93," *The China Quarterly* 142 (June 1995): 388–422.

66. According to Bo (Bo Kong, *China's International Oil Diplomacy* [Santa Barbara: Praeger Security International, 2010], 60), the severe national power shortages that China experienced between 2003 to 2006 were the result of Chinese domestic oil production declining twenty years previously and an inability of the Chinese central bureaucracy to mobilize fast enough in order to address the impending crisis of demand due to artificially low fuel prices.

67. Fred C. Bergsten, et al., *China's Rise: Challenges and Opportunities* (Washington: United Book Press, 2008), 151.

68. Shaofeng Chen, "Motivations behind China's Foreign Oil Quest: A Perspective from the Chinese Government and the Oil Companies," *Journal of Chinese Political Science* 13, no. 1 (2008): 79–104.

69. Hirschman, "Beyond Asymmetry," 46.

70. Carine Kiala, "China-Angola Aid Relations: Strategic Cooperation for Development?" *South African Journal of International Affairs* 17, no. 3 (2010): 313–31.

71. SDR are "special drawing rights," a unit of international reserve assets defined and maintained by the IMF. It is weighted against four currencies: the US dollar, the Japanese yen, the British pound, and the Euro.

72. This ceiling is contained in Article 12 of the Technical Memorandum of Understanding, and further elaborated upon in the Memorandum of Economic and Financial policies, submitted with a letter of intent by the Angolan government. See: IMF, "Angola: Letter of Intent, Memorandum of Economic and Financial Policies, and Technical Memorandum of Understanding," November 3, 2009, 117.

73. Sogge, "Angola: 'Failed' yet 'Successful,'" and de Oliveira, "Business Success, Angola-Style."

74. Cecile de Comarmond, "China Lends Angola $15 bn, but Few Jobs Are Created," *Mail and Guardian*, March 6, 2011,http://mg.co.za/article/2011-03-06-china-lends-angola-15bn-but-few-jobs-are-created.

75. Alves, "The Oil Factor in Sino-Angolan Relations"; Ricardo Gazel, "Macro-Brief: Angola," World Bank, February 2010, 1–3.

76. *Angola Press*, "Angola e China rubricam acordos de cooperação," November 19, 2009, http://www.portalangop.co.ao/motix/pt_pt/noticias/politica/2010/10/46/Angola-China-rubricam-acordos-cooperacao,00047b9c-b809-48a8-ae71-fd280c46b116.html.

77. Interview, senior diplomat, Angolan embassy, Beijing, October 28, 2009.

78. Ricardo Soares de Oliveira (2007) points out that the IMF cannot afford to disengage with the Gulf of Guinea states, as this will marginalize its role globally.

79. IMF, "Angola: Letter of Intent, Memorandum of Economic and Financial Policies, and Technical Memorandum of Understanding," 4.

80. Christine Messiant, *L'Angola postcolonial: Guerre et paix sans democratisation* (Paris: Karthala, 2008), 275.

81. Messiant, *L'Angola postcolonial*, 389.

82. William Reno, "The (Real) War Economy in Angola," in *Angola's War Economy: The Role of Oil and Diamonds*, edited by Jackie Cilliers and Christian Dietrich (Pretoria: Institute for Security Studies, 2000), 219–38.

83. Vasco Martins, "Keeping Business In and Politics Out: Angola's Multi-Vector Foreign Policy," *Portuguese Institute of International Relations and Security (IPRIS)*, October 2010, 1–2.

84. There is some controversy as to the ownership of the remaining 45 percent shareholding in SSI. Although it was initially widely reported on its formation that Sinopec held 75 percent and Sonangol 25 percent, this appears to have changed. Vines et al. (2009:42) report the shareholding as Sinopec (55 percent), Beiya (now Dayuan) International Development Ltd. (31.5 percent), and China Sonangol (13.5 percent). *Wall Street Journal* (2011) reports that China Sonangol owns the entire remaining 45 percent shareholding. Alex Vines, Lillian Wong, Marcus Weimer, and Indira Campos, "Thirst for African Oil: Asian National Oil Companies in Nigeria and Angola," Chatham House, August 2009.

85. *Financial Express*, "China Beats ONGC, Gets Angola Block," July 15, 2006,http://www.financialexpress.com/news/Sinopec-beats-ONGC,-gets-Angola-block-/171139/

86. Christopher Burke, Lucy Corkin, and Nastasya Tay, "China's Engagement of Africa: Preliminary Scoping of African Case Studies: A Scoping Exercise Evaluating China's Engagement of Six African Case Studies," prepared for the Rockefeller Foundation (Stellenbosch: Centre for Chinese Studies, Stellenbosch University, 2007), 37.

87. David Winning and Benoit Faucon, "Sinopec, CNOOC to Agree on $1.8B for Angola Asset," *Dow Jones Newswires*, October 1, 2008,http://www.rigzone.com/news/article.asp?a_id=67348.

88. The stake was later reportedly awarded by Sonangol to China Sonangol (Interview, Western Oil Company, Luanda, May 4, 2010).

89. Erica Downs, "The Fact and Fiction of Sino-Africa Energy Relations," *China Security* 3, no. 3 (Summer 2007): 46–47.

90. Even if China Sonangol's stake in SSI is 45 percent as reported by the *Wall Street Journal* (2011) this would give Sonangol an indirect 13.5 percent in SSI, less than half of its shareholding in China Sonangol if the latter owns oil equity directly.

91. Laura Murray et al., "African Safari: CIF's Grab for Oil and Minerals," *Caixin*, October 17, 2011 http://english.caixin.cn/2011-10-17/100314766.html.

92. Aslak Orre, Who's to Challenge the Party-State in Angola? Political Space and Opposition in Parties and Civil Society," paper presented at CMI and IESE conference "Election Processes, Liberation Movements and Democratic Change in Africa," Maputo, April 8–11, 2010, 1–20.

93. Lara Pawson, "The Angolan Elections: Politics of No Change," *Open Democracy*, September 25, 2008,http://www.isn.ethz.ch/isn/Current-Affairs/Security-Watch/Detail/?ots591= 4888CAA0-B3DB-1461-98B9-E20E7B9C13D4&lng=en&id=91981.

94. Messiant, "The Mutation of Hegemonic Domination," 106.

95. Abdul R. Mustapha, "States, Predation and Violence: Reconceptualizing Political Action and Political Community in Africa," Panel on State, Political Identity and Political Violence. 10th General Assembly of CODESIRA, Kampala, Uganda, December 8–12, 2002.

96. Rafael Marques de Morais, "The Angolan Presidency: The Epicentre of Corruption," *Pambazuka News* 493 (2010): 73.

97. Rafael Marques de Morais, "The New Imperialism: China in Angola," *World Affairs* March/April 2011, 71.

98. Personal correspondence, Angolan activist, October 18, 2011.

99. Interview, senior official, Angolan Embassy, Beijing, October 28, 2009.

100. Hodges, *Angola: Anatomy of an Oil State*, 169.

Chapter Five

Ethiopia: Toward a Foreign-Funded "Revolutionary Democracy"

Aleksandra W. Gadzala

Like so many other African states, Ethiopia has since the early 2000s taken concerted steps toward strengthening its relations with China. Unlike other African states, however, Ethiopia's ties to China have until recently escaped much academic and mainstream literature; as it is not a resource-rich country, Ethiopia exports little that is of strategic importance for Beijing. Yet Ethiopia is important in other ways. With a population of around ninety million people, it is the second most populous market on the continent, second to Nigeria. It is the seat of the African Union, and a hub for international organizations. Because of its strategic location in the Horn, it is also a crucial link in the global chain of defenses against global terror—an area in which China is gradually becoming increasingly active.

Owing to Ethiopia's unique makeup, Chinese engagement in the country diverges from that in other states. Unlike in Angola or Nigeria, for instance, where Chinese interests are concentrated in a single sector, they are in Ethiopia disbursed across a plethora of industries. China invests in infrastructure, manufacturing, mining, and, to limited degree, agriculture. Between 2000 and 2011, the majority of Chinese projects in Ethiopia were registered in the manufacturing sector; the largest volumes of capital were invested in the infrastructure and mining sectors—particularly in cement production. In 2013, China invested more in Ethiopia than any other country, followed only by Turkey. Cumulative Chinese investments by year-end 2013 reportedly reached $1.1 billion.

Yet Chinese enterprises do not foray into the Ethiopian market uninvited. Government decisions to fortify relations with Chinese public and private actors are precisely that—*decisions*. Ethiopian leaders actively choose Chinese financiers and dictate the terms and conditions of their operations. To understand Sino-Ethiopian relations, appreciation of these decisions therefore becomes important: how decisions are made, who makes them, and why do those individuals decide to do what they do. This is ultimately a question of agency and, in particular, of Ethiopian, rather than Chinese, agency. The objective of this chapter is to begin to unpack these dynamics. In the process, we come to see that political relations in Ethiopia are made by a circumscribed group of political elites within the ruling Ethiopian People's Revolutionary Democratic Front coalition. We also see that the ideals held by these individuals are the unique product of Ethiopian history and culture, which together inform a "revolutionary democratic" ideology. This ideology underpins Ethiopia's contemporary foreign affairs, including those with China.

The remainder of this chapter consists of three sections; the first elaborates on the historical and cultural foundations of the Ethiopian state as they relate to its present-day decision makers. It further unpacks the notion of "revolutionary democracy" and its relevance to government objectives of rapid economic development, in which China plays a critical role. The second section in turn explores how revolutionary democracy as an ideology informs the way in which Ethiopian leaders manage Chinese investments to reflect their revolutionary democratic ideals. Evidence from the telecommunications and infrastructure sectors suggests that investments often serve ideologically predicated motivations first, and economic or developmental considerations second; all considerations are filtered through an ideological lens. This is true not only in Ethiopia's relations with China but, indeed, in most of the country's foreign dealings. Land investments made by Asian and Arab investors since 2008—the so-called land grabs—likewise reflect this reality. These investments are examined in the chapter's third section. They reveal that it is the Ethiopian government, rather than foreign speculators, that is the ultimate "land-grabber": it organizes deals for its own benefit at the expense of the majority of people.

At a minimum, inquiry into Ethiopian ties to China points to the need to dig deeper, and to unpack the anatomy of the decisions being made.

IDEOLOGY AND THE ETHIOPIAN STATE

An appreciation of decisions undertaken by Ethiopia, or indeed, any state, vis-à-vis China and other foreign actors demands an understanding of the individuals whose responsibility it is to make such decisions, as well as the factors that influence their mind-set. As Lucy Corkin argues in this volume—and as is generally accepted in the wider foreign affairs literature—foreign affairs is a two-level game in which actors operate on national and international levels. In the former, political actors pursue policy goals through domestic bargaining processes. In the latter, they maximize those goals "while minimizing the adverse consequences of foreign developments."[1] Foreign policy "decisions and actions of governments are [therefore] intranational political resultants."[2] Resultants in the sense that outcomes derive "from compromise, conflict, and confusion of officials"; political insofar as the process from which they emerge "is best characterized as bargaining [. . .] among individual members of the government."[3] Robert Putnam and other scholars have likewise noted this multilayer nature of foreign affairs. For example, Robert Axelrod has advanced a paradigm in which the Cold War policies pursued by the United States' president vis-à-vis the Soviet Union were motivated by the objective of maximizing his domestic popularity.[4] Similarly, Glenn Snyder finds that prediction of foreign policy outcomes is improved by an appreciation of internal state bargaining and domestic politics, "including their ideological and ethnic makeup."[5]

In the two-level game of Ethiopia's foreign affairs, policy decisions are made by the ruling coalition, the Ethiopian People's Revolutionary Democratic Front (EPRDF)—specifically by a circumscribed group of political elites from the Tigray People's Liberation Front (TPLF), which has since 1991 held leadership of the coalition. Because of the dominant role of the TPLF in the EPRDF coalition, the hyphenated acronym TPLF-EPRDF is used throughout this chapter. Indeed, despite the nominally coalition structure of the EPRDF, the TPLF provides the leadership and ideological direction of the Ethiopian government. While policy decisions are formally made by the thirty-six-member EPRDF executive committee, political outcomes are the de facto consequence of choices made by nine TPLF central committee members who also occupy executive committee roles. Under former prime minister Meles Zenawi, these members included: Zenawi himself; Abadi Zemo (Chief Executive Officer, Endowment Fund for the Rehabilitation of Tigray); Abay Woldu (TPLF Deputy); Tsegay Berhe (president of Tigray); Beyene Mikru (Tigray Educational Bureau); Azeb Mesfin (wife of Meles); Tedros Adhanom (Health Minister); Debretsion Gebremichael (head of Ethiopia's Information and Communication Technology Development Agency); and Tewodros Hagos (head of Political Affairs, Tigray). Foreign affairs decisions also sometimes involved former foreign affairs minister Seyoum Mesfin, and Getachew Assefa, director of Ethiopia's National Intelligence and Security Service.

Under Prime Minister Hailemariam Desalegn, and on the back of the latest party elections in May 2013, members include old-timers Abay Woldu; Debretsion Gebremichael; Beyene Mikru; Tewodros Hagos, and Azeb Mesfin, as well as newly elected officials Tedros Adhanom (Minister of Foreign Affairs); Gebremeskel Tareke (Tigray State Disaster Prevention and Preparedness Bureau); Tirfu Kidanemariam (Tigray Women's Association); and Alem Gebrewahid. All nine TPLF central committee/EPRDF executive committee members under Meles and Desalegn are from Tigray. Of those who served under Meles, all were involved in the uprising against the Derg regime. Their contemporary political beliefs have to a large extent been shaped by the underlying objectives of that experience, which in turn inform their views of Ethiopian statehood and its foreign relations.

In his work on political ideologies, theorist Michael Freeden shrewdly argues that individuals do not exist as a tabula rasa, but rather are products of their culture—of "temporally and spatially bounded social practices, institutional patterns, ethnical systems, technologies, influential theories, discourses, and beliefs."[6] Culture is the context within which decision makers are embedded. Yet while culture is spatially bounded, it also "bear[s] the accumulative burdens of its past."[7] The culture, as well as the history, of the TPLF as vanguard of the ruling EPRDF is therefore central to understanding its contemporary domestic and foreign relations. This is all the more true given that when the TPLF-EPRDF seized power in 1991, it upended the institutions of previous regimes and inaugurated what then prime minister Zenawi called a "new era of democracy."[8] Jon Abbink notes that "traditional structures [were] recast,"[9] and realities "which did not previously exist"[10] were created. All structures and policies are thus in some way instrumental to TPLF-EPRDF objectives.

The TPLF emerged in 1975 under, and in opposition to, the Derg regime—the military junta led by Mengistu Haile Mariam that took power with the ousting of Emperor Haile Selassie in 1974. The TPLF was an outgrowth of the Marxist-oriented Tigray University students' movement at Haile Selassie University (today Addis Ababa University). According to Sarah Vaughan, its emergence was a "function of the juxtaposition of the aspirations and experience of educated Tigrayans [. . .] with their awareness of life in an [. . .] underdeveloped and stagnant Tigray." These problems were seen as the "result of a deliberate and ethnically-motivated government policy of discrimination against the northern region."[11] Indeed, both the Derg and Haile Selassie before it were ethnically Amhara; each sought to establish a unitary state with Amharic as the official language and Amhara culture as the foundational Ethiopian identity. Haile Selassie's *Amharisation* policy, for example, campaigned for the elimination of the identities of the frontier non-Amhara peoples, which were to be supplanted by an Amhara orientation. Under Selassie, the Amhara elite became the primary political authority.

Few changes occurred under the Derg. Aregawi Berhe, among the TPLF's founding members, argues that "Mengistu's regime in no time revealed itself as no different from the previous regime towards the assertive ethnic-nationalities, only this time accompanied by the harshness of military dictatorship."[12] The Derg saw Ethiopia as a monolithic Amharic society; any ethnically predicated grievances or requests were therefore regarded as threats to "Ethiopian unity and interests,"[13] and were quickly, and violently, suppressed. The Derg's policies were especially damaging for the population in Tigray—not least owing to their ethnic suppression. The household economies of Tigray's farmers were jeopardized by the regime's prohibition of work in urban areas, as well as by a national ban imposed against the hiring of agricultural laborers. Because the land in Tigray was not able to support the region's citizens, an estimated two hundred thousand Tigrayans either sought periodic work in urban areas or "follow[ed] cash crop harvests around Ethiopia."[14] With these practices forbidden, Tigray's population became impoverished and isolated—both ethnically as well as economically.

Within this context, the TPLF waged a national armed struggle. The objectives of the struggle, as described in 1989 by Gebre Medhin Araya, a TPLF defector who had been with the group for twelve years, were to "separate Tigray from Ethiopia and set up a government of its own," and "'help' all nationalities desiring to break away from the Motherland and form their own governments through armed struggle."[15] Paulos Milkias similarly notes that the TPLF "manifesto was drafted clearly as referring to a Tigrayan ethnic struggle for independence, not as one seeking the political liberation of Ethiopia from the dictatorship of the Derg."[16] This objective was recorded in a two-page TPLF dossier written in 1974,[17] as well as in the 1976 "Manifesto of the TPLF." The Manifesto argued that the "first task of [the] national struggle will be the establishment of an independent democratic republic of Tigray."[18] It has not been updated since it was first written.

The Maoist Influence

Early TPLF documents often referenced the teachings of Mao Zedong, especially in the context of the group's armed struggle against the Derg. While the TPLF's uprising was largely driven by ethnic motivations, it was ultimately a peasant-based revolt; the physical insecurity of Tigray's peasantry, caused by the repressive policies of the Derg, enabled the TPLF to mobilize an armed rebellion. In this context, the TPLF's early reliance on Mao is most apparent in its emphasis on mass organization, self-reliance, and protracted warfare between 1975 and 1991. This early reliance on Mao suggests an early ideological affinity to the Chinese state. It further suggests that Ethiopia's contemporary ties to China may be an extension of—or a return to—earlier relations. As Daniel Kaheman argues, (historical) associations of ideas may influence how individuals perceive, and make, decisions.[19]

The TPLF's ability to develop a mass movement on the back of peasant discontent—as well as the character of the uprising itself—indeed illustrated a debt to Mao and his dictum that "in order to make a revolution the party must first find an army."[20] This was the most influential of Mao's revolutionary tactics; it called on leaders to assume the social and political grievances of the masses, and to interpret them in terms that would advance the revolutionary consciousness. Mao, like the TPLF, emphasized the peasantry as the primary revolutionary force. In his 1927 "Report on an Investigation of the Human Peasant Movement," Mao wrote:

> Being the most revolutionary, the poor peasants have won the leadership [. . .]
> Without the poor peasants there can be no revolution. To reject them is to
> reject the revolution.[21]

The Maoist emphasis on the peasantry differentiated Maoism from other revolutionary agendas, and rendered it attractive for the TPLF; in 1970s Ethiopia, the peasantry comprised the majority of the Tigrayan population.[22] For example, in classic Marxism the communist revolution was defined as one led by the working class, the "proletariat," and not the peasantry. Marx had little regard for the peasants, believing them to be "incapable of enforcing their class interests in their own name,"[23] and requiring others to act on their behalf politically. In Marxist doctrine, peasants are thus futile revolutionaries. Yet like Mao, TPLF leaders "emphasized the importance of the peasants to the armed struggle."[24] In the early years of the uprising, TPLF leaders provided Tigray's peasantry with primary education, health care, and agricultural inputs. This, as Kaatje Segers notes, played an "important role in forging loyalty with the movement and consolidating its legitimacy in a society affected by drought and war."[25] As more of Tigray came under TPLF control, more farmers threw their support behind the group's revolutionary project. By the time the TPLF-EPRDF claimed political victory in 1991, nearly all of its armed forces consisted of peasant farmers from Tigray.

It is not entirely clear how Maoist precepts came to be accessed by the TPLF. Equally unclear is the extent to which Maoist thought informed TPLF ideology. Insofar as ideology is "packed with past associations, debates, and prejudices,"[26] however, the TPLF's exposure to Maoism can be said to have at minimum played some role in the formation of the group's ideology, though the exact weight of its influence may be unknown. A possible conduit for the transmission of Maoist ideas was the Eritrean People's Liberation Front (EPLF), which between the 1960s and 1980s served as a mentor to the TPLF and helped to train its forces.[27] The *New Statesmen* in 1982 claimed that as many as four thousand TPLF fighters were sent to be trained by the EPLF, but many informants believe this figure to be too high. The EPLF had been primed by Chinese revolutionaries in the 1960s, who saw the then-Eritrean struggle against Ethiopia as an opportunity to force Ethiopia to recognize Peking and to accept China's admission to the United Nations, which was at the time blocked by the US and other Western member states. TPLF rebels were encouraged to read *Lun Chi'ih-chui Chan* (*On Protracted Warfare*) and other accounts of Chinese peasant guerilla movements; special emphasis was placed on attaining the kind of endurance and revolutionary discipline exhibited by Chinese fighters. [28]

Unpacking "Revolutionary Democracy"

The history of the TPLF as a revolutionary, peasant-based, and partly Maoist-influenced organization shaped its guiding ideology, "revolutionary democracy." Revolutionary democracy is an ambiguous ideology that escapes clear definition. Meles once explained it by stating:

> When Revolutionary Democracy permeates the entire society, individuals will start to think alike and all persons will cease having their own independent outlook. In this order, individual thinking becomes simply part of collective thinking because the individual will not be in a position to reflect on concepts that have not been prescribed by Revolutionary Democracy. [29]

Sarah Vaughan and Kjetil Tronvoll define revolutionary democracy as an ideology founded on "communal collective participation" and "consensus forged through discussion led by the vanguard organization,"[30] which exists absent a negotiated basis. That is, the ideology of the state is in Ethiopia distinct from the ideology of the populace. Owing to the disconnect in party and popular ideology, the TPLF-EPRDF suffers from a persistent crisis of internal legitimacy. The regime must therefore persistently work to validate itself as the rightful owner of power by providing the population with material payoffs; its legitimacy is tied to progress toward economic growth and development.

As an ideology, revolutionary democracy consists of a collection of concepts that work in tandem to lend it meaning; the meaning of each concept also exists only insofar as it relates to the others. For example, *democracy* can only be properly understood when qualified by the term *revolutionary*. On its own, *democracy*, as such, is meaningless. Central among the concepts implicit in revolutionary democracy are, indeed, notions of democracy, revolution, and self-determination, as well as broader ideas of equality, centralism, state, and autonomy. Ideologies, of course, are not static but evolve to reflect the temporal and contextual realities of those who hold to them. Revolutionary democracy as an ideology has likewise evolved over time. Yet as Alexander de Waal argues, while Meles's thinking progressed, his basic principles and sensibilities remained constant. [31]

The TPLF-EPRDF's understanding of "democracy," for example, has always been predicated on the "inclusive participation of the people."[32] It emphasizes *all* the people, as opposed to *every* person. As conceived by revolutionary democracy, the communalism implicit in "democracy" is further bound up with wider notions of revolution and ethnic self-determination—this is a product of Tigrayan history. Indeed, a key assumption of the

TPLF-EPRDF leadership is that "democracy can only be established *through* ethnicity."[33] A 1982 TPLF document submitted before the UN General Assembly noted that the ultimate vision for Ethiopia is a "democratic multinational Ethiopia based on equality where there are no oppressor and oppressed nations."[34] This ideal is reflected in the structure of the state itself and its system of ethnically based federalism. Under Ethiopia's constitution, each of the country's nine regions has a full measure of self-government, replete with rights to independent lawmaking, executive, and judicial powers. Ethnic federalism is thus an expression of that equality that is to guarantee Ethiopia's ethnicities a sense of autonomy and security. Eshete Andreas argues, "Ethnic communities [. . .] have inherited Ethiopia . . . not *vice versa* [sic.]"[35] In reality, however, relations between the central government and the regions are so centralized that the federal division of power is severely undermined. Ultimately, ethnic federalism is a mode of "divide and conquer."

Over the years, the TPLF-EPRDF's understanding of self-determination has also come to embrace socioeconomic equality. Meles, and Desalegn after him, both speak of a "democratic developmental state," the objectives of which are rapid economic growth and the elimination of poverty. The TPLF-EPRDF emphasizes such development as a means of vindicating its rule in the eyes of the public, at times comparing the struggle for development to the struggle against the Derg. Like in the struggle against the Derg, too, the TPLF-EPRDF similarly perceives itself as the responsible vanguard for the oversight of the developmental process—the state, as Meles often argued, requires autonomy. Once economic development is attained, the state "will undermine its own social base to be replaced by a social democratic or liberal democratic coalition."[36] The "community [will] speak with one voice, and dissent [will be] ruled out."[37] This "one voice," of course, will belong to the state.

CHINESE INVESTMENTS AND REVOLUTIONARY DEMOCRACY

The central tenets and influences of revolutionary democracy underpin, and are apparent in, policy decisions taken by the TPLF-EPRDF. This is apparent, too, in Ethiopia's relations with China. While Chinese state and private actors make investments in; establish businesses in; and forge political, economic, and cultural ties with, Ethiopia, their governing conditions and, to an extent, outcomes are determined by how the activities are managed by Ethiopia. In its ties with China, as with other actors, the TPLF-EPRDF leverages activities to uphold and advance the underlying principles of revolutionary democracy. Investment options that advance the ideals of revolutionary democracy are thus regarded as gains, while those that undermine it are regarded as losses—this, irrespective of the associated developmental and economic gains and losses. While economic development is pursued, it is pursued only insofar as it does not compromise party ideology.

ZTE Corporation's $1.5 Billion Ethiopian Telecommunications Agreement

In September 2006 the Ethiopian Telecommunications Corporation (ETC, now Ethio-Telecom), Ethiopia's sole state-owned telecommunications provider, signed a $1.5 billion agreement with China's ZTE Corporation to roll out and expand telecommunications services in the country. The agreement, signed between ZTE, ETC, and Ethiopia's Ministry of Transport and Communication, is the largest telecommunications investment in Africa. It is also among the more peculiar as it gave a single supplier, ZTE, the right to supply and install all telecoms equipment in Ethiopia over a three-year period. Finance was offered on vendor finance terms under which funds provided by ZTE to ETC were used to buy ZTE technology and services. The repayment period on the loan was thirteen years with a fixed rate of Libor + 1 percent. Nine equipment packages were placed with ZTE.

The agreement adopted the objectives of ETC's 2006 to 2010 strategic plan, implicit in which were provisions for the rollout of a ten-thousand-kilometer fiber transmission network; the expansion of 3G services to rural areas outside of Addis Ababa, where less than 1 percent of the population has mobile coverage (in Tigray, 6 percent of the population had mobile coverage in 2010); the expansion of Ethiopia's mobile subscriber base to ten million with 85 percent national coverage; and an increase in operational fixed lines to 4.4 million by 2010. The policy objective, as stated by the plan, was to "improve the social and economic well-being of the peoples of Ethiopia through the exploitation of the opportunities created by ICT for achieving rapid and sustainable socio-economic development, and for sustaining a robust democratic system."[38] This objective, of course, was to be attained exclusively via the strategic direction of the TPLF-EPRDF, which, perceiving telecommunications infrastructure to be a public good, believes that "the government is best placed to promote universal access."[39]

ETC officials allege that ZTE was selected from a group of eight global bidders among which were Ericsson, Nokia, Alcatel, and Siemens. ETC officials further allege that ZTE was selected due to its "willingness to meet [ETC] requirements and enter into a long-term relationship with the telecom."[40] What these requirements were is unclear. There is no evidence that would point to any commercial justification for such a large tender to be placed with a single supplier, and it is hard to imagine the kind of stipulations that would necessitate such an arrangement. At no point in the procurement process, too, were ETC's financial needs made known to any competing supplier. That an open and competitive procurement process took place is also in doubt; the price and quality of the equipment to be supplied were agreed upon only after the agreement was signed. In general, ZTE prices itself 30 to 40 percent lower than its major foreign competitors, which is also at least 15 percent lower than its primary Chinese competitor, Huawei.[41] Whether such low pricing was offered in 2006 is unclear—though not unlikely.

Vendor finance is an altogether not uncommon form of telecommunications finance: it was a catalyst behind the emerging markets telecoms boom in the 1990s and 2000s. For underdeveloped providers like ETC, such financing can provide needed capital for network startup and operations. Yet it is also a risky form of lending that, if not properly managed, can have destabilizing economic effects for borrowers. Because vendor finance requires that borrowers purchase equipment exclusively from the lender, it can produce a kind of "lock in," binding the borrower to a single vendor—in this case ETC to ZTE and other Chinese suppliers. What is curious about the 2006 agreement is that the TPLF-EPRDF willingly acquiesced to such a shut-in; as Lishan Adam then noted, the ETC "will not have any choice but to continue to borrow from Chinese banks to maintain its massive network."[42]

Upon the signing of the 2006 agreement, ZTE regional president Yin Zhang remarked ZTE had "achieved [its] long-term plan in Ethiopia."[43] Between 2006 and 2013, ZTE enjoyed a near-monopoly over Ethiopia's telecoms sector, being able, too, to "dictate the level of infrastructure and the quality of service."[44] Yet quality remains low, and the deal, as well as those that have followed—a known five ZTE deals in total—have done little to improve and expand Ethiopia's telecoms infrastructure. By 2013, ZTE had built upward of two thousand mobile transmission lines and had laid five thousand miles of fiber optic; an estimated twelve million mobile subscribers have been registered, up from one million in 2005. Such limited progress temporarily bolsters regime legitimacy under the veneer of development.

Still, telecommunications in Ethiopia is among the least developed in the world. Only 2.5 percent of Ethiopians have Internet access; mobile-phone penetration, which averages 70 percent in most of Africa, was 25 percent in 2013. Despite the uptick in mobile subscribers, too, the mobile annual revenue per user has been declining since 2007, from an average $12 per month to $2 per month in 2012. While partly a reflection of the increase in base-of-pyramid subscribers, the decline in revenue also underscores ETC's persistent inefficiencies—and its function as an instrument of TPLF-EPRDF ideology.

The TPLF-EPRDF began repaying the $1.5 billion loan in 2008. As of early 2014 it had repaid $300 million in principal. Under the terms of the finance agreement, ETC pays ZTE by issuing promissory notes; it then pays the capital plus interest on the note. Included in the agreement, too, is a proviso that allows for repayment in the form of sesame exports to China, akin to the "oil-for-infrastructure" arrangements signed between China and other African states; Ethiopia is the world's fourth largest producer of sesame (the largest in Africa), with China its main export destination. Foreign currency earned from the sesame sales is passed to the state-owned Commercial Bank of Ethiopia and, at least in principle, used to repay financing extended by Chinese banks. Yet the currency is also inevitably used to resource the TPLF-EPRDF's revolutionary democratic goals. As an arm of the government, ETC has complete control over all phone, mobile, and Internet services; its general manager as well as CEO are appointed by Ethiopia's Ministry of Transport and Communication. Essentially, ETC is an instrument of government policy—a cash cow—and a reflection of the concepts of state and centralism that are key to the TPLF-EPRDF's attainment of a "robust democratic system."

In January 2008, Ethiopia's Federal Ethics and Anti-Corruption Commission brought charges against twenty-seven former ETC executives for allegedly procuring $154 million in low-quality equipment from suppliers that should have been rejected on the basis of Ethiopia's procurement regulations. In August that same year, the Commission arrested a senior ETC executive after it was discovered that he openly accepted bribes from an international supplier. In 2011, former ETC CEO Tesfaye Birru and sixteen former employees were found guilty of mismanaging Birr 1.54 billion ($89 million) in a contract awarded to Swedish telecom giant, Ericsson. According to individuals familiar with the matter, funds supplied by the 2006 agreement have also been subject to TPLF-EPRDF mishandling; a 2013 World Bank report found ZTE not to have been complicit in any wrongdoing.[45] Rather than leveraging Chinese telecommunications investments such that they might engender genuine progress, the TPLF-EPRDF instead leverages them to reinforce its role as the vanguard of development. And as it is guided by revolutionary democracy, it remains convinced of the righteousness of its ways.

The Case of Norinco Lalibela Engineering and Construction Company (Nori-La)

Among the concepts informing revolutionary democracy, that of "revolution" is seldom addressed; how the TPLF-EPRDF today understands "revolution" is often difficult to grasp. Under the Derg, the notion implied an ethnic, peasant-based revolt, the objective of which was to rid Ethiopia of the vestiges of prior, Amharic regimes. Referencing the Maoist precept of protracted warfare, the TPLF-EPRDF then emphasized the extensiveness and gravity of its struggle, and the consequent need to fight along many divergent fronts. John Young notes, the TPLF "remained preeminently a guerrilla movement until the final stages of the war."[46] For the TPLF-EPRDF, however, the overthrow of the Derg did not signify the victorious culmination of its insurrection. Rather, it marked a milestone on the way to the realization of a revolutionary democratic state, characterized by the self-determination of Ethiopia's ethnicities and their collective participation in state political and economic processes.

For the TPLF-EPRDF, this objective has not yet been realized: the revolution is ongoing. In the area of foreign affairs, relations must therefore be subversive insofar as they hasten the realization of such a federation. The actualization of such a federation, too, demands the autonomy—and by extension, security—of the state against domestic and foreign threats. This is today represented by the stalwart security and military control that the government has over its population, and the profound strength of its armed forces. The TPLF-EPRDF, too, leverages foreign investments to advance this purpose, of which the Norincio Lalibela Engineering and Construction Company is one example.

Nori-La was established in 2004 as a joint venture company between Ethiopia's Lalibela Engineering and Construction Enterprise and Norinco International Corporation (Norinco). Other shareholders to the venture included Kality Construction (Ethiopia), Branna Printing Enterprise (Ethiopia), China Wanbao Engineering Corporation, and Yu Dewei (China). The joint venture agreement called for an initial investment of $32.9 million, with Norinco taking a 12.5 percent stake.[47] Officially, Nori-La was set up to manage "building construction; real estate development; equipment leasing; and other related civil construction business."[48] Unofficially, it appears to have been a front company established for the exchange of military technology and strategy between China and the Ethiopian National Defense Forces (ENDF).

Of the firms party to the Nori-La venture, all had ties to their respective defense industries. Norinco, for instance, is the Shenzhen-listed arm of China North Industries Corporation, a Chinese military weapons and engineering firm and a leading supplier to the People's Liberation Army (PLA). As the commercial arm of the PLA, Norinco's acquisitions have generally been controversial. In 1996, for instance, the company was implicated in "Operation Dragon Fire," believed to be the largest seizure of fully operational and automatic weapons in United States' history; the United States has sanctioned Norinco three times: once in 2003 and twice in 2004. In 2006, Norinco entered into a joint venture with the Zimbabwe Defense Industries and Zimbabwean Mining Development Corporation to explore for chromite in the Great Dyke. Implicit in the transaction were military sales for which it is believed that Zimbabwe paid in chromium concessions.[49] Norinco forayed into the Ethiopian market in 1998 when "there was a general boom in the construction industry."[50] By the time Nori-La was established in 2004, the company had allegedly completed three successful Ethiopian road construction projects.

Wanbao Engineering Corporation, the other Chinese party to Nori-La, is Norinco's engineering and construction arm, engaged in the construction of "military and civil engineering products" including "factories to manufacture rocket and missile propellants."[51] Little else is known about the company. Even less is known about Yu Dewei, other than that he at the time held a senior position in Norinco. Whether he acted privately or in his capacity as a Norinco employee in the joint venture is unclear.

On the Ethiopian side, all entities signatory to the Nori-La venture had ties to the ENDF and, by extension, the TPLF-EPRDF leadership. Branna Printing Enterprise is one of seven known enterprises headed by the Ethiopian Defense Industry Sector (DIS), an office under the Ministry of Defense responsible for the administration of Ethiopia's military-industrial complex; DIS is mandated to supply and support the ENDF. Little is known about Lalibela and Kality Construction, other than that both firms are controlled by the Ethiopian Ministry of Defense. Kality in particular was established especially to "satisfy national defense construction needs."[52] As such, and as part of Nori-La, it between 2004 and 2009 undertook an alleged fifteen defense-sector projects. Known undertakings included construction of residential and commercial buildings for the Mekele Regional Hospital in Tigray; the construction of low-cost housing in Addis Ababa; as well as the construction of various army camps, airfield works, and recreational facilities for the Ethiopian Air Force (EAF).[53] Nori-La in 2006 additionally secured a $25 million contract to refurbish EAF's fighter plane hangars and construct a maintenance center in Debre Zeit, thirty miles southeast of Addis Ababa.[54] While Nori-La officials maintain that projects were won in competitive tender processes, the company's ties to the highest echelons of the TPLF-EPRDF cast doubt on such auspicious assertions.

Nori-La unexpectedly liquidated in 2009. Company profits were transferred to Ethiopia's Ministry of Defense, though the exact sums are unknown; members of Nori-La's senior management claim the firm was never profitable. They further maintain that no profits accrued to Norinco or to Wanbo. This is rather unusual. Under articles 20(1) and 21(3) of Ethiopia's Investment Proclamation, foreign investors have the right "to take profits and dividends accruing from investment out of Ethiopia in convertible foreign currency at a prevailing rate of exchange" (this applies to "proceeds from the sale or liquidation of an enterprise" as well as to "proceeds from the transfer of share or of partial ownership of an enterprise to a domestic investor"), and to "remit compensation paid to them out of Ethiopia in convertible foreign currency." That neither Chinese firm capitalized on these stipulations is strange. In interviews, Chinese shareholders would often refer to Nori-La as a "bridge" between China and Ethiopia, further observing that the market was "golden"[55] for business. What they failed to specify, however, is the business to which they were referring.

Additionally transferred from China to Ethiopia's Ministry of Defense at the time of liquidation were an alleged several hundred items of machinery and equipment, including 122 dump, courier, fuel trucks, and trailers; twenty-six concrete vibrators; thirty loaders; twenty-seven graders; and small and light weapons including artillery guns, ammunition, WMZ-551 6 feet x 6 feet wheel-armored vehicles, and an undisclosed amount of 155 millimeter propulsion howitzers. With the exception of the vehicles, all items were imported into Ethiopia duty free, as sanctioned by the investment proclamation.[56] Article 5(2) of the proclamation further allows for the manufacture of weapons and ammunition in joint venture with the TPLF-EPRDF. Although unconfirmed, Nori-La's structure and exploits portend that such activity may have indeed transpired. In a rare moment of candor, a member of Nori-La's senior management professed that the core aim of the company was the supply and upgrade of Ethiopia's defense sector.

The Ethiopian defense sector is monopolized by the TPLF, with most senior military commanders former TPLF fighters. This remained the case in 2008 when Meles promoted a dozen senior military officials to lieutenant, brigadier, and major general. Eight of those promoted were Tigrayans, including the ENDF's Chief of Staff, Samora Yunis.[57] Overall, between 60 to 80 percent of the ENDF is from Tigray[58]—approximately 80 percent is said to be from the same village.[59] Amhara and Oromo officers in the country's armed forces thus recognize that their primary duty is to pander to the Tigrayan elite, rather than serve the wider interests of the de jure Ethiopian state.[60] The security and autonomy of Ethiopia is tantamount to the security and autonomy of the TPLF-EPRDF. ENDF troops stationed around the country are therefore another way by which the TPLF-EPRDF ensures perpetuation of its revolutionary democratic cause; partnerships like those forged under the umbrella of Nori-La advance this aim. Such partnerships, and their inherent transfer of finance to the TPLF, also tangentially advance the self-determination of Tigrayans and of Tigray region. As Paulos Chanie notes, it is an open secret in Ethiopia that "the EPRDF channels a larger amount of [. . .] funding to Tigray than to the other regions, under the pretext of reconstructing the war-affected region."[61]

Yet Ethiopia has relations with other foreign defense contractors who also supply it with military equipment, finance, and know-how. In 2003, the ENDF acquired sixty modern Russian T-72 main battle tanks that were transferred via Yemen. In 2011, it signed a $100 million contract with Ukrspetsexport, a Ukrainian state-owned vehicle manufacturer, for the supply of two hundred upgraded T-72 tanks.[62] That same year, it signed an agreement with the Israeli manufacturer BlueBird Aero Systems for the purchase of drones. The transfer of military equipment through operations like Nori-La therefore suggests the transfer of potentially illicit goods. It further underscores the intensity with which the TPLF-EPRDF regards the objective of a revolutionary democratic end-state.

AN INVESTOR BY ANY OTHER NAME

It is of course undeniable that Chinese engagement in Ethiopia diverges from that of other foreign actors; the chapters in this volume underscore the point. Yet what seldom diverges is the way foreign investments are managed by the TPLF-EPRDF, with few exceptions. This is true not only in the case of Chinese investments but also in nearly all foreign engagements Ethiopia.

Much has, for instance, been made of foreign land deals in Ethiopia—dubbed by some as a new form of colonization, land "grabs," or indeed, theft. Since 2008, the Ethiopian government has embarked on a supercharged process of awarding millions of hectares of land to foreign and national investors. It is estimated that by the end of 2011, nearly 3.5 million hectares were ceded to foreign investors,[63] most from capital-rich but food-poor countries like India, Saudi Arabia, and the Gulf Cooperation Council states. The TPLF-EPRDF claims that such investments will allow for much-needed foreign currency, and will facilitate long-term food security through the transfer of technology to small-scale farmers. By couching the deals in developmental terms, the TPLF-EPRDF hopes to legitimate them, and thereby itself, in the eyes of the public—especially in regions where the deals are enforced. Gambella, Benishangul-Gumuz, Afar, Somali, and the Southern Nations, Nationalities, and People's Region (SNNPR) receive the bulk of investments; firms that invest in these regions receive additional tax exemptions, on top of the already favorable investment climate forged by the TPLF-EPRDF.

Between 2000 and 2011 the investment office in Gambella, western Ethiopia, registered an estimated 896 agriculture investments, approximately half of which were made by Indian firms. At the end of 2011, there were about twenty-five to thirty Indian firms that between them held 450,000 and 500,000 hectares of land in various parts of the country.[64] Perhaps the most well known is Karuturi, a company based in Bangalore, India. Karuturi forayed into the Ethiopian market in 2004 with a $5 million investment and one hundred hectares of land; by 2010 its total invested capital was $150 million with three hundred hectares of land in Itang and Jikawo in Gambella (this was subsequently reduced to one hundred thousand hectares). The land is harvested to grow cereals, palm oil, rice, and sugar and, according to documents from the Ethiopian Ministry of Agriculture and Rural Development, is leased for a fifty-year period with the option of renewal. The cost of land is Birr 20 ($1.19) per hectare per year, at a price of Birr 100 million ($5.6

million) for the contract period. In line with the Investment Proclamation, Karuturi is exempt from import duties and tariffs on goods shipped overseas.[65] The company additionally leases eleven thousand hectares of land in Bako, Oromia, for the production and export of flowers—its core competency.

Most of the crops harvested on the leased land are cash crops grown for export: rice, oil seeds, maize, palm oil, sugar cane, and cotton.[66] The earned revenues constitute a critical source of foreign exchange for the TPLF-EPRDF. Moreover, among the perceived benefits of cash crop farming are the employment opportunities created by such ventures; Karuturi suggested that it would require between four thousand and five thousand workers. Yet most of these jobs are laborer positions that offer low wages, and seasonal and short-term contracts. So far, it is therefore the TPLF-EPRDF that stands to reap the greatest gains from the land lease arrangements, boosting not only its foreign reserves but also further concentrating power over territory—and the biodiversity and peoples that occupy it.

In October 2010, Saudi Star Agriculture Development Plc., a food company part of the MIDROC group of companies owned by the Saudi-Ethiopian billionaire Mohammed Al-Amoudi, similarly acquired ten thousand hectares of land along the Alwero River in Gambella; the area is in close proximity to, and partly overlaps with, Gambella National Park. Land is leased for a sixty-year period at an annual cost of Birr 158 ($9.42) per hectare. Land prices in Ethiopia range depending on the land's distance from the capital: farmland located seven hundred kilometers (435 miles) from Addis Ababa costs Birr 111 ($5.41) per hectare, per year. As land moves closer to the capital, the price increases by Birr 4.05 ($0.19) per kilometer; as it moves away, it declines by Birr 0.45 per kilometer. For irrigation farming, the annual cost of land is Birr 158 ($7.71) per hectare; the price increases or decreases by Birr 4.17 ($0.20), contingent on the land's distance from Addis.[67] Average annual land prices in sub-Saharan Africa are between $800 and $1,000 per hectare. This means that the TPLF-EPRDF leases land at prices that are well below some of the lowest, globally.

Implicit in the Saudi Star deal—as in most land investments in Ethiopia— is the forced relocation and "villagization" of local populations, including pastoralists, agropastoralists, and peasant cultivators. Several small villages—among them, Oriedhe and Oridge—within the lease area were relocated to the one-thousand-person village of Pokedi, across the Alwero River. By the end of 2013, the TPLF-EPRDF aimed to relocate upward of 1.5 million Ethiopians to make way for land investments, including 225,000 individuals in Gambella alone.[68] How many people have been transferred is unclear. What is clear, however, is that while some finger wagging at firms like Karuturi and Saudi Star is warranted, these firms act upon conditions and opportunities that are set and sanctioned by the TPLF-EPRDF; foreign investors in Ethiopia lease land on terms dictated by the TPLF-EPRDF, not on terms that they themselves determine. Dessalegn Rahmato notes, "The state [is] the sole actor through the various stages of the land 'grabbing' process, from the initial task of publicity and investor attraction to the final stage of allocation of specific farm plots. This is an important point to bear in mind."[69]

Indeed, Ethiopia's constitution stipulates that land is a public good that can be expropriated by the federal state for the common benefit and development of the population; Ethiopia's investment proclamation additionally prioritizes foreign speculators in obtaining lease for land. Since 2009, the state is mandated to carry out all aspects of foreign land investment for land over five thousand hectares—the baseline for nearly all foreign land leases. The Agricultural Investment Support Directorate under the Ministry of Agriculture and Rural Development identifies potential land for investments, receives land from Ethiopia's regions, and transfers it to international investors. Ultimately, it is the TPLF-EPRDF that is the chief "land-grabber," with foreign investors as ready beneficiaries.

Like the ZTE agreement and Nori-La, the leasing out of large tracts of land is intended to advance the objectives of revolutionary democracy. The deals are, as René LeFort notes, "part of a process of re-concentration"[70] of state power. Implicit in the *Amharization* policies of Selassie and the Derg was the assimilation of periphery cultures into the Amharic Ethiopian state. Although itself a periphery culture, this policy was taken up by the TPLF-EPRDF when it assumed power in 1991; it reflects its adherence to notions of centralism and state implicit in revolutionary democracy. Indeed, the bulk of the investments are concentrated in areas where the process of political and economic assimilation is still ongoing; only few deals have so far been recorded in Tigray. The TPLF-ERPDF's approach to the land leases also encapsulates contradictions inherent in Ethiopia's system of ethnic federalism. Although state structures give equal rights to all ethnic groups, historical legacies and contemporary perceptions create a situation where mistrust and (Tigrayan) dominance prevail. The TPLF-ERPDF's desire for land is associated with the likely marginalization and disempowerment of frontier peoples.

CONCLUSION

How revolutionary democracy manifests itself is not always discernible *ex ante*. Yet the cases explored in this chapter demonstrate that the TPLF-EPRDF pursues foreign investment decisions in which there is a clear benefit to the concepts encompassed by the ideology. The TPLF-EPRDF leadership reasons not in economic or developmental terms first and ideological terms second, but vice versa: economic and developmental considerations are to support ideology, not ideology economics. This renders Ethiopia distinct from other African states where the weight of the ideological influence is limited or else curbed by other considerations. At minimum, the uniqueness of the Ethiopian context encourages a focus on bilateral relations in discussions of "China-in-Africa," and nuanced appreciation of the historical, cognitive, and institutional variables that inform African settings. Insofar as China can be said to be taking advantage of, of pilfering from, African states, this is often done within states' conventional and legal frameworks, and often with African governments as willing parties to the transactions. In Ethiopia, institutions and policies have been crafted by the TPLF-EPRDF such that they champion the aims of revolutionary democracy with little benefit to the vast majority of Ethiopians.

A fundamental question is therefore one of how to assure positive outcomes of China's Ethiopian ventures, militating against their capture by ideological agendas. China's investment in Ethiopia, as in Africa, has already proven beneficial—issues of corruption and backdoor dealings notwithstanding. The first phase of the Addis Ababa Ring Road, built by the China Road and Bridge Corporation and completed in 2004, for example, allows for heavy vehicles entering the city to bypass the city center, in this way reducing traffic congestion and limiting pollution. It also connects previously isolated neighborhoods to marketplaces, schools, and other key services. Local residents refer to the road as the "Ethiopia First Road," or the "Milestone Road" (some, more crudely, "China Road")—a testament to the benefits that it has brought city residents. For the TPLF-EPRDF, the project gave a boost to its popular legitimacy and reinforced, if temporarily, its role as the rightful vanguard of Ethiopia's development. Still, completion of the road—the third and final phase of which is due to be finished in 2015—has encountered significant delays, with the final cost over five times the expected budget. Chinese contractors dominate the market, and procurement processes are often anything but competitive.

What are needed are sound political institutions that can not only serve as a check on government behavior but can also engender inclusive development. In the world of African politics, this is hardly a startling proposition; problems associated with the lack of independent and accountable institutions reign perennial. Indeed, analyses of Ethiopian foreign affairs remain concerned with the cognitive biases of the TPLF-EPRDF precisely because independent institutions are lacking. Existing state structures are the result of the Tigrayan experience under prior regimes, and the TPLF's exposure to Maoist precepts during its uprising against the Derg. These events have shaped the government's ideology, of which Ethiopia's political institutions are both the manifestation and active vehicles.

Such a reality casts doubt on the near-term potential for institutional reform, and leaves to the imagination the makeup of the evolved structures. There is, of course, no recipe for how institutional development should happen or what effective institutions should look like. Still, a few observations are warranted. Needed in Ethiopia are structures that not only accommodate the country's ethnicities but also elevate them to decision-making roles. This would disperse Tigrayan political influence and its associated monopoly over Ethiopian history, further challenging—or, indeed, refashioning—the central tenets of revolutionary democracy. Needed, too, are strengthened local and participatory institutions. When agricultural plots are leased to foreign speculators, individuals resident on the land are usually not consulted and learn of the developments only after their fate has been sealed. The formal inclusion of local communities into the land lease process would not only safeguard Ethiopian livelihoods but could result in more financially viable and productive contractual agreements; surely those resident on the land are those best suited to assess the potential of its harvest. The cases of ZTE and Nori-La also point to the need for independent auditing agencies; this is especially critical as Ethiopia continues to court foreign investors and absorb significant volumes of foreign exchange.

Ultimately, what is needed in Ethiopia are multiple formal and informal avenues through which agency vis-à-vis China and other foreign actors can be expressed. Now there is but one.

NOTES

1. Robert Putnam, Diplomacy and Domestic Politics: The Logic of Two-Level Games," *International Organization* 42, no. 3 (1988): 434.
2. Graham Allison and Philip Zelikow, *Essence of Decision: Explaining the Cuban Missile Crisis*, 2nd ed. (New York: Longman, 1999 [1971]), 294.
3. Allison and Zelikow, *Essence of Decision*, 295.
4. Robert Axlerod, *The Complexity of Cooperation: Agent-Based Models of Competition and Collaboration* (Princeton: Princeton University Press, 1997).
5. Glenn H. Snyder, *Alliance Politics* (Ithaca, NY: Cornell University Press, 1997), 129.
6. Michael Freeden, *Ideologies and Political Theory: A Conceptual Approach* (Oxford: Clarendon Press, 1996), 69–70.
7. Freeden, *Ideologies and Political Theory*, 98.
8. "Acting President Promises 'New Era of Democracy,'" *F.B.I.S*, June 3, 1991.
9. Jon Abbink, "Breaking and Making the State: The Dynamics of Ethnic Democracy in Ethiopia," *Journal of Contemporary African Studies* 13, no. 2 (1995): 149.
10. Jon Abbink, "Ethnicity and Constitutionalism in Contemporary Ethiopia," *Journal of African Law* 41, no. 2 (1997): 160.
11. Sarah Vaughan, "Ethnicity and Power in Ethiopia," PhD, The University of Edinburgh, 163.
12. Aregawi Berhe, "Ethiopia: Success Story or State of Chaos?" in *Post-Modern Insurgencies: Political Violence, Identity Formation and Peace-Making in Comparative Perspective*, edited by Ronaldo Munck and Purnaka de Silva, 99 (New York: Palgrave MacMillan, 2000).
13. Aregawi Berhe, "The Origins of the Tigray People's Liberation Front," *African Affairs* 103, no. 413 (2004): 569–92.574.

14. Berhe, "The Origin of the Tigray People's Liberation Front," 222.
15. Yohannes Lakew, "Defector Describes Inner Workings of TPLF," *F.B.I.S* (1989).
16. Paulos Milkias, "Ethiopia, the TPLF, and the Roots of the 2001 Political Tremor," *Northeast African Studies* 10, no. 2 (2003): 13
17. See: Berhe, "The Origins of the Tigray People's Liberation Front," 579. This two-page guideline is located in the archives of the TPLF as a classified document. Access to this and other classified TPLF documents is possible only with the permission of Meles Zenawi.
18. On the TPLF Manifesto see, among others: Matthew J. McCracken, "Abusing Self-Determination and Democracy: How the TPLF Is Looting Ethiopia," *Case Western Reserve Journal of International Law* 36 (2004); Milkias, "Ethiopia, the TPLF, and the Roots of the 2001 Political Tremor"; John Young, *Peasant Revolution in Ethiopia: Tigray People's Liberation Front, 1975–1991* (Cambridge: Cambridge University Press, 1997).
19. See: Daniel Kahneman, *Thinking, Fast and Slow* (New York: Farrar, Straus and Giroux, 2011), part I, chapter IV.
20. Mao Zedong quoted in: Young, *Peasant Revolution in Ethiopia*, 33.
21. Mao Tse-Tung, "Report on an Investigation of the Hunan Peasant Movement," in *Sources of Chinese Tradition*, edited by W. T. De Bary, Wing-Tsit Chan, and Burton Watson (New York: Columbia University Press, 1960 [1927]), 209.
22. Kaatje Segers et al., "Be Like Bees—The Politics of Mobilizing Farmers for Development in Tigray, Ethiopia," *African Affairs* 108 (430): 91–109.
23. Karl Marx, "The Eighteenth Brumaire of Louis Bonaparte (selections)," in *Karl Marx: Selected Writings*, edited by Lawrence H. Simon (Indianapolis: Hackett Publishing, 1994 [1852]), 200.
24. Personal interview, former EPRDF cabinet minister and member of the legislature of the government of Ethiopia (1991–1993), Addis Ababa, June 2010.
25. Segers et al., "Be Like Bees," 96.
26. Freeden, *Ideologies and Political Theory: A Conceptual Approach*, 98.
27. John Young, "The Tigray and Eritrean Peoples Liberation Fronts: a History of Tensions and Pragmatism," *The Journal of Modern African Studies* 34, no. 1 (1996): 105–20.
28. Aregawi Berhe, "A Political History of the Tigray People's Liberation Front (1975–1991): Revolt, Ideology and Mobilisation in Ethiopia," Doctor of Philosophy, Faculty of Social Sciences, University of Amsterdam, 2008, see especially page 87.
29. Meles Zenawi, as cited in Paulos Milkias, "The Great Purge and Ideological Paradox in Contemporary Ethiopian Politics," *Horn of Africa* 19 (2001): 59.
30. Sarah Vaughan and Kjetil Tronvoll, *The Culture of Power in Contemporary Ethiopian Political Life*, SIDA Studies, No. 10 (2003): 15.
31. Alexander De Waal, *Evil Days: Thirty Years of War and Famine in Ethiopia* (New York: Human Rights Watch, 1991), 148.
32. Ethiopian People's Revolutionary Democratic Front (EPRDF), "Action Plan of the EPRDF for Development, Peace and Democracy," 1995, 12.
33. Abbink, "Breaking and Making the State: The Dynamics of Ethnic Democracy in Ethiopia," 152. Italics in original text.
34. From the TPLF's 1982 submission to the UN General Assembly, regarding the Tigray people's struggle for self-determination, as quoted in: Sarah Vaughan, "The Addis Ababa Transitional Conference of July 1991: Its Origins, History and Significance," Edinburgh: Centre of African Studies, Edinburgh University, 9.
35. Eshete Andreas, "The Protagonists in Constitution-Making in Ethiopia," in *The Experience of Constitution-Making in Africa: Ethiopia, Uganda and South Africa* (Africa Institute, Pretoria, May 26–28, 1997), 20.
36. Meles Zenawi quoted in de Waal, "The Theory and Practice of Meles Zenawi," 155.
37. Vaughan and Tronvoll, *The Culture of Power in Contemporary Ethiopian Political Life*, 117. Also see: Jean-Nicolas Bach, "*Abyotawi* Democracy: Neither Revolutionary nor Democratic, a Critical Review of EPRDF's Conception of Revolutionary Democracy in Post-1991 Ethiopia," *Journal of Eastern African Studies* 5, no. 4 (2011).
38. Federal Democratic Republic of Ethiopia, "The National Information and Communication Technology Policy and Strategy," 2009.

39. Lishan Adam, "Ethiopia ICT Performance Review 2009/2010: Toward Evidence-Based ICT Policy and Regulation," ed. Research ICT Africa (2010), 7.

40. Noted in personal interviews with Senior Official, Ethiopian Telecommunications Corporation, August 15, 2010.

41. The Wharton School Lauder Institute, "Huawei Technologies: A Chinese Trail Blazer in Africa," in *Lauder Global Business Insight Report 2009: Firsthand Perspectives on the Global Economy* (Philadelphia: University of Pennsylvania, 2009), 3.

42. Wharton School Lauder Institute, "Huawei Technologies," 16.

43. Anon., "With New Deals, ETC Bidders Offer Financing," *Addis Fortune*, September 19, 2006. Retrieved from LexisNexis on August 23, 2011.

44. Adam, "Ethiopia ICT Performance Review 2009/2010: Toward Evidence-Based ICT Policy and Regulation," 16.

45. Janelle Plummer (ed.), *Diagnosing Corruption in Ethiopia: Perceptions, Realities, and the Way Forward for Key Sectors* (Washington DC: World Bank, 2013).

46. Young, *Peasant Revolution in Ethiopia*, 6. For a detailed account of the TPLF as a guerrilla organization, see: Berhe, "A Political History of the Tigray People's Liberation Front (1975–1991): Revolt, Ideology and Mobilisation in Ethiopia."

47. "China Norinco Unit to Invest US$4.1M in Engineering JV," *Business Daily Update, Asia Africa Intelligence Wire*, April 28, 2004.

48. Norinco-Lalibela Engineering and Construction Share Company, "Nori-La: Norinco-Lalibela Engineering and Construction Share Company since September 1st 2004."

49. See: Deborah Bräutigam, "China's Resource-Backed Weapons Exports: Norinco," *China in Africa: The Real Story*, December 27, 2010, http://www.chinaafricarealstory.com/2010/12/chinas-resource-backed-weapons-exports.html; Philip M. Mobbs, "The Mineral Industry of Zimbabwe," in *U.S. Geological Survey Minerals Yearbook 2006*.

50. Deputy General Manager (Chinese) Norinco-Lalibela Engineering and Construction Share Company, Interview by author, Addis Ababa., July 5, 2010.

51. For a company snapshot see: "China Wanbao Engineering Corp.," *Bloomberg/Businessweek* (2011), http://investing.businessweek.com/research/stocks/private/snapshot.asp?privcapId=24572176.

52. Federal Democratic Republic of Ethiopia, "Regulation No. 149/2008 Kality Construction and Construction Materials Production Enterprise Establishment Council of Ministers Regulation," Article 5.

53. Norinco-Lalibela Engineering and Construction Share Company, "Nori-La: Norinco-Lalibela Engineering and Construction Share Company since September 1st 2004."

54. The Indian Ocean Newsletter, "A Contract for a Chinese Firm in Ethiopia," January 28, 2006.

55. Personal Interview, Deputy General Manager (Chinese), Norinco-Lalibela Engineering and Construction Share Company.

56. The import of computers and vehicles is excluded from duty-free benefits.

57. "Tigrayans at the Army Top," *Indian Ocean Newsletter*, September 3, 2008.

58. Wikileaks, "Ethiopia: Purged Air Force Commander Says Military Suffers from Ethnic Division," May 14, 2008, http://www.wikileaks.org/plusd/cables/08ADDISABABA1324_a.html.

59. Personal interview, Researcher, African Conflict Prevention Programme, Institute for Security Studies.

60. Wikileaks, "Ethiopia: Purged Air Force Commander Says Military Suffers from Ethnic Division."

61. Paulos Chanie, "Clientelism and Ethiopia's Post-1991 Decentralisation," *Jouranl of Modern African Studies* 45, no. 3 (2007): 380.

62. Jane's Sentinel Security Assessment—North Africa, "Procurement (Ethiopia)," June 29, 2012.

63. Dessalegn Rahmato, "The Perils of Development from Above: Land Deals in Ethiopia," *African Identities* 12 no. 1 (2014): 33.

64. Dessalegn, "The Perils of Development from Above."

65. Federal Democratic Republic of Ethiopia, "Land Rent Contractual Agreement Made Between Ministry of Agriculture and Rural Development and Karuturi Agro Products PLC," Article 2(1).

66. See: T. Lavers, "Land Grab" as Development Strategy? The Political Economy of Agricultural Investment in Ethiopia," *Journal of Peasant Studies* 39 (2012): 105–32; F. Malik, "Power and Property: Commercialization, Enclosures, and the Transformation of Agrarian Relations in Ethiopia," *Journal of Peasant Studies* 39 (2012): 81–104.

67. Andualem Sisay, "Ethiopia to Introduce New Agricultural Land Lease Price," *New Business Ethiopia*, April 13, 2010, http://community.businessfightspoverty.org/profiles/blog/list?user=smtb7niduuy6.

68. The Oakland Institute, "Unheard Voices: The Human Rights Impact of Land Investments on Indigenous Communities in Gambella," Oakland, CA: The Oakland Institute, 2013. http://www.oaklandinstitute.org/sites/oaklandinstitute.org/files/OI_Report_Unheard_Voices.pdf.

69. Rahmato, "The Perils of Development from Above," 33.

70. René LeFort, "The Great Ethiopian Land-Grab: Feudalism, Leninism, Neo-Liberalism...Plus Ça Change," *openDemocracy.net*, December 2011, https://www.opendemocracy.net/rené-lefort/great-ethiopian-land-grab-feudalism-leninism-neo-liberalism-plus-ç-change.

II

African Agency Beyond the State

Chapter Six

Making Space for African Agency in China-Africa Engagements

Ghanaian and Nigerian Patrons Shaping Chinese Enterprise

Ben Lampert and Giles Mohan

The dominant assumption in much literature on the Chinese presence in Africa is that the monolithic entity "China"—and the Chinese state in particular—is able to set the terms of engagement with African states and to unilaterally determine events. This is problematic for two linked reasons that we examine in this chapter. First, it privileges unitary states as the key players in these relationships. Second, it underplays the role that African actors, both within and beyond the state, play in brokering and shaping the terms on which these relationships unfold. A ramification of this tendency to attribute all the power to one side is a reactive "anti-China" response since Africans are assumed to be the helpless victims. Indeed, we have seen some African political actors playing up this negative portrayal of the Chinese, which produces a potentially dangerous xenophobia. While we are not arguing that China is only a beneficial force in Africa, in this chapter we examine how African agency can shape these relationships, many of which lie outside official interstate channels. While African agency in China-Africa relations takes many forms, involves a wide array of actors, and operates at a range of levels,[1] here we argue that the state-society interface is a key arena in which African agency is exercised, particularly by African patrons who utilize their state connections to encourage and support Chinese enterprise. While these actors may be based in or connected to the state, their interest in facilitating Chinese activities often appears to have more to do with their own political and economic interests than wider state agendas. The result is a

109

more mixed and contradictory analysis than one in which coherent state interests intersect and "China" drives the relationship.

The chapter begins with an overview of how we can think about African agency and the linkages between "state" and "society." We argue against the Weber-inspired theories that locate African practices in long-standing cultural predispositions that often lack the empirical support for their claims. In arguing for a more empirically informed analysis of patronage and networks, we use data from our West African case studies of Ghana and Nigeria. We frame this around three "scales" of patronage ranging from relatively petty graft up to elite politics.

REINSERTING AFRICAN AGENCY

In making a case for reinserting African agency into the China-Africa debates, we are reminded of older discussions around dependent development. The neo-Marxist accounts of the 1970s were a useful corrective to ideas of developmental catch-up. The limitations of this neo-Marxist approach were soon realized,[2] and in seeing African development as ultimately determined by capitalism they tended to reduce the specificity of the political process in Africa. That said, these approaches usefully focused on what they termed *comprador elites*, who brokered the entry of foreign capital into Africa.[3]

As noted, analysis of Africa's contemporary engagements with China repeat these older debates in that it underplays African agency. Where African agency is noted, the focus is overwhelmingly on formal bilateral relations between Chinese and African state actors.[4] However, the "black box" nature of these state-to-state deals often makes it difficult to specify the precise role of African agency in determining their nature and outcomes. Nonetheless, such work does at least demonstrate that African state agency creates a political context that Chinese actors have to negotiate.[5]

Approaches to the African state that seek to blur its boundaries with wider society is not simply a theoretical exercise but an empirical imperative given that China-Africa relations incorporate an increasingly diverse range of actors beyond the formal realm of the state. As China's renewed engagement with Africa has developed, we see a growing presence of private Chinese multinationals and a profusion of Chinese small- and medium-scale enterprises,[6] all of which are associated with increasing flows of Chinese professionals, entrepreneurs, and workers. It is estimated that there are now in the region of a million Chinese migrants in Africa, and evidence is emerging of how they interact with a wide array of African actors, from customers and employees to colleagues and partners.[7] Consequently, there is growing recognition that the everyday Sino-African encounters this brings about in the social realm are a key factor in determining how China-Africa relations unfold. [8]

Theorizing African Agency within and beyond the State

Given that China-Africa relations are clearly international, a starting point for thinking about African agency is in international relations (IR). Particularly helpful here is Wight's attempt to construct "a structurally aware, although non-structuralist, theory of IR." [9] While Wight is primarily concerned with the realm of the state, his three-layered account of agency [10] is profoundly social and usefully avoids an artificial separation between the two spheres. His first meaning of agency relates to the commonsense view in which agents have accountability, intentionality, and subjectivity. This Wight terms "agency$_1$." However, as we are all reflexive and embedded actors, there is no pure "I" unencumbered by social forces, even if we are able to act. This notion of "embodied intentionality" [11] relates to Wight's second dimension— "agency$_2$,"—in which agents are "an agent of something." This social context refers to "the socio-cultural system into which persons are born and develop." [12] There is a recursive aspect to this since individuals can reproduce or transform these collective identities, although Wight acknowledges "not all agents are equally placed or positioned." [13] The third dimension of Wight's framework is the roles that agents inhabit, although Wight prefers the term *positioned practices* to reflect the non-normative aspect of this. However, these positioned practices—or agency$_3$—are structural insofar as they refer to properties that "persist irrespective of the agents that occupy them," [14] and Wight uses the figure of the diplomat as an example. For Wight any invocation of agency requires all three dimensions; that is, they are "co-constituted" and can only be analyzed empirically.

A key analytical implication of Wight's tripartite approach to agency, especially agency$_2$ and agency$_3$—the social context and roles—is to radically diversify what we might mean by politics and hence political action. Here the work of Hagmann and Péclard [15] is instructive, in which their "analytic of statehood" concerns the dynamic and always undetermined, but not random, process of state (de)construction that is a multilevel phenomenon. Their heuristic framework comprises diverse actors, many of whom lie outside formal political structures, and the resources and repertoires they deploy in shaping their political authority. Similarly, Jessop's strategic-relational theory of the state contends that the state is an ensemble of institutions that can never achieve full separation from society. [16] Hence the boundaries between "state" and "society" are porous, and the operations of states "depend on a wide range of micro-political practices dispersed throughout society."

These "state in society" approaches seek to retain the state as an actor in society but also to see society shaping the state. They bring us away from the abstract level of global "structures" and coherent "states" to a more emergent and messy process of materialist politics. Here the role of social networks and intersections of social identity becomes key, and it is to this that we now turn.

Actors, Networks, and Intersections

In the context of Africa, "state in society" approaches have a long lineage and include debates on neopatrimonialism,[17] prebendalism,[18] and the Weberian turn of Bayart and others.[19] These analyses refute "the very notion that there exists a clear frontier between private and public spheres."[20] The Weberian group of authors argue that the state is a western invention and has been artificially imposed on African societies and so masks "the realities of deeply personalized political realities."[21] Their historicism traces these "realities" back and so implies that African societies are somehow predisposed to such practices, without looking at how transnational forces undermined and shaped African political agency. Moreover, given the clandestine nature of these networks there is very little evidence of how they function politically, so that we need, in the vein of Wight and Jessop, to "integrate the analysis of social dynamics with a closer examination of African state logics."[22]

This social network analysis of the state overlaps with literature on informalism and ethnic entrepreneurship.[23] Kate Meagher traces how social network analysis sought to transcend the unhelpful dualism of in/formality, but—and echoing the critique of Bayart and those working in the same vein—these remained culturally essentialist, ahistorical, and undertheorized. As a result they tend to flatten the diversity of different networks, and in doing so lose "focus on institutional content, power relations and the nature of relations with the state."[24]

Meagher's critique of broad-brush social network analysis concludes that "[S]pecific realities of occupational history and class as well as ethnic origins are shown to shape the embedded values and practices of a given network."[25] This usefully points to a contextual and intersectional understanding of the relationship between class, cultural capital, gender, and ethnicity[26] and their connection to development impacts. Here the spatiality of intersections is key, and we have to understand place-based processes of political, economic, and cultural positioning. Valentine's work[27] focuses on the experiential aspects of intersectionality, which is fluid and malleable. It changes in different spaces and in relation to those occupying those spaces such that the same person in one space may be subject to very different powerful positionings and openings in another. That said, the smaller Chinese firms we examine are capitalist, and so we have to acknowledge the accumulation imperative in any relationship with African actors and the possibility of exclusion, marginalization, and exploitation. We also need to examine how different networks intersect. Norman Long[28] uses the notion of the "interface" to highlight the "critical points of intersection between multiple life-worlds or domains where discontinuities exist based on discrepancies in values, interests, knowledge and power." He sees the resultant processes of negotiation occurring in "arenas,"[29] which, being highly contextual, can only be investigated empirically.[30]

In terms of the networks and values involved in Chinese migrant business, much of the literature has taken a Weberian line,[31] which tends to posit cultural closure and the essentializing of "groups."[32] Here we get closed communities and "ethnic" economies built around *guanxi*. However, Meagher[33] argues that Chinese firms can play a brokerage role between enterprises. Here she uses Bräutigam's work on "flying geese industrialization,"[34] where the Chinese presence can kick-start local economic development. By contrast, when Meagher examines Hart's work on Taiwanese firms in South Africa,[35] we get a political economy of casualization and undercutting, which is anything but developmental. Meagher usefully argues that when Chinese networks "touch ground" in Africa they become more like African networks. By this she means that in the period after many African countries gained independence, Chinese firms enjoyed supportive and regularized relations with African states, but more recently newly arriving firms encounter a less supportive environment and enter various "irregular activities," such as clientelism, illegal foreign exchange transactions, and bribery.

As various authors note, we can only really understand the dynamics of such processes through contextual, empirical study. This chapter is based on ethnographic fieldwork with Chinese migrants in Ghana and Nigeria, as well as with Ghanaians and Nigerians connected to or affected by their presence. The research[36] was conducted between July 2010 and September 2011 and involved participant observation, a local attitude survey, and semistructured interviews with 102 Chinese migrants and 61 Ghanaians and Nigerians. All respondents and associated companies have been anonymized, and where names have been used, these are pseudonyms.

AFRICAN AGENCY IN ACTION

Our analysis focuses primarily on the role of individuals and networks that transcend a "state" or "society" location. Rather than fixed "locations," we focus on the "arenas" and "intersections" where state-based and more social forms of agency interact. A key arena in which African agency comes to the fore in China-Africa relations is at the interface between Chinese enterprises and African actors with positions in, or connections to, the state. Across this interface, we see the emergence of what can be described as patron-client relations. In these relationships, a patron "uses his [*sic*] own influence and resources to provide protection or benefits" to a client "who, for his [*sic*] part, reciprocates by offering generous support and assistance, including personal service."[37] Such relationships are generally structured around distinct power asymmetries, with the patron in the privileged position of possessing resources to which the client requires access.[38] Significantly, in the relations we describe below, it is the African actors who occupy the ascendant role of the patron, utilizing their locally embedded social, economic, and political resources to facilitate and support the activities of their Chinese clients, who in turn reciprocate with financial rewards, the provision of services, and mutually beneficial business opportunities. In this way, Chinese migrant entrepreneurs are not only incorporated into the blurred realm between public and private interests that defines the neopatrimonialism observed in many African states, but also become dependent on local bureaucratic and political elites for their economic survival and success.

We structure our exploration of the role of African patrons in furthering Chinese enterprise around a scaling of patron-client relations that encompasses different motivations, forms of agency, and strategy. The first emerges out of everyday graft in which African officials exact payments, or local brokers control imports. Here agency is very much with the African actors, and the Chinese businesses often experience the demands involved as an operational inconvenience, albeit a serious one that can shape business decisions and social activities. However, the prevalence of these relations can also create opportunities for Chinese entrepreneurs to navigate bureaucratic procedures and restrictions, and this can lead to the development of ongoing, reciprocal relations with African officials who then become critical to sustaining Chinese enterprise. The second set of patron-client relations revolves around a more proactive and convivial form of networking for "smoothing" business relations and accessing contracts, and is not necessarily dependent on direct, unofficial payments. While more even in terms of power, the Africans able to participate in such negotiations tend to be local business and bureaucratic elites, and so both sides use these relationships to reinforce their status and positions. Finally are the more purposive uses of Chinese investment by high-level African state-based and state-connected elites for grander political and economic projects. These shade into those state-based accounts of agency we identified as being the most studied in terms of China-Africa relations, but we show that these projects are often entwined with the personal interests of the African patrons as much as wider state agendas. While Chinese businesses actively seek and knowingly benefit from these high-level relationships, they nonetheless become vulnerable to the vicissitudes of local politics.

Everyday Graft

For Chinese entrepreneurs in Ghana and Nigeria, African agency most often manifests itself at the state-society interface in the form of pervasive petty corruption by African state officials. While there is some acknowledgment that a good number of their conationals may not be fully compliant with local regulations, there is a strong and widespread sense among Chinese respondents that the frequent attention of local officials tends to be motivated primarily by a desire to extract unofficial and often unjustified payments rather than enforce the law. For example, a Chinese entrepreneur based in Lagos remarked:

> The cost for Chinese to stay here, the cost is too high. [. . .]. I used to go outside with car. When police catch me they will hold my driving licence, he will now ask for, even I don't have any problems, he will ask for money [. . .]. That's why I will always be afraid if I see police or LASTMA [Lagos State Traffic Management Authority], [. . .], what they want is money, big money.[39]

Significantly, these experiences of apparent corruption are felt to have a notable effect on the social lives and investment decisions of Chinese entrepreneurs. As a Kano-based Hong Kong Chinese entrepreneur contended:

> The immigration, they always come out to catch people. Even go to restaurant, so the Chinese scare to come out. Sometimes they catch them, ask 500, 5000 US dollar. [. . .] So people scared to come out so their lifestyle change. They go to this family's house, gather together and limit the times come out.[40]

The Chinese manager of an electrical equipment outlet in Kano concurred, and added that such actions on the part of officials also "block social development" by discouraging foreign investors.[41]

However, African actors' utilization of state roles and connections to exploit the Chinese presence can also further Chinese enterprise by establishing ongoing relations of mutual benefit. As some Chinese respondents admitted, making unofficial payments can help negotiate bureaucratic hurdles such as obtaining the necessary immigration documents or permits to undertake particular economic activities. "[Y]ou have to identify those who can be useful to you," argued an Accra-based Chinese shop manager, "and if it means you have to spend some money to them for them to get what you want and to pave a way for you, we do that, that's life."[42] Some well-established Chinese entrepreneurs in Ghana and Nigeria support McNamee et al.'s[43] argument that recent Chinese migrants are predisposed to deploy financial incentives in these ways because there is a strong culture of corruption around business in China. However, other long-standing Chinese entrepreneurs suggest that newcomers simply lack the confidence and linguistic skills to stand up to the intimidation and demands of local officials in what they see as a system of corruption very much driven by African actors. Indeed, recently arrived Chinese entrepreneurs tended to assert that low-level business corruption has been much reduced in China in recent years and that it was a major challenge to adapt to its prevalence in Ghana and Nigeria. Whatever the main drivers, established and recent Chinese migrants generally agreed that having to engage local systems of corruption was unavoidable. As the Chinese manager of a Chinese company's Ghana outlet contended, "If you don't follow [the system], you can't stay here!"[44]

Mutually beneficial relationships with African state-based and state-connected actors are especially important for Chinese entrepreneurs who wish to circumvent local regulations. In both Ghana and Nigeria there have been complaints from some local traders and manufacturers about the growing influx of Chinese-made goods, particularly textiles, and this has prompted government action to stem the flow, including the imposition of import bans and then prohibitive tariffs in Nigeria.[45] However, it is widely recognized that such measures have been undermined by local and Chinese traders engaging in large-scale smuggling facilitated by unofficial payments to enforcement officials. As a senior figure in the Lagos business community contended of government attempts to reduce Chinese imports, "The Customs are making good money from it because it creates room for corruption" (Interview, Lagos, February 2011). Indeed, a respondent who has been closely involved in the Lagos "China Town" retail complex, which housed several hundred Chinese traders at the height of its activity in the early to mid- 2000s and became a key channel for the importation of Chinese goods to Nigeria, suggested that making regular payments to local customs officials enabled the complex's traders to evade import bans and openly sell substantial volumes of contraband goods. This echoes Chalfin's[46] work on members of Ghana's Customs, Excise and Preventive Service, who are key actors that both represent the state at its borders and so endow the territory with legitimacy but who also subvert this by withholding the release of goods in return for "unofficial" payments. As Boone[47] argues in her study of trade liberalization in Senegal and Côte d'Ivoire, "fraud and contraband pit "state agents against the state."

While this arrangement was severely disrupted in 2005 to 2006 when the growing agitation of Nigeria's manufacturing lobby prompted high-profile customs raids and the temporary closure of "China Town," some of the traders who remained in the complex were able to reestablish their connections with officials, and continue trading in contraband goods. In these relationships, a central role is played by local clearing agents, as a Nigerian involved in a Chinese-founded trading business in the Lagos "China Town" detailed:

> Now the agents and the customs officers they are, you know, into good rapport. Like the agent we're using, [. . .], the man is good. If he tells you today your goods is coming, it is coming. [. . .] So you know customs have to meet money. Now, in 24 hours, [. . .], you can clear goods. [. . .]. They know that it's contraband, all these are contraband. But then because of their rapport together, so no problem. (Interview, Lagos, September 2010)

Similarly, in Kano, where many Chinese traders attempted to relocate after the Lagos "China Town" was temporarily shut down, a Chinese textile wholesaler described how a local agent maintains what has become a major alternative route for smuggling Chinese products:

> There is more Custom [in Lagos] but for Kano they find another way. They ship the container [to] Cotonou or Lomé then they take the goods to Niger, a city called Maradi [near the border with Nigeria]. There is one people if he allow, normally there is one day in each week he allow this day take all the goods to Kano. (Interview, Kano, December 2010)

This agent appears to have become well known in the city, a representative of the local business community bemoaning his activities and highlighting the importance of his high-level political connections in enabling him to facilitate the lucrative illicit trade in Chinese goods:

> Here in Kano we have somebody that we don't like because he is a party to the smuggle of most of these textile goods. He is the one that clears the goods through the border with Niger Republic. He clears them in the guises of another product inside the container but unfortunately it was a contraband but because he is a very strong man in politics, he is a strong man in the ruling party, [he is able to do this]. The Chinese are hiding behind this man. This man can bring anything to this country as far as import is concerned. Whatever you want him to bring to this country he can bring it for you. He is just a clearing agent but he is so strong because at one time he had a very strong relationship with the former leadership [of the country] and he takes that advantage up to this leadership and he is still using it. (Interview, Kano, February 2011)

Such a critical brokering role echoes Walther's[48] more general and historical point about how mobility and trade have been central to Sahelian economies. This trade, he argues, is mediated by patrons who are the wealthy and powerful merchants who control border flows and distribution channels, and who mark their status with ostentatious investments in local society (e.g., building mosques). Distributionally, and echoing Bayart, these patrons are "a small number of operators who enjoy privileged relationships within the states."[49] As such, these networks tend to enhance the position of elites, something that can merge with their wider political aspirations. Indeed, Tidjani Alou[50] details how large-scale traders in Niger are intimately linked to political office holders, providing them with financing for their political parties in return for protection from the customs authorities.

Convivial Connections

As noted above, some argue[51] that given the nature of China's "nomenklatura" capitalism, patronage and graft are part of Chinese business life. The argument goes that when Chinese migrants come to Africa they slot in because such practices are familiar. While this has some value, it is important to avoid a simplistic argument that "the Chinese" simply export the capitalism they know best since this is a restatement of the China agency versus African victim dynamic rather than a relational one. It is clear that such patronage networks need to be seen in a more complex way that recognizes the interplay of capitalist imperatives, dynamic racial and ethnic positionings, and state power. Nyíri,[52] using Bonacich,[53] argues that Chinese migrants operate as "middlemen minorities" in economic frontiers, ranging from Eastern Europe after the fall of communism through to contemporary Africa and South-East Asia. He argues that "seeking the patronage of local political elites in exchange for protection against xenophobic attacks and the vulnerability created by legal discrimination was typical of colonial 'middleman minorities' and persisted in some postcolonial states . . . But the rise of China as a coveted market and the increase of its clout as a world power have made the power dynamics of such patronage networks more complex."[54] A corollary of this in his Hungarian study[55] is that Chinese migrants "have been largely uninterested in enfranchisement as a group, cultivating instead personal relationships with officials and recruiting middlemen who broker between them and agents of the state."

Such patronage has been identified in relations between African elites and Chinese business migrants. Haglund[56] and Dobler[57] both identify such relationships as important, though they lack specific examples. For example, Haglund states "political elites secure financial or other support by providing external capital interests with protection."[58] Dobler argues "the more established migrants form alliances with influential members of the host society in order to secure their status in an increasingly hostile environment."[59] He contends that this also enables the longer-established migrants to act as migration brokers for subsequent in-migrants from China.

While unofficial financial transfers such as those described above often appear to underpin such relationships, particularly at the state-society interface, our data suggest that they can also emerge out of less instrumental but nonetheless proactive "networking" between Chinese entrepreneurs and African officials and state-connected business elites. Interpersonal Sino-African relationships are often framed as being dominated by tensions and conflict,[60] but, as we have argued elsewhere,[61] they can also involve more convivial relations, and it is out of these that both formal and informal cooperation can develop. This is particularly apparent around well-established Chinese entrepreneurs who often enjoy a high degree of local embeddedness, being well known within local business circles and having a wide range of local, often state-connected contacts who are happy to help them overcome challenges in what is often seen as a difficult business environment. As a Chinese shop worker in Accra reported of his Chinese employer:

> My boss like eighteen years ago he come to Ghana so he knows a lot [of local people]. That time when he come he knows a lot of big guys. Because like 18 years ago there is only a few Chinese people in Ghana, so and at that time [. . .], that company he worked for is very big, so he have a chance to contact with the many big guys in Ghana. So even the chief policeman is his friend [. . .]. If [he] ha[s] any problems, [he] can solve [them]." (Interview, Accra, May 2011)

Similarly, a member of a Chinese family business in Tema detailed how the firm was established in 2000 after his uncle was introduced to Ghana by a "Ghanaian friend" he had met while working in South Africa and who helped the company develop convivial and ultimately useful local relationships:

> It is the same friend who introduce us here, he helped us to show us the place where we can register and they introduce us to some [government] officer. We also get some Ghanaian friends. For maybe the business partners or the government officers, why we get help from them, [it's because] we know each other. (Interview, Tema, August 2011)

Like a number of the more established Chinese entrepreneurs engaged in our study, both of these respondents argued that the assistance they are able to access through their extensive and influential local networks means that there is little or no need for them or their bosses to be members of the Chinese business associations established in Ghana and Nigeria. As the Tema-based responded asserted, "Because we are here long we know most of the government office so any problem, it is not very serious, we just sort it ourselves."[62] This very much resonates with Nyíri's[63] point that Chinese migrant entrepreneurs are often more interested in developing personal relationships with state-based and state-connected actors than in securing group-based interests.

Local contacts built through networking and convivial interactions can not only help Chinese entrepreneurs overcome the challenges of the local business environment but can also enable them to pursue new economic opportunities and develop their enterprises. This can be seen in the case of Mrs. Lu, a Hong Kong Chinese entrepreneur based in Kano. She reports that she was only able to secure her nascent business selling beverages produced

by a Lagos-based Chinese company when two of her Nigerian contacts offered to lend her the necessary finance to pay for the exclusive distribution
rights for northern Nigeria. One of these local patrons was a long-standing
customer of her existing fashion business, and the other was a man she had
known for five years from a casino they both frequented. Mrs. Lu was deeply
grateful for what she saw as their "kindness" and "generosity," noting that
they freely lent the money without demanding a share of the business or
setting a time scale for repayment (interview, Kano, February 2011). To
demonstrate her gratitude, Mrs. Lu made them "partners" in the business and
paid them handsome returns. For Mrs. Lu, an added benefit of this relationship is that a close relative of one of the local partners is a senior police
officer. He not only helped her when a local landlord attempted to defraud
her but has also enabled her to take business risks she might not have done
without his support. "I feel very secured," she revealed, "even I give credit in
the market because all the people know in the back is the [police officer].
Nobody thief my money."

The decisive role that state-connected and state-based local patrons can
play in furthering Chinese enterprise is especially apparent in the case of Dr.
Sheng, a Chinese medical doctor based in the Greater Accra region who
established a private clinic there in the mid-1990s having first come to Ghana
in the mid-1980s as part of a health cooperation between the Chinese and
Ghanaian governments. A Chinese entrepreneur who claimed to be familiar
with Dr. Sheng's story argued that he had been able to establish his clinic
because he had successfully treated the persistent knee problem of a very
senior political officeholder, who in return "gave" Dr. Sheng the land to
build his clinic (interview, Tema, June 2011). Certainly, Dr. Sheng very
much emphasized the role of this prominent figure in facilitating his career in
Ghana, highlighting that at the end of each of his three successive three-year
official postings at a Ghanaian military hospital, the official personally re-
quested that he stayed on to continue working in Ghana. When he recounted
his decision to establish his own private clinic at the end of his third posting,
Dr. Sheng recalls that he was able to overcome tight restrictions on foreign-
trained private practitioners because he had worked closely with the Ghanaian government for nine years and "they made an exception," enabling him to
become what he believes to be the first foreigner to open a private medical
clinic in Ghana (interview, Greater Accra Region, August 2011). He clearly
remained very grateful to his contacts in government, who had given him this
opportunity to build a life and business in a country to which he expressed a
strong attachment, particularly the leading political figure who had supported
him since his early years in Ghana and with whom he appeared to have
developed something of an enduring friendship.

Elite Politics

The case of Dr. Sheng illustrates how the local connections of Chinese entrepreneurs in Ghana and Nigeria can reach the highest echelons of the state, and can play a critical role in the establishment and expansion of Chinese enterprise. While some of these high-level links appear to be grounded principally in convivial relationships, they tend to emerge out of the conscious efforts of African elites to develop direct connections with ambitious Chinese entrepreneurs in order to further their own economic and political interests. Bayart[64] argues that extraversion requires "active intermediation" and that this has been a continuity from precolonial, through colonial, and onto more recent "rentier" political economies. The outcome is that this role adds "to the personal fortunes of whichever person or group was the gatekeeper of the system."[65] This suggests that African elites capable of acting as patrons use their relationship with foreign businesses to cement this position, potentially perpetuating neopatrimonial practices among those based in or connected to the state. Furthermore, building on Long's work, it is important to recognize not only how external interventions are mediated and transformed by local actors, but also how these actors can actively reach out and initiate interventions that might at first appear to be purely "external."

This is clearly demonstrated in the case of Mr. Daniel, a Lagos-based Nigerian entrepreneur who since the mid-2000s developed an explicit strategy of encouraging Chinese companies to partner with him in establishing enterprises in Nigeria. His aim is to become *the* person Chinese investors go through and partner with when entering Nigeria, and he plans to end up with a stake in a range of enterprises with Chinese partners—the proceeds from which he can live on when he retires. In addition to employing four Chinese craftsmen in his high-end furniture business, who he recruited from the China-based furniture supplier he imported from prior to undertaking his own production, Mr. Daniel entered into a joint venture with a Chinese construction company that was about to leave Nigeria following the completion of a contract. He initially approached the company in Nigeria to propose the partnership and, having received an encouraging response, traveled to its headquarters in China to seal the deal. With the Chinese company providing equipment and "know-how" in the form of skilled labor, Mr. Daniel's contribution was to provide accommodation, manage in-country logistics, and, most importantly, use his local knowledge and contacts to secure contracts. As he contended, "You can only give what you have, what I have in Nigeria is that the country is my country, I understand it very well, so I have to make use of it" (interview, Lagos, October 2010).

What appear to be particularly important in this case are Mr. Daniel's political connections, not least to his brother who had recently held a senior state office and remained influential in the national political scene. Indeed, the first project undertaken by Mr. Daniel and his Chinese partner was to convert a building divested by the arm of the state his brother had run into a hotel aimed at Chinese business visitors. Mr. Daniel was excited that he had followed this up by winning a very lucrative government contract to construct a new state building. Seeking to further expand his business collaborations with Chinese companies, Mr. Daniel had recently initiated joint-venture discussions with a Chinese medical equipment firm, representatives of which he had first met when they stayed at his hotel while visiting Lagos for a trade exposition, and the following week he was traveling to China to "search for companies that are ready to come and partner in Nigeria." He contended of his links with Chinese companies, "I see the potential of running into hundreds upon hundreds of millions of US dollars business partnering with them." It would seem that by using his local knowledge and connections, particularly to the state, and by actively courting Chinese investment, Mr. Daniel has not only been able to significantly advance his own commercial interests, but has also enabled his Chinese partners to access opportunities that might otherwise have been beyond their reach.

Similarly, in the case of the Lagos "China Town" shopping complex, it was Chief Oladipo, a prominent Nigerian businessman and politician, who first brought over Mr. Wu, the Chinese founder, as a business partner. While Chief Oladipo's political exile in the early 1990s curtailed the development of their joint venture, his return in 1998 and assumption of an important political position the following year saw him support Mr. Wu's establishment of "China Town" in Lagos—first in the upmarket Ikoyi district and, from 2002, at a larger site in Ojota on the eastern edge of the city. A political ally of Chief Oladipo argued that his intention in supporting the project was to attract Chinese entrepreneurs who would go on to establish factories in Lagos, thereby generating local employment and supporting economic development. However, another respondent closely involved with the complex pointed out that it became a useful outlet for close relatives of Chief Oladipo involved in the large-scale importation of Chinese textiles. Whatever Chief Oladipo's intentions, he has seemingly remained a vital supporter of "China Town," respondents claiming that it is only with his backing that the complex has been able to remain open in the face of the protests and clampdowns it has attracted. It would again seem that an African patron has been central to the establishment and survival of a notable Chinese enterprise.

CONCLUSION

In terms of the ongoing effects of these complex engagements, Chinese businesses do not radically alter preexisting networks or practices of patronage in Africa. Indeed, they often reinforce the pervasiveness of patron-client relations and wider practices of neopatrimonial governance. While there are some spinoffs for smaller-scale entrepreneurs and skills gains for rising professionals,[66] it is often about African elites cementing their positions, not just in relation to the narrow confines of state power, but also in the wider realm of economic enterprise: this, in turn, has thrown up forms of African "resistance." This resistance is not explicitly "anti-Chinese" but rather moves beyond the cynical xenophobia of some responses to Chinese investments. For example, in 2010 in Nigeria there was a demonstration against the Dangote Group—the largest Nigerian industrial conglomerate headed by (reputedly) the wealthiest Nigerian—and its use of imported Chinese workers. The tenet of the protest was that Nigerian elites were being unpatriotic rather than a complaint against "the Chinese" per se. Such an appeal speaks to the complex intersection of neoliberal globalization, state-business relations, patronage, and ethnicity that have been the focus of this chapter.

In seeking to move the analysis of China-Africa relations away from abstract or interstate levels, we focused on social networks and particularly forms of patronage where African agency is key. While African Studies has a history of theorizing patronage-based politics, we found that many of these approaches tended to flatten the specificity of embedded social relations. As such, our analysis revealed that networked relations and agency are not uniform but incorporate multiple actors, interests, and processes, which can only be specified empirically. We also showed that social networks are tied to accumulation and the state as much as they are "cultural." Too much of the existing China and Africa work is posited on cultural essentialism and/or lapses lazily into arguing that "the Chinese" are only concerned with profit. While we retained a focus on the materiality of these social relations, we also showed that motivations of both African and Chinese actors are multiple and interlinked.

NOTES

1. Giles Mohan and Ben Lampert, "Negotiating China: Reinserting African Agency into China-Africa Relations," *African Affairs* 112, no. 446 (2013): 92–110.

2. Theda Skocpol, "Bringing the State Back In: Strategies of Analysis in Current Research," in *Bringing the State Back In*, edited by P. Evans, D. Rueschemeyer, and T. Skocpol, 3–43 (New York: Cambridge University Press, 1985).

3. C. Leys, *The Rise and Fall of Development Theory, EAEP* (London: Indiana University Press and James Currey, 1996).

4. J. Holslag, "China and the Coups: Coping with Political Instability in Africa," *African Affairs* 110, no. 440 (2011): 367–86; D. Large, "China's Sudan Engagement: Changing Northern and Southern Political Trajectories in Peace and War," *The China Quarterly* 199 (2009): 610–26.

5. P. Carmody, and I. Taylor, "Flexigemony and Force in China's Geoeconomic Strategy in Africa: Sudan and Zambia Compared," *Geopolitics* 15, no. 3 (2010): 495–515; Holslag, "China and the Coups."

6. J. Gu, "China's Private Enterprises in Africa and the Implications for African Development," *European Journal of Development Research* 21, no. 4 (2009): 570–87.

7. G. Mohan, B. Lampert, D. Chang, and M. Tan-Mullins, *Chinese Migrants and Africa's Development: New Imperialists or Agents of Change?* (London: Zed Books, 2014).

8. C. Alden, *China in Africa* (London: Zed Books, 2007).

9. C. Wight, "State Agency: Social Action without Human Activity?" *Review of International Studies* 30 no. 2 (2004): 270.

10. C. Wight, "They Shoot Dead Horses Don't They? Locating Agency in the Agent-Structure Problematique," *European Journal of International Relations* 5, no. 1 (1999): 109–42.

11. Wight, "They Shoot Dead Horses Don't They?" 132.

12. Wight, "They Shoot Dead Horses Don't They?" 133.

13. Wight, "They Shoot Dead Horses Don't They?"

14. Wight, "They Shoot Dead Horses Don't They?"

15. T. Hagmann, and D. Péclard, "Negotiating Statehood: Dynamics of Power and Domination in Africa," *Development and Change* 41, no. 4 (2010): 539–62.

16. B. Jessop, *State Theory: Putting Capitalist State in Its Place* (Cambridge, Polity Press, 1990), 342.

17. See, for example: G. Hyden, *No Shortcuts to Progress: African Development Management in Perspective* (London: Heinemann, 1983); D. Bach, "Patrimonialism and Neopatrimonialism: Comparative Receptions and Transcriptions," in *Neopatrimonialism in Africa and Beyond*, edited by D. Bach and M. Gazibo, 25–45 (London: Routledge, 2012); M. Bratton, and N. Van de Walle, "Neopatrimonial Regimes and Political Transitions in Africa," *World Politics* 46, no. 4 (1994): 453–89; J. F. Médard, "The Underdeveloped State in Tropical Africa: Political Clientelism or Neopatrimonialism," in *Private Patronage and Public Power: Political Clientelism in the Modern State*, edited by C. Clapham, 162–92 (London: Frances Pinter, 1982).

18. See, for example: R. Joseph, *Democracy and Prebendal Politics in Nigeria: The Rise and Fall of the Second Republic* (Cambridge: Cambridge University Press, 1987); E. Obadare, and W. Adebanwi, "Introduction—Democracy and Prebendalism: Emphases, Provocations, and Elongations," in *Democracy and Prebendalism in Nigeria: Critical Interpretations*, edited by W. Adebanwi and E. Obadare, 1–22 (Basingstoke: Palgrave Macmillan, 2013).

19. J. F. Bayart, *The State in Africa: The Politics of the Belly* (Harlow: Longman, 1993); B. Hibou, "The 'Social Capital' of the State as an Agent of Deception," in *The Criminalization of the State in Africa*, edited by J. Bayart, S. Ellis, and B. Hibou, 69–113 (Oxford: James Currey, 1999).

20. J. F. Bayart, "Africa in the World: A History of Extraversion," *African Affairs* 99, no. 395 (2000): 243.

21. P. Chabal, and J. P. Daloz, *Africa Works: Disorder as Political Instrument* (London: James Currey, 1999), 16.

22. P. Nugent, "States and Social Contracts in Africa," *New Left Review* 63 (May–June 2010), 37.

23. K. Meagher, *Identity Economics: Social Networks and the Informal Economy in Nigeria* (Suffolk: James Currey, 2010).

24. Meagher, *Identity Economics*, 23.

25. Meagher, *Identity Economics*, 24.

26. R. Ellis, "The Politics of the Middle: Re-Centering Class in the Postcolonial," *ACME* 10, no. 1 (2011): 69–81.

27. G. Valentine, "Theorising and Researching Intersectionality: A Challenge for Feminist Geography," *Professional Geographer* 59 (2007): 10–21.

28. N. Long, "Exploring Local/Global Transformations: A View from Anthropology," in *Anthropology, Development and Modernities: Exploring Discourses, Counter-Tendencies and Violence*, edited by A. Arce and N. Long, 197–98. London: Routledge, 2000).

29. N. Long, and M. Villarreal, "Exploring Development Interfaces: From the Transfer of Knowledge to the Transformation of Meaning," in *Beyond the Impasse: New Directions in Development Theory*, edited by F. J. Schuurman, 140–68 (London: Zed Books, 1993); N. Long,

and J. D. van der Ploeg, "Heterogeneity, Actor and Structure: Towards a Reconstitution of the Concept of Structure," in *Rethinking Social Development: Theory, Research and Practice*, edited by D. Booth, 62–89 (London: Longman, 1994).

30. See also: W. Brown, "A Question of Agency: Africa in International Politics," *Third World Quarterly* 33, no. 10 (2012): 1889–1908; M. de Bruijn, R. van Dijk, and J. B. Gewald, "Social and Historical Trajectories of Agency in Africa," in *African Alternatives*, edited by P. Chabal, U. Engel, and L. de Haan, 9–20 (Leiden: Brill, 2007).

31. A. Portes, and J. Sensenbrenner, "Embeddedness and Immigration: Notes on the Social Determinants of Economic Action," *American Journal of Sociology* 98, no. 6 (1993): 1320–50.

32. K. Meagher, "Weber Meets Godzilla: Social Networks and the Spirit of Capitalism in East Asia and Africa," *Review of African Political Economy* 39, no. 132 (2012): 261–78; S. Greenhalgh, "De-Orientalizing the Chinese Family Firm," *American Ethnologist* 21, no. 4 (1994): 742–71.

33. Meagher, "Weber Meets Godzilla."

34. D. Bräutigam, "Close Encounters: Chinese Business Networks as Industrial Catalysts in Sub-Saharan Africa," *African Affairs* 102, no. 408 (2003): 447–67.

35. G. Hart, "Global Connections: The Rise and Fall of Taiwanese Production Network on the South African Periphery," Working Paper No. 6, *University of California*, California, Institute of International Studies, 1996.

36. The research on which this chapter is based was funded by the UK Economic and Social Research Council (Grant Reference RES-062-23-1893)

37. J. Scott, "Patron-Client Politics and Political Change in Southeast Asia," *American Political Science Review* 66 (1972): 92, quoted in A. Hicken, "Clientelism," *Annual Review of Political Science* 14 (2011): 292.

38. S. N. Eisenstadt, and L. Roniger, "Patron-Client Relations as a Model of Structuring Social Exchange," *Comparative Studies in Society and History* 22, no. 1 (1980): 42–77; G. Erdmann, and U. Engel, "Neopatrimonialism Reconsidered: Critical Review and Elaboration of an Elusive Concept," *Commonwealth and Comparative Politics* 45, no. 1 (2007): 95–119; Hicken, "Clientelism."

39. Interview, Lagos, September 2010.

40. Interview, Kano, February 2011.

41. Interview, Kano, December 2016.

42. Interview, Accra, May 2011, interpreter translation from Chinese.

43. T. McNamee, with G. Mills, S. Manoeli, M. Mulaudzi, S. Doran, and E. Chen, "Africa in Their words—A Study of Chinese Traders in South Africa, Lesotho, Botswana, Zambia and Angola," *The Brenthurst Foundation Discussion Paper*, Lesotho, March 2012.

44. Interview, August 2011.

45. For the Ghanaian case, see: L. Axelsson, *Making Borders: Engaging the Threat of Chinese Textiles in Ghana* (Stockholm: Acta Universitatis Stockholmiensis, 2012).

46. B. Chalfin, "Cars, the Customs Service and Sumptuary Rule in Neoliberal Ghana," *Comparative Studies in Society and History* 50, no. 2 (2008): 424–53.

47. C. Boone, "Trade, Taxes, and Tribute: Market Liberalizations and the New Importers in West Africa," *World Development* 22, no. 3 (1994): 462.

48. O. Walther, "A Mobile Idea of Space: Traders, Patrons and the Cross-Border Economy in Sahelian Africa," *Journal of Borderlands Studies* 24, no. 1 (2009): 34–46.

49. Bayart, "Africa in the World."

50. M. Tidjani Alou, "Monitoring the Neopatrimonial State on a Day-to-Day Basis: Politicians, Customs Officials and Traders in Niger," in *Neopatrimonialism in Africa and Beyond*, edited by D. Bach and M. Gazibo, 142–54 (London: Routledge, 2012).

51. McNamee et al., "Africa in Their Words," 22.

52. P. Nyíri, "Chinese Entrepreneurs in Poor Countries: A Transnational 'Middleman Minority' and Its Futures," *Inter-Asia Cultural Studies* 12, no. 1 (2011): 145–53.

53. E. Bonacich, "Theory of Middleman Minorities," *American Sociological Review* 38 (1973): 383–94.

54. Nyíri, "Chinese Entrepreneurs in Poor Countries," 148.

55. P. Nyíri, "Global Modernisers or Local Subalterns? Parallel Perceptions of Chinese Transnationals in Hungary," *Journal of Ethnic and Migration Studies* 31, no. 4 (2005): 668.

56. D. Haglund, "Regulating FDI in Weak African States: A Case Study of Chinese Copper Mining in Zambia," *Journal of Modern African Studies* 46, no. 4 (2008): 5487–5575; D. Haglund, "In It for the Long Term? Governance and Learning among Chinese Investors in Zambia's Copper Sector," *The China Quarterly* 199 (2009): 627–46.

57. G. Dobler, "Solidarity, Xenophobia and the Regulation of Chinese Businesses in Namibia," in *China Returns to Africa: A Rising Power and a Continent Embrace*, edited by C. Alden, D. Large, and R. S. de Oliveira, 237–55 (London: Hurst, 2008); G. Dobler, "Chinese Shops and the Formation of a Chinese Expatriate Community in Namibia," *The China Quarterly* 199 (2009): 707–27.

58. Haglund, "In It for the Long Term?" 639.

59. Dobler, "Chinese Shops and the Formation of a Chinese Expatriate Community in Namibia," 708.

60. See: A. Y. Baah, and H. Jauch, (eds.), *Chinese Investments in Africa: A Labour Perspective* (Windhoek: African Labour Research Network, 2009); A. Brooks, "Spinning and Weaving Discontent: Labour Relations and the Production of Meaning at Zambia-China Mulungushi Textiles," *Journal of Southern African Studies* 36, no. 1 (2010): 113–32; K. Giese, "Same-Same but different: Chinese Traders' Perspectives on African Labor," *China Journal* 69 (2013): 134–53; C. Lee, "Raw Encounters: Chinese Managers, African Workers and the Politics of Casualization in Africa's Chinese Enclaves," *The China Quarterly* 199 (2009): 647–66; M. Lee, "Uganda and China: Unleashing the Power of the Dragon," in *China in Africa*, edited by H. Melber (Uppsala: Nordiska Afrikainstitutet, 2007).

61. Mohan et al., *Chinese Migrants and Africa's Development: New Imperialists or Agents of Change?*

62. Interview, Tema, August 2011.

63. Nyíri, "Global Modernisers or Local Subalterns?" 668.

64. Bayart, "Africa in the World."

65. Bayart, "Africa in the World," 261.

66. See G. Mohan, and B. Lampert, "Negotiating China: Reinserting African Agency into China-Africa Relations," *African Affairs* 122, no. 446 (2013): 92–110.

Chapter Seven

Racialization as Agency in Zambia-China Relations

Barry Sautman

The recent counter by scholars to the long-standing erasure of Africans' agency in works on international politics[1] is reflected in analyses of African relations with China. Lucy Corkin writes that "certain African countries have been able to 'play the China card' well," leveraging ties with China to alter relationships with other states. Corkin notes that Angolan elites in particular "have actively shaped the nature of negotiations with China and [the] Angolan government plays an important role in the outcomes," including through rhetoric constitutive of Angola-China relations.[2] Giles Mohan and Ben Lampert find agency through and beyond the state that protects African petit-bourgeois class privileges in relations with Chinese entities.[3] Along these lines, Aleksandra Gadzala decries "the near-constant depiction of African states as pliant third-world clients" and holds that "with impressive growth rates, abundant natural resources, and increasingly favorable business environments, African states today exercise significant leverage over their foreign affairs. In their relations with China, they deftly maneuver weaker positions into tactical advantages."[4]

The denial of African agency has been embedded in a racialized discourse of Afropessimism—a predominantly Western view that Africans lack the ability to push for their development.[5] This discourse overlooks the harm done to development by the International Monetary Fund and World Bank–backed structural adjustment in Africa and shifts the continent's development problems entirely onto Africans. African agency is still largely denied in the more recent Western notion of "Chinese neo-colonialism" that attributes a negative superagency to China.[6] American president Barack Obama and then-US Secretary of State Hillary Clinton, alluding to China, have spoken of an ongoing colonial relationship with Africa.[7] American journalist Howard French claims that China's presence in Africa has "striking parallels with imperial patterns of the past."[8] Africa scholar Gloria Emeaglwali has written that "[Chinese] neo-colonialism embraces all aspects of classic colonialism except for occupying foreign lands . . . the exploiting power (China) controls weaker states' economic resources and political systems and exploits their wealth."[9] While most Africa-China specialists reject this view as an unsupported imaginary, it nevertheless continues to exert a hold through the idea that Africa's divided and misgoverned states cannot influence a more unified and effectively ruled China.

Within this discourse, expressions of African agency usually boil down to supposed acts of resistance against "the Chinese." All the while, other expressions of agency are made invisible. In the case of Zambia, the Chinese state, like others, crafts policies to serve its own perceived interests; Chinese firms, like others, exploit Zambian workers for profit. Yet the Zambian state and various Zambian nonstate organizations have agency in dealings with Chinese entities in ways that scholars have found generally for Africa: they sometimes elicit from Beijing and from Chinese firms beneficial economic relations and regard for Zambian state sovereignty, even if in accordance with Jean-Francois Bayart's concept of Africa's extroversion, that may also involve Zambian elite management of dependence through rents.[10] At any rate, Zambian officials are convinced that they have at least as much agency in their interactions with the Chinese state as they have with other foreign entities. A former top executive of Zambia's state mining company and telecommunications firm noted that he preferred to deal with Chinese because:

> [O]ne company that we own 100% is being re-capitalized. The [Western] bank told us that the condition of the loan is that we put up our shares as security and it pushed this demand until we turned down the loan. It made us feel that "I'm a slave because I borrowed from you." Financing from China does not impose conditions and is based on the capacity to pay the interest and repay the loan. Chinese are more respectful. Western banks derive their benefits to the exclusion of other stakeholders.[11]

The state-to-state relationship is, however, only one way that agency has been exercised by Zambians. Racialization is another strategy through which Zambian and some other African actors have exercised agency vis-à-vis Chinese entities. Zambia's relations with China have received hugely disproportionate attention in global media and academic works precisely because, since 2004, the erstwhile oppositional Patriotic Front (PF), trade unions, and merchants have discursively racialized the Chinese presence. Scholars have assumed that this agency leveraged Chinese entities into changing their practices.[12] PF head Michael Sata claimed as much when he became Zambia's president, stating that the Chinese "had adjusted before we even decided to introduce any laws to force them to adjust."[13]

We take issue with this assessment. In this chapter, racializing rhetoric and associated events in Zambia are regarded as an exercise of agency, and their effects on the practices of Chinese entities are analyzed. Zambia alone is considered, even though "racialization-as-agency" might be claimed for several other African states, and it is seen by some as a factor in a putative contest between the West and China in Africa.[14] Racialization-as-agency, however, is like agency in general: it does not always have the consequences intended or claimed for it. Though positive aspects or improvements in the Chinese presence in Zambia exist—contradicting the mainstream "negative narrative" of "China-in-Africa"[15]—they were not necessarily attained through the exercise of racialization-as-agency. That is because the racializers have consistently mischaracterized Chinese practices, and because such changes in Chinese practices that have occurred have been in the interests of the Chinese entities that made them. In fact, we cannot even be certain that the chief racializers, the PF leaders, were as concerned about changing Zambia's relationship with China as they made out; instead, they may have seen racialization mainly as an electoral tactic. We thus do not know that racialization-as-agency altered the practices of the Chinese state or firms in Zambia, but we can be confident of other, ascertainable consequences: it helped the PF attain power in 2011 and entrenched the racialization of Chinese among Zambians, thereby inhibiting solidarity between Chinese and Zambians.

AGENCY AND RACIALIZATION

It is perhaps ironic, in light of condemnations of Chinese practices in the "China-in-Africa" discourse, that China more obviously recognizes African agency than do Western states. South African analyst of Africa-China relations Richard Poplak has argued that Chinese business never regards Africa as an "economic basket case" and thus "respects African agency in a way that the West never, ever has and still doesn't."[16] Not surprisingly, the Chinese government holds a similar view: its Special Envoy to Africa has stated that "we always regard Africa as Africans' Africa . . . We never override what they have decided"[17]—a statement inconceivable from any Western official.

But what is the "agency" that some now recognize Africans possess? Social scientists define agency in several ways, but here we mean a capacity for intentional action to alter outcomes (see the introduction in this volume). Agency is "composed of variable and changing orientations within the flow of time . . . by actors capable of formulating projects for the future and realizing them, even if only in small part, and with unforeseen outcomes, in the present."[18]

Some claims of agency have been rejected as "false."[19] In the African context, the agency asserted by "Kony 2012," a campaign to stimulate military intervention to curb the depredations of the Lord's Resistance Army in Uganda, has been characterized as illusory because the movement's American organizers promoted the idea that "by donating, by calling representatives and by spreading awareness they can actually end the targeted conflict."[20] Whether or not agency can be only apparent, it is always exercised, as Michel Foucault noted, within a field of power relations.[21] It is embedded in, but sometimes used to change, structures, but its existence does not guarantee desired outcomes. Even if such outcomes occur and are credited to actions by A with respect to B, there still may be a question of whether that outcome would have happened anyway, not due to A's agency, but to B's.

Agency vis-à-vis the Chinese presence in Africa partly derives from Africans knowing that the Chinese state view of its relations with Africa is borne out of need; the recognition that "China needs Africa. It needs Africa for resources to fuel its development goals, for markets to sustain its growing economy, and for political alliances [and] in its aspirations to be a global influence."[22] Chinese Africa specialists go further, by recognizing that "China needs Africa more than Africa needs China."[23] African scholars are likewise aware of this. Ghanaian Africa-China specialist Adams Bodomo has argued that "even though China is a permanent UN Security Council member, Africa-China relations are asymmetrical in favor of Africa on the political front because of Africa's massive voting clout at the UN and other international bodies."[24] An analyst of Africa in Chinese foreign policy has observed that:

> China seeks Africa's support for the Chinese Communist Party's domestic political legitimacy and for China's foreign policy agenda internationally, especially in multilateral forums, given the size of the African voting bloc . . . As China pushes for "democratization of international relations," the success of the so-called China Model and relations with non-Western and non-democratic African countries have become an increasingly important goal for China, both for domestic and foreign policy purposes.[25]

South African economist Tony Twine has made a similar point—about China needing Africa more than Africa needs China—with respect to trade and investment.[26]

That China has a greater need for Africa than vice versa is not mere importuning.[27] It is an appraisal of African agency. Chinese media, after all, also reckon that, for political and economic reasons, the United States also needs Africa more than Africa needs the United States.[28] Chinese media do so even though the leaders of the "greatest country in the history of the world" do not themselves acknowledge a need for Africa. When Obama visited Tanzania in 2013, the American need for Africa was voiced—not by him, but by Tanzania's president Jakaya Kikwete, who stated that "Africa needs the United States. The United States needs Africa."[29]

Racialization—giving a racial character to a group or relationship—has often been part of the global exercise of agency; for example, "The historical agency of white colonizers in orchestrating the encounter of multiple racial groups in the Caribbean . . . "[30] Racialization is overgeneralization; for example, a study found that in Lusaka's Kamwala Market, "Chinese traders were grouped in one social category, separate from their occupation, social status, length or purpose in Zambia."[31] In this chapter we argue that when African elites exercise agency by racializing "the Chinese," they may mainly aim to alter domestic politics, not relations between Chinese and locals, but even if that is so, racialization is nevertheless consequential for the Chinese relationship with the host government and people, as starkly seen in the Zambian example.

RACIALIZING "THE CHINESE" IN ZAMBIA: THE PATRIOTIC FRONT IN OPPOSITION (2005–2011)

The PF has been the main racializer in Zambia, although merchants, unions, and others have been slotted into the discourse of "resistance" to Chinese employers or competitors.[32] The PF used racialization as one means to conquer power, and it was assumed that through that power it would leverage relations with China and Chinese firms. Yet after becoming Zambia's president, PF head Michael Sata wryly admitted, "When we were campaigning . . . I promised I will sort the Chinese out. They are also going to sort me out."[33] Reuter's Africa Bureau chief, asked after Sata's death in 2014 about his "relationship with the Chinese," replied that "there was really nothing concrete that emerged from his rhetoric, in terms of policy toward China."[34]

The PF formed in 2001 when Sata, a minister in the arch-neoliberalist Movement for Multi-Party Democracy (MMD) government of Frederick Chiluba (1991–2001), failed to receive Chiluba's nod as successor. Sata received only 3 percent of the 2001 presidential vote. From 2005, however—after an accident at a Chinese-owned explosives plant killed scores of Zambians—Sata's great constant, through losing presidential bids in 2006 and 2008 and a win in 2011, was his rhetorical savaging of "the Chinese." In that he was joined by his deputy, Guy Scott, and by PF National Youth Leader, MP and future minister, Chishimba Kambwili.

During the PF's rise, the six thousand to ten thousand Chinese were a tiny part of Zambia's twelve to thirteen million people. Sata claimed there were eighty thousand Chinese[35] —a typical racializing gambit in which an overestimate of Chinese creates an environment of Yellow Peril. As the eminent twentieth-century Chinese writer Lao She, who lived in London in the 1920s, observed, "If there were 20 Chinese living in Chinatown, [UK media] accounts would say 5,000. [And] every one of those 5,000 yellow devils would certainly smoke opium, smuggle arms, murder people . . ."[36]

American journalist Howard French has noted that "Zambia was one of the first African countries where the role of China and of Chinese people in the country became an explicit and potent political issue."[37] By 2004, Sata was telling Zambian traders that "the MMD government is removing you from the markets and bringing the Lebanese and Chinese because they think you are fools."[38] In the 2006 elections, he promised to deport Chinese investors[39] and said that "Zambia has become a province—no, a district—of China . . . The Chinese are the most unpopular people in the country because no one trusts them. The Chinaman is coming just to invade and exploit Africa. We need investors not infesters."[40]

Sata's critics called him a Hitler or Idi Amin.[41] After his 2006 defeat, PF supporters sacked Lusaka and Copperbelt province Chinese-owned shops[42] and attacked Chinese traders.[43] Sata charged that "Chinese investors have employed 20,000 dehumanized Zambian workers"[44]; in building an economic zone in Copperbelt, "[Chinese] will have their state within a state, and will truly be able to do as they please"[45] ; and Zambia had "become a labor camp. Most of the Chinese are prisoners of conscience. I want any investment but not Chinese human beings."[46] He averred that China's "interest is exploiting us . . . They have simply come to take the place of the West as the new colonizer of Africa."[47] Sata judged that "Chinese investment had not benefited Zambians at all," as "Chinese investors were just plundering everything in Zambia" and "for every dollar, the Chinese bring one Chinaman."[48] He exclaimed that "the Chinese are very unpopular around the world and people have to fight them wherever they are"[49] and threatened to expel Zambia's largest Chinese investor, the China Nonferrous Metals Mining Company (CNMC).[50]

In the 2008 election, Sata opined that "the Chinese are not here as investors, they are here as invaders . . . it is not only Zambia, it's the whole Cape to Cairo where the Chinaman is."[51] After losing, Sata said that Chinese practiced "slave labor" in Zambia,[52] and "the Chinaman is the rider, the African is the horse."[53] He judged that Chinese enterprises are not engaged in investment, but merely corruption,[54] and asserted that "if 100 Chinese come, 20 of them are skilled and the other 80 are unskilled prisoners."[55]

PF Secretary General Guy Scott has said of Chinese that "they're not here to develop Zambia, they're here to develop China"[56] and queried where the benefit was from Chinese mining investment.[57] He constructed a racial hierarchy that complimented colonialism by ranking mining investors in a country where most mines have been run by "white" foreign firms but that also has Indian and Chinese mining firms: "People are saying: 'We've had bad people before. The whites were bad, the Indians were worse, but the Chinese are worst of all.'"[58] Scott also claimed "the Chinese are no longer welcome. They are seen as cheats,"[59] and that the Chinese turn African governments into "client factions"; they "are out to colonize Africa economically";[60] and they have no Zambian supporters.[61] As vice president of Zambia, Scott averred "The Chinese . . . have a reputation for being somewhat . . . inhumane" and "are terrible managers."[62]

Although mine unions supported selling to China's CNMC the Luanshya Mine after it was shuttered by its Swiss-based owner during the global financial crisis, the PF opposed it.[63] Chishimba Kambwili noted that in his Luanshya parliamentary constituency, people were "now wallowing in abject poverty,"[64] yet he "led a fierce opposition to Chinese running the mine"[65] and sought a UK investor to take it over.[66] When CNMC did arrive in Luanshya, Kambwili continued to attack it[67] and criticized the government for awarding construction projects to Chinese firms.[68]

In the 2011 elections, Sata again made inaccurate charges: "The Chinese bring excessive laborers, unskilled people, which is not the case with other Western investors"; Zambia's buildings were all left by Westerners, while Chinese had not constructed a single one; Chinese came to Zambia "to seek refuge"; and Westerners developed everything in Copperbelt, while "There isn't anything the Chinese have developed." He added that earnings through Chinese investors' exports from Zambia go only to Chinese, while with Westerners, "everything they sold came back to Zambia." Sata concluded that "the Chinese are very crafty," "extremely aggressive economically," and live sixty to a room.[69]

The PF leaders' anti-Chinese agitation, although largely inventions, motivated many voters and placed Chinese on edge about whether they might be expelled.[70] Chinese were so demonized that Scott admitted in 2012 that the "mild intimidation" of "anti-orientalism" had even forced the Catholic Church "to send elsewhere priests from the Philippines who had been working in Zambia."[71] Mob physical attacks on Chinese occurred in the PF's Copperbelt strongholds.[72]

RACIALIZING "THE CHINESE" IN ZAMBIA: THE PATRIOTIC FRONT COMES TO POWER

After the PF took power in 2011—with Sata as president, Scott as vice president, and Kambwili as minister of Foreign Affairs and then minister of Labor—Zambia's government had "correct" relations with its Chinese counterpart. China is a major investment source, and Sata conceded that in infrastructure building, Chinese work hard, often in harsh, remote conditions.[73] Criticized for government tenders going to Chinese firms to build roads, he replied, "When our friends [local road contractors] start working properly I'll not be importing Chinese. But me what I want is the road; I don't care who is building the road, whether it is Chinamen."[74] Yet PF anti-Chinese campaigns continued from just before the 2011 election to after it; one concerned the Chinese-owned Collum Coal Mine (CCM) and another was the Chinese Defilement Case.

A defunct, remote, unprofitable mine was revived as Collum Coal Mine in the mid-2000s by an ethnic Chinese Australian. Pay was low and working conditions harsh and unsafe. Worker unrest, at times violent and even murderous, was directed against about seventy Chinese employed alongside six hundred to one thousand Zambians. In late 2010, a misunderstanding over pay led to a protest in which Zambians stoned and chased Chinese at the mine. Two supervisors responded by firing a shotgun and wounding thirteen miners, one seriously. The supervisors were arrested, but the Chinese Embassy pressured CCM to apologize and pay compensation. Zambia's chief prosecutor then dropped the case because the compensated shooting victims were unwilling to testify. Guy Scott portrayed the shooting as a gratuitous act of "the Chinese." A PF MP, who was to become Minister of Mines, claimed "the Chinese" would continue to shoot Zambians. Soon after the PF took power in 2011, a wave of strikes and "inspections" particularly targeted Chinese-owned enterprises. Another misunderstanding over pay at CCM in 2012 resulted in a riot. This time, the beleaguered Chinese were—on company orders—unarmed and a Chinese surveyor was murdered and a half-dozen Chinese injured.[75]

The Chinese Defilement Case arose during the wave of strikes and inspections of Chinese firms. Two Chinese workers were charged, in Kambwili's home base of Luanshya, with having sex with two underage prostitutes, although no Zambian had ever been prosecuted for defiling a prostitute. While the workers languished in prison, their accusers tried to extract a payment that the Chinese Embassy and defendants' company refused as extortionate. Politics were central to the case. Foreign Minister Kambwili plunged into it from the outset, though a law bars Zambians from public comment on ongoing court proceedings. He demanded the defendants' company assemble its workforce to be lectured on how to behave, thereby spreading the idea that Chinese are key abusers of underage girls, a fanciful notion, as there have been no other reported arrests of Chinese for defilement among the thousands made in Zambia annually. After a trial, the judge acquitted the defendants, indicating they had not even been properly identified and that there was no convincing evidence of guilt. The judge jailed one accuser for perjury and found that the other "defiled" girl was a *virgo intacta*. Despite the acquittal, a subsequent survey indicated that Zambians had indeed come to associate Chinese with immorality, a link similar to what anti-Chinese forces in Western countries forged in the late nineteenth and early twentieth centuries.[76]

After the Chinese Defilement Case acquittals and deadly CCM riot, both in 2012, PF anti-Chinese campaigns abated. Not all PF leaders abandoned their anti-Sinicism however. In 2014, Kambwili, by then Minister of Youth and Sports, was the racializing point man. A Zambian media article recounted that China Luanshya Mine (CLM) awarded Kambwili a contract in 2012 to decommission a mineshaft, allowing him to garner about US$500,000 in scrap. But after he wrote to CLM CEO Luo Xingeng in February 2014 demanding that lists of potential hires at the mine be channeled through him as PF National Youth Chairman, CLM told Kambwili that his current contract would be his last. Kambwili met in April with CLM miners about their grievances, some concerning CLM's Human Resources Department. Its Zambian head Frederick Chola then told Kambwili to stop being malicious. Kambwili sought a meeting with CEO Luo, bringing along the Copperbelt Provincial Minister, the District Commissioner, Luanshya's mayor, another Luanshya MP, and an intelligence officer. Luo declined to intervene in a "personal matter" between Kambwili and Chola, and Kambwili claimed Luo was attacking the PF.[77] He later gave a speech in which he stated that he does not appreciate Chinese investors in the mines and faulted Chinese for not renting from local landlords and instead living "40-60 to a house" in company accommodations. Kambwili closed by saying, "I don't deal with, sorry to say, Chinese . . . If I bounce back as labor minister, I am coming for you Chinese . . . I am warning [the] CLM CEO that he should not dismiss a single worker, because the moment he does that . . . he will be deported."[78]

Kambwili won nothing in his latest racializing of Chinese, and his remarks drew a riposte from a key elite bastion, the Zambia Federation of Employers. Its head said "[Kambwili's] statement that he hates Chinese investors is a serious threat to employment creation," as "it took the Chinese to . . . bring life to Luanshya Copper Mines and Luanshya town in particular," by upping mine employment from 1,700 to 3,000.[79] Indeed, soon after his threats to come for "you Chinese," Kambwili, as Minister of Youth and Sport, was reduced to asking visiting Chinese Vice President Li Yuanchao for help to maintain two Chinese aid-built stadiums in Zambia and requesting from First Secretary of China's Communist Youth League Qin Yizhi help in training Zambian youth skills instructors and setting up agricultural-processing industries in rural youth resettlement centers.[80]

Racialized Issues

Claims that racializing mobilizations, as exercises of agency, have ameliorated issues arising from the Chinese presence in Zambia—particularly issues of mining employment, taxes, wages, and safety—are inapt. While these mobilizations result from agency, the claims are based on mischaracterizations of the actual practices of the main Chinese mining firm in Zambia, CNMC. There is, moreover, no necessary causal link between positive or ameliorative aspects of CNMC's practices and the exercise of racializing agency. Zambian state-level agency may have played a role in shaping these practices and, of course, since CNMC is a national-level, state-owned enterprise (SOE), Chinese state-level agency certainly did as well.

As already discussed, sweeping distortions have been made by US politicians and media with regard to employment by Chinese in Africa. They have been made for CNMC specifically with regard to wages and safety by US-based NGO Human Rights Watch, and these distortions themselves contributed to racialization. There is, however, no evidence that any positive aspects of CNMC practice resulted from PF racialization; the evidence instead suggests that CNMC decisions were made for its own benefit. We discuss that evidence with regard to the effect of CNMC's "three no's" policy on mining employment, the company's unique acceptance of taxes, the wage gap between its employees and those of other foreign mining companies, comparative safety records, and the localization of workforces at Chinese companies in Zambia.

Three No's

During the 2008 to 2009 global financial crisis, Lusanshya Copper Mine's Swiss-based owner abandoned it. Almost all other non-Chinese-owned mines massively laid off workers. No reductions occurred at Chinese facilities. CNMC adopted a countercyclical "three no's" (三不) policy: no layoff of workers, no cutbacks in investment, no abandonment of expansion plans. CNMC asserts that the policy, which contradicts market ideology, was taken by the firm because "state-owned enterprises generally don't put profit as the only target" and "for Chinese companies, strategic thinking is more important . . . Short-term profit is not so important."[81] According to the CEO of CNMC's other mine-owning Zambian subsidiary, Nonferrous Company Africa (NFCA), the "three no's" were first enunciated

> when a CNMC CEO visited to inspect the work in 2008. He also met with
> Zambian officials at a high level. When talking with them, he promised it. He
> didn't think of it on his own; there had to be some discussion and deliberation
> about it. Had the crisis lasted a bit longer, [Swiss-based Glencore's] Mopani

Copper Mine was ready to apply for bankruptcy. CNMC was already planning to buy it.[82]

CNMC's CEO himself stated that he concluded that "Chinese are hardworking and demand in the world has not changed, nor the market . . . so the price drop would not last long." There was also a need to dispel concerns Zambians might have:

> The three no's policy shows that we have ability and confidence. It was announced at a ceremony at which the [Zambian] Ministry of Commerce had an official in attendance. The announcement was to enhance confidence of the Zambian people and government in CNMC. About 500 people attended the conference and applauded the announcement.[83]

CNMC proposed the three no's in early 2009. Soon after it bid for the Luanshya mine, copper prices regained precrisis levels. The three no's policy also impacted non-Chinese mines: they had to rehire many of the workers that they had laid-off[84] to not lose face with Zambia's government in comparison with CNMC, and to avoid having their laid-off skilled workers being hired by Chinese-owned mines.

The "three no's" policy, as an aspect of China's politics of "mutual benefit," is of a piece with a more recent Chinese action taken to show support for an African government during another crisis. In 2013, a violent South Sudan–Sudan border dispute led South Sudan to expel Sudanese oil industry employees and ask China to train South Sudanese to replace them. While training was underway, civil war broke out in South Sudan. Its government then asked China to keep its three hundred Chinese oil workers in South Sudan to maintain operations. China's Special Envoy for Africa has stated that

> the [South Sudan] government requested us not to close down the oilfields. We made a pretty difficult decision to maintain a minimum number of Chinese workers in the field to maintain production. Losing that interest would not significantly affect any Chinese peoples' lives. Losing that interest for South Sudan could be life and death. That's why we risk our peoples' lives to be there.[85]

That episode, like the "three no's policy," illustrates that African states may appreciate that they can exercise agency with the Chinese state in ways not available to them in relation to Western states that do not influence business decisions of their citizen corporations.

Tax Acceptance

Mohan and Lampert state that "recent moves by the Sata government in Zambia to double mining royalties highlight how African states are acting to leverage benefits from Chinese investment."[86] Unlike other foreign mining companies, however, Chinese firms have not resisted Zambian government efforts to increase revenues from mining taxes and royalties. The Zambian state has moreover magnified the revenue benefits it receives from Chinese investment by having the Chinese state, if not on its side, then at least not actively opposing it on taxation issues, thereby obviating a united tax resistance by mining companies.

In 2007, the MMD government responded to super-low revenues from foreign-owned mines resulting from Development Agreements (DAs) it negotiated when privatizing mines[87] by increasing royalties from 0.6 percent to 3 percent.[88] Yet in 2008, Zambia president Levi Mwanawasa stated that the effective mining tax rate was still the lowest in the world.[89] He imposed a windfall profits tax. It was scuttled soon after his death and the onset of the global financial crisis. Both the ruling MMD and opposition PF renounced reimposing the windfall profits tax, despite copper prices rising again from 2009.[90] In 2012, royalties were doubled from 3 percent to 6 percent. In early 2015, the 30 percent corporate income tax was dropped, but royalties temporarily rose from 6 percent to 20 percent for open cast (OC) mines and from 6 percent to 8 percent for underground (UG) mines.[91]

An ex-minister of mines and mining economist argued in 2010 that mining firm claims against Zambia's general fund for Value-Added Taxes (VAT) rendered negative their contribution to Zambia's budget and that the only mining firms paying taxes were Chinese.[92] Several non-Chinese firms had, in 2008 to 2009, refused to pay any higher taxes, so that only a third of a predicted revenue boost from the windfall and other taxes occurred.[93] The United States and other Western states endorsed these owners' efforts to escape added taxes by upholding the DAs' fifteen-to-twenty-year "stability periods." Canada-based First Quantum Minerals (FQM) led most owners—but not CNMC—to threaten to sue the Zambian government.[94] Chinese investors said they wanted a stable Zambian tax regime that comports with "international terms,"[95] likely meaning taxes that approach the level elsewhere.

CMNC firms did not object to new taxes,[96] and unlike Glencore's MCM, they have not been accused of evading taxes.[97] Unlike Glencore and FQM (Kansanshi Mine), CNMC has not scaled back expansion plans to protest Zambian government withholding of tax refunds until firms present import certificates from countries to which they export copper.[98] Unlike Canada-based Barrick Gold (Lumwana Mine), CNMC will not suspend output to resist increased royalties.[99] In short, tax issues have not required any special Zambian exercise of agency against Chinese firms.

Closing the Wage Gap

A 2011 report by US-based NGO Human Rights Watch (HRW) erroneously claimed that Chinese copper mining firms offer base salaries about one-fourth of their competitors for the same work.[100] The two best-paying Zambian mines have been MCM and UK-Indian-owned Konkola Copper Mine (KCM),[101] but only if comparison is limited to direct employees. The CEO of NFCA, the CNMC subsidiary that owns Chambishi Mine, stated in 2011 that average basic pay for miners there was about half of KCM's,[102] and a vice CEO of CNMC subsidiary CLM said its wages were 80 percent of KCM's.[103] Such estimates were based on comparing wage scales for permanent workers in 2011 union contracts. CNMC stated in 2011, before that year's election, that in 2012 it would narrow the gap by giving larger wage increases than other companies; it did so, and the Chinese-owned mines lowest wage rose to 82 percent of that at KCM.[104]

NFCA and CLM workforces in 2011 were almost all permanent employees, while some half of MCM's and KCM's workforces were "contractors," who earned one-fourth to one-half of what permanent workers did.[105] If pay for the whole NFCA/CLM workforce was compared to the whole MCM/KCM workforce, the former may have earned on average more than the latter. That belies claims that "NFCA's salary level for the general workforce has been about 30% lower than KCM . . . and 15% lower than MCM" and that NFCA "wages remain the lowest on the Copperbelt."[106] Such comparisons also consider only wage scales in union contracts, not how the workers' distribution within scales affects average pay. That has been done, however, through a mid-2014 survey by anthropologist Yan Hairong and me of fifty miners each at NFCA, CLM, MCM, and KCM. It showed average pay at NFCA/CLM of K3970 (US$640) and at MCM/KCM K4392 ($708). Thus, wages at Chinese-owned mines were 90 percent of those at the "best-paying" non-Chinese foreign-owned mines.

Because, however, we sampled only MCM/KCM direct employees, the MCM/KCM pay figure was higher than the actual average. If contractors working at MCM/KCM were also taken into account, the pay difference between the "best payers" and CNMC mines would likely disappear. Workers at the Chinese-owned mines might on average even be better paid, despite the non-Chinese-owned mines having lower production costs and much greater profits. The workers at CNMC Zambia mines, incidentally, earned more than the two hundred workers at China's largest (SOE) copper mine who we surveyed in mid-2014. They averaged RMB3450 (US$555), a result at odds with claims that "China is exporting poor labor conditions to Africa."[107] Rather, all mining firms in Zambia pay low wages, so that Zambian miners' living conditions are far below counterparts in the developed countries from which most mining firms in Zambia hail. For example, miners in Canada average US$5,300 a month.[108]

Safety

It has been alleged, notably by HRW, that CNMC facilities in Zambia are the least safe copper mines there. When CNMC first came to Zambia, established NFCA, and rehabilitated the long-dormant Chambishi Mine, from 1998 to 2001, safety conditions may have been problematic. Chambishi Mine was the Chinese state's first investment in Africa, and mine rehabilitation is dangerous work. In any case, available statistics are only from 2001 onward. From 2001 to 2011, CNMC's mining deaths were proportionate to its workforce numbers among Zambian copper miners.[109] In 2012 to 2013, the four deaths at CNMC mines were one-sixth of the industry total, while CNMC employees were one-seventh to one-sixth of Zambia's copper miners.[110] Mining death rates, moreover, are highly correlated with serious injury rates.

CNMC death rates were proportional to workforces even though UG mines are much more dangerous than OC mines and both CNMC mines (until 2012) were entirely UG, while other foreign-owned firms had only OC or mixed UG/OC mines. A fatalities study at UG/OC KCM showed a 7:1 UG:OC ratio.[111] Zambia Mine Safety Department 2006 to 2011 data indicate a ratio of 7.7:1.[112] Thus, given the difference in the kind of mines owned, CNMC mines were at least as safe, if not safer, than other foreign-owned mines.

Localization

President Sata has been remembered "for demanding China up the number of their Zambian workers."[113] He and Kambwili constantly and erroneously spoke of Chinese being imported to "push wheelbarrows."[114] The implication was that Chinese are so ethnocentric that they would rather pay the hugely higher costs of bringing Chinese than employ Zambians.

In Zambia, Chinese firms are most active in mining and construction. They are highly and increasingly localized. CNMC is the largest Chinese firm in Zambia. In 2012, it had 379 Chinese and 5,815 Zambian direct employees (94 percent localization).[115] JCHX, a Chinese mine operations firm attached to CNMC, had 126 Chinese and 1,800 Zambians in 2012 (93 percent localization);[116] in 2014, it had 60 Chinese and 3,440 Zambians (98 percent localization).[117] Provincial SOE Jinchuan is the largest non-CNMC Chinese-owned copper firm in Zambia. Its Chibuluma Mine had 779 employees in 2013; two were Chinese (99.9 percent localization).[118] The largest

Chinese construction firm in Zambia is provincial SOE China Jiangxi. In 2013, its workforce included four thousand locals and sixty Chinese direct employees (98.5 percent localization). If the three hundred Chinese short-term contract workers laboring there are counted, localization was still 91 percent, the same as for China Jiangxi subsidiary Wah Kong, which in 2013 had 1,500 Zambians and 150 Chinese.[119]

Sata once stated that "instead of creating jobs for the local workforce, they bring in Chinese workers to cut wood and carry water. We don't want Zambia to be a dumping ground for their human beings."[120] Claims that Chinese are brought to Zambia to "push wheelbarrows" continue to appear in Zambia,[121] pressed by opposition political parties that now use the issue to attack the PF.[122] Such assertions are often based on Chinese skilled workers, engineers, or even managers being observed helping out through manual labor when needed, a Chinese socialist-era custom.[123] In any case, the idea that most Chinese enterprise employees in Zambia are Chinese is refuted by well-known Zambian economist Dambisa Moyo, who has put the local-to-Chinese ratio at 13:1[124] or 15:1.[125] Zambia is not an outlier: our database, currently including about six hundred Chinese enterprises and projects in Africa, indicates that across most sectors, Chinese firms' localized work-forces average well over 80 percent.

CONCLUSION: CONSEQUENCES OF TWO KINDS OF AGENCY IN CHINA-ZAMBIA RELATIONS

Agency exercised does not always have its intended consequences, nor does it necessarily result in influence. State-level agency has generally had its intended consequences and a modicum of influence with regard to the Zambian-Chinese interface. That has not necessarily been so for the racializing discourse of the Chinese presence. It has had two ascertained consequences, however: it helped the PF come to power,[126] as party leaders intended, and entrenched racialization of Chinese among many Zambians, a consequence that has made it difficult for a sense of Zambian/Chinese solidarity to develop. These two consequences come together in the effect of racialization on how Chinese view their place in Zambia, as vulnerable, particularly during election campaigns.[127] Four months before his death, Sata told a reception for Li Yuanchao that "Zambia and China are 'twin brothers' and Chinese people is the 74th ethnic group of Zambia."[128] That was cold comfort, how-ever, for Chinese who experienced PF racializing mobilizations; most cannot regard Zambia as their home, but only as a place of sojourning.[129] The mobilizations also gave labor relations at Chinese firms a racial character; many local employees speak not of their bosses, but of "the Chinese," which also contributes to the perception of vulnerability.[130] In contrast, Zambia's forty thousand whites have been almost entirely spared from invidious racialization and indeed live in a country which, from 2011-2014, had a white vice president. [131]

Racialization coincided with the three no's policy, CNMC abstention from mining firm antitax efforts, a narrowed wage gap, passable Chinese mining safety, and a high and increasing enterprise localization rate. It is plausible to assume that racialization as an exercise of agency induced these positive phenomena, but whether that is so is not evident. Because correlation, but not causation, is apparent, we must avoid the philosophers' "post hoc, propter hoc fallacy"—"the cock crows, the sun rises; the sun has risen because the cock crowed"—or obviate the social scientists' "endogenity bias" of unobserved confounders driving a correlation of independent and dependent variables. Here the omitted variable, as it were, is the agency of the very Chinese entities supposed to have been positively affected by the racializers' agency. It may well be that the Chinese state and firms conducted themselves according to what they regarded as beneficial, rather than acting in response to the racializers.

The changes in Chinese activities that we have noted do, after all, benefit the Chinese state and the firms that made them. Three no's allowed CNMC to gain a mine, other firms' laid off skilled workers, and a reputation for standing by employees and the host government. Accepting tax hikes has not been onerous for CNMC firms, as they are not high-profit operations like FQM, MCM, and KCM, so there is much less to tax. A narrowed wage gap creates a more stable workforce, retains skilled labor, and has gradually proceeded as CNMC firms developed. Improved safety means less down time in production, fewer compensatory payouts, and more contented workers. Our interviews with scores of Chinese managers in a dozen African states indicate that all favor localization, which saves on labor costs and provides access to otherwise recondite local information. Claims that racialization made the difference in any of these matters remain speculative. Instead of racialization inducing changes by Chinese entities, it may have merely provided short-term political advantages for Zambian racializers, so that only those who equate a party (PF) and a people can feel assured that racialization produced anything of value for average Zambians.

The two kinds of agency in China-Zambia relations are experienced differently. State agency of the kind scholars allude to derives from Zambia's leading role among African states and its resources, most notably the copper that the Chinese "workshop of the world" so abundantly uses. State agency allows, for example, Zambia to get good terms on Chinese SOE-built infrastructure [132] and for more than one thousand Zambian students to study in China in 2014. [133] State agency can also become a collective agency of African states, if they together seek certain benefits through the Chinese government; for example, a generalized three no's policy, continentwide localization guidelines, and more.[134]

Agency exercised via racialized mobilization is another matter. Those subjected to such campaigns pay attention to them, but racialized mobilizations may not have gained anything for the nations in whose name they are carried out. Instead, many of those who rally to them and oppress others themselves end up disillusioned. Anti-Chinese moves in Zambia have also been counterproductive: they have steered many Zambians away from taking action against corrupt and oppressive foreign and domestic forces that in practice have much more agency in Zambia than "the Chinese."

NOTES

1. William Brown and Sophie Harman, eds., *African Agency in International Politics* (London: Routledge, 2013).

2. Lucy Corkin, *Uncovering African Agency: Angola's Management of China's Credit Lines* (Farnham: Ashgate, 2013), 5–7.

3. Giles Mohan and Ben Lampert, "Negotiating China: Reinserting African Agency into China-African Relations," *African Affairs* 112, no. 446 (2013): 92–110.

4. Aleksandra Gadzala, "The Silliness of 'China-in-Africa,'" *National Interest*, November 19, 2013,http://nationalinterest.org/commentary/the-silliness-china-africa-9422.

5. Noah Bassil, "The Roots of Afropessimism: the British Invention of the 'Dark Continent," *Critical Arts* 25, no. 3 (2011): 377–96.

6. Barry Sautman and Yan Hairong, *East Mountain Tiger, West Mountain Tiger: China, the West, and "Colonialism" in Africa* (Baltimore: University of Maryland, 2007).

7. "Remarks by President Obama at Young African Leaders Initiative Town Hall," White House, June 29, 2013,https://www.whitehouse.gov/the-press-office/2013/06/29/remarks-president-obama-young-african-leaders-initiative-town-hall; "Clinton 'Concerned' by Chinese Trade Practices in Africa," States News Service, June 14, 2011.

8. Howard French, *China's Second Continent: How a Million Migrants Are Building a New Empire in Africa* (New York: Random House, 2014).

9. Gloria M. Emeagwali, "Intersections between Indigenous Knowledge and Economic Development in Africa," in *Indigenous Discourses of Knowledge and Economic Development in Africa*, edited by Edward Shizha and Ali Abdi, 31–45 (London: Routledge, 2013).

10. Jean-Francois Bayart, "Africa in the World: A History of Extraversion," *African Affairs* 99 (2000): 217–67.

11. Interview, Mukela Muyunda, Lusaka, August 11, 2011.

12. Laura Spilsbury, "Can Michael Sata Tame the Dragon and Channel Chinese Investment towards Development for Zambians?" *Journal of Politics & International Studies* 8 (2012–2013): 238–78 (260); Alastair Fraser, "Conference Report: MineWatchZambia, September 19–20, 2008,http://orenga.politics.ox.ac.uk/materials/funding_reports/Fraser_Conf_Report.pdf.

13. Gemma Ware, "Zambia: Sata Sets the Record Straight," *The Africa Report*, February 10, 2012,http://www.theafricareport.com/News-Analysis/zambia-sata-sets-the-chinese-straight.html.

14. Steven Hess and Richard Aidoo,"Charting the Roots of Anti-Chinese Populism in Africa: A Comparison of Zambia and Ghana," *Journal of Asian and African Studies* 49, no. 2 (2013): 129–47.

15. Te-Ping Chen, "China in Africa Podcast: Understanding the 'Negative Narrative,'" China Talking Points, June 12, 2010,www.chinatalkingpoints.com/china-in-africa-podcast-the-negative-narrative/.

16. Lucas Powers, "Why Obama Is Making an African Power Play against China," CBC News, July 2, 2013.

17. Susan Seligson, "China and Africa: A Love Story?" *BU Today*, October 2, 2012,http://www.bu.edu/today/2012/china-and-africa-a-love-story/.

18. Mustafa Emirbayer and Ann Mische, "What Is Agency?" *American Journal of Sociology* 103, no. 4 (1998): 962–1023 (964).

19. Lilian Hughes, "The Real Housewives of Postfeminism: False Agency and the Internalization of Patriarchy on Reality TV," MA thesis, Georgetown University, April 23, 2012, 6,https://repository.library.georgetown.edu/bitstream/handle/10822/557535/   Hughes_georgetown_0076M_11826.pdf?sequence=1&isAllowed=y.

20. Nyuol Tong, "Kony 2012: An African Perspective," *The Chronicle* (Duke University), March 15, 2012,http://www.dukechronicle.com/articles/2012/03/16/kony-2012-african-perspective -.VLuhi4f9mUk.

21. Michel Foucault, "Afterward: The Subject and Power," in Michel Foucault: Beyond Structuralism and Hermeneutics, edited by Hubert Dreyfus and Paul Rabinow, 208–26 (Chicago: University of Chicago Press, 1982).

22. Bates Gill et al., *China's Expanding Role in Africa: Implications for the United States"* (Washington: CSIS, 2007), 5, quoted in Victor Ojakorotu and Ayo Whetho, "Sino-African Relations: The Cold War Years and After," *Asia Journal of Global Studies* 2, no. 2 (2008): 35–43 (37).

23. "刘贵今、李安山谈习近平主席出访非洲与中非关系" (Liu Guijin, Li Anshan Talk of Xi Jinping's Africa Trip and China-Africa Relations), 人民网，March 26, 2013,http://fangtan.people.com.cn/n/2013/0326/c147550-20924046.html.

24. Adams Bodomo, "Africa-China Relations: Strengthening Symmetry with Soft Power," *Pambazuka News* 440 (July 2, 2009),www.pambazuka.net/en/category/africa_china/57385.

25. Sun Yun, "Africa in China's Foreign Policy," Brookings Institution, 2014, 3,http://www.brookings.edu/~/media/research/files/papers/2014/04/africa-china-policy-sun/africa-in-china-web_cmg7.pdf.

26. "China's Hold on SA," *New Age* (South Africa), October 6, 2011.

27. Sarah Raine, *China's African Challenges* (London: Routledge, 2013), 45.

28. "王慧卿 '希拉里访非'力不从心'" (Hillary Clinton's Africa Visit 'Did Not Meet Her Expectations'"), 第一财经日报 (Shanghai), August 7, 2009.

29. "Remarks by President Obama and President Kikwete of Tanzania at Joint Press Conference," White House Documents and Publications, July 1, 2013.

30. Keith Sandiford, *Theorizing a Colonial Caribbean-Atlantic Imaginary: Sugar and Obeah* (London: Routledge, 2011), 146.

31. Kari Stien, "Kamwala Shopping World: Competition and Cooperation among Zambian and Chinese Traders in Lusaka," Master Thesis, Norwegian University of Science & Technology, 2013, 72,http://brage.bibsys.no/xmlui/handle/11250/271441.

32. John Kapwmbwa, "Jury Out on How Zambia's New Leader Will Deliver on Promises," *Sunday Independent* (South Africa), September 25, 2011; Han Wei and Shen Hu, "China's Harsh Squeeze in Zambia's Copperbelt," *Caixin*, November 10, 2011,http://english.caixin.com/2011-11-10/100324752; Thula Kaira, "The Chinese and Unfair Competition: Part 2," *The Post* (TP, Zambia), March 8, 2010.

33. "Sata's U-Turn on China," *Lusaka Times* (LT Zambia), October 30, 2011.

34. "Zambia's King Cobra Spits No More," Biznews.com, October 29, 2014.www.biznews.com/video/2014/10/29/   zambias-king-cobra-spits-no-more-bequeaths-free-africa-its-first-white-president/.

35. "Cold Reception for China's President," Integrated Regional Information Networks (IRIN), February 5, 2007.

36. Yo Zushi, "Sympathy for the Devil Doctor," *New Statesman* (UK), November 28, 2014, 64–65.

37. Howard French, "In Africa, an Election Reveals Skepticism of Chinese Involvement," *Atlantic* (online), September 29, 2011,www.theatlantic.com/international/archive/2011/09/in-africa-an-election-reveals-skepticism-of-chinese-involvement/245832/.

38. Sheikh Chifuwe, "Sata Needs to be Tamed, Says Nalumango," *TP*, August 17, 2004.

39. "Electoral Commission Summons PF President over Remark," *TP*, August 17, 2006.

40. Mary Fitzgerald, "Zambia Becomes Shorthand for What Can Go Wrong," *Irish Times*, August 25, 2008.

41. Neo Simutanyi, "Why I Won't Vote for Sata," *TP*, September 25, 2006.

42. "Sata Visits Taiwan," *TP*, February 6, 2007; Rohit Negi, "Beyond the 'Chinese Scramble': The Political Economy of Anti-China Sentiment in Zambia," *African Geographical Review* 27, no. 1 (2008): 41–63 (48).

43. Terence McNamee, "Africa in Their Words: A Study of Chinese Traders in South Africa, Lesotho, Botswana, Zambia and Angola," Brenthurst Foundation, Discussion Paper 2012/03, March 2012, 37.

44. Brighton Phiri, "Sata Explains Why He Stayed Away from SADC Summit," August 20, 2007.

45. Andreas Lorenz and Thilo Thielke, "Age of the Dragon: China's Conquest of Africa," Spiegel Online, May 30, 2007,http://www.spiegel.de/international/world/the-age-of-the-dragon-china-s-conquest-of-africa-a-484603.html.

46. Bivan Saluseki, "I'm Not Ashamed to Deal with Taiwan, Says Sata," *Maravi* (Zambia), November 2007.

47. Lydia Polgreen and Howard French, "China's Trade in Africa Carries a Price Tag," *New York Times*, August 21, 2007.

48. Chibaula Silwamba, "Sata Condemns Chinese Investments in Zambia," *TP*, July 5, 2007.

49. Joseph Mwenda, Bivan Saluseki and Patson Chilemba, "Sata Loses Passport, U-turns from London," *LT*, October 24, 2007.

50. Brian Chama, "Economic Development at the Cost of Human Rights: China NonFerrous Metal Industry in Zambia," *Human Rights Brief* 17, no. 2 (2010): 1–6 (4).

51. Ofeibea Quist-Arcton, "Chinese-Built Zambian Smelter Stirs Controversy," National Public Radio (NPR, US), July 31, 2008,http://www.npr.org/templates/story/story.php?storyId=93081721.

52. "Sata Accuses China and Malaysia Investors of Slavery," *LT*, January 21, 2010.

53. "The China Man Is the Rider, the African Is the Horse: Sata," *Times of Zambia* (TOZ), December 18, 2009.

54. Howard French, "The Next Empire," *The Atlantic* 305, no. 4 (May 2010).

55. Quoted in Aaron Sikombe, "Should the Trade between Africa and China Be Regulated?" *Tumfweko, Zambia*, April 20, 2012,http://tumfweko.com/2012/04/20/should-the-trade-between-africa-and-china-be-regulated/.

56. "Chinese President Takes His African Tour to Copper-Rich China," Associated Press, February 4, 2007.

57. "China's Goldmine," *Guardian* (UK), March 28, 2006.

58. Chris McGreal, "Chinese Influx Revives Colonial Fears," Guardian (UK), February 9, 2007.

59. "African Protests Show China That Investment Comes with Heavy Price," *The Times* (UK), February 3, 2007.

60. Colin Freeman, "Africa Discovers the Dark Side of its New Colonial Master," *Sunday Telegraph* (UK), February 4, 2007.

61. "Cold Reception for China's President," IRIN, February 5, 2007.

62. Lucy Bannerman, "Dr Scott, I Presume?" *Spectator* (UK), March 10, 2012.

63. "Pastors Counsel Kambwili," TOZ, November 20, 2009.

64. Karen Brulliard, "Global Woes Imperil African Nations' Gains," *Chicago Tribune*, March 29, 2009.

65. Kelvin Kachingwe, "Controversial Chinese Firm Given Another Copper Mine," Inter Press Service, June 2, 2009.

66. "Nesawu Counsels Kambwili," TOZ, April 15, 2009.

67. Zumani Katasefa, "'Rupiah Banda Should Stop Protecting Chinese Nationals Who Violate Zambian Laws': MP," UKZambians, January 20, 2012, http://www.ukzambians.co.uk/home/2011/01/20/rupiahs-banda-stop-protecting-chinese-nationals-violate-zambian-laws-mp/.

68. "Government Defends Chinese Contractors," TOZ, October 1, 2009.

69. "Transcript of Sata's Controversial Interview," LT, March 22, 2011.

70. McNamee, "Africa in Their Words," 38; Interview, Chinese ambassador Zhou Yuxiao, Lusaka, August 3, 2012.

71. Rowan Callick, "Zambia's Test: to Bridge Gap with Chinese," *The Australian*, March 31, 2012.

72. "Zambia KCM Launches Drive to Boost Skills of Local Miners," Dow Jones Commodity News, March 25, 2010; "Two Chinese Nationals Beaten by Unemployed Youths Languishing in the Streets," UK Zambians, April 12, 2012,www.ukzambians.co.uk/home/2011/04/12/zambia-chinese-nationals-beaten-unemployed-youths-languishing-streets/.

73. "Dinner with His Excellency Michael Sata in London, 6/6/12," YouTube,https://www.youtube.com/watch?v=eg4QPg3DmGs.

74. "Enjoying Good Health: Sata," TP, March 31, 2013.

75. Barry Sautman and Yan Hairong, "Bashing 'The Chinese': Contextualizing Zambia's Collum Coal Mine Shooting," *Journal of Contemporary China* 23, no. 90 (2014): 1073–92.

76. Barry Sautman, "The Chinese Defilement Case: Racial Profiling in an African 'Model of Democracy,'" *Rutgers Race and the Law Review* 14, no. 1 (2014): 87–134.

77. "Kambwili, LCM CEO in Bitter Exchange," Open Zambia, May 10, 2014,www.openzambia.com/2014/05/ kambwili-lcm-ceo-in-bitter-exchange/.

78. "Kambwili Says Shamenda Is Incompetent, Ridicules Chinese Investors," *Zambia Reports* (ZR), May 19, 2014.

79. "ZFE Raises Concerns over Kambwili's Handling of Industrial Ties," TendersInfo, 26 May 2014.

80. "Kambwili Asks China to Help Address Youth Unemployment," *Daily Mail* (Zambia), June 20, 2014; "Chinese Veep Visits Heroes National Stadium," TOZ, June 20, 2014.

81. Interview, CLM CEO Luo Xin'geng, Luanshya, June 24, 2013.

82. Interview NFCA CEO Wang Chunlai, Chambishi, August 15, 2011.

83. Interview CNMC CEO Luo Tao, Beijing, October 18, 2011.

84. Interview, Delax Chilumbu, Chief Mining Engineer, Zambia Ministry of Mines, Lusaka, August 10, 2011.

85. "China Plays Peacemaker in Africa," *Sunday Independent* (South Africa), November 2, 2014.

86. Mohan and Lampert, "Negotiating China," 92.

87. Open Society Institute of Southern Africa (OSISA) et al., "Breaking the Curse: How Transparent Taxation and Fair Taxes Can Turn Africa's Mineral Wealth into Development," 2009, 37–38, 50; John Lungu, "Contextualising Mining in Zambia," *ZIPPA Journal* (January–March, 2011): 1–3,http://www.scribd.com/doc/46873541/ZIPPA-Journal-Jan-March-2011-Taxing-the-Mines.

88. "Zambia: Mineral Tax Increase Holds No Benefits for Citizens," IRIN, February 21, 2007.

89. Cho, "Mining Reflections: a People Betrayed," *Zambian Economist*, November 22, 2009.

90. "Zambian Miners Want Windfall Tax Back," *Southern Times* (Zambia), June 14, 2010.

91. Shihoko Goto, "Tax Hikes, Violence Not Hurting Zambia's Copper for Now," *Copper Investing News*, August 22, 2012,http://copperinvestingnews.com/12157-tax-hikes-violence-zambia-copper-africa-first-quantum-china.html; "Zambia Issues 2015 Budget Proposals," *EY Global*, October 17, 2014,http://www.ey.com/GL/en/Services/Tax/International-Tax/Alert--Zambia-issues-2015-Budget-proposals.

92. "Mining Firms Are Claiming Tax Refunds from ZRA," TP, June 29, 2010.

93. Duncan Green, "A Copper-Bottomed Crisis? The Impact of the Global Economic Meltdown on Zambia," Oxfam GB, March 2009, 2,http://www.oxfam.org.uk/resources/policy/economic_crisis/impact_on_zambia.html.

94. "US Impressed by Zambia's Corruption Fight," LT, April 4, 2010.

95. "China Seeks Stable Tax Policies in Zambia," Reuters, September 3, 2009.

96. Ching Kwan Lee, "The Spectre of Global China," *New Left Review* no. 89 (2014): 29–65 (39).

97. Naomi Rovnick, "Glencore Denies Tax Evasion over Mine in Zambia," *South China Morning Post* (Hong Kong), May 13, 2011.

98. Nicholas Bariyo, "Glencore Suspends Zambia Copper Projects over Tax Row," *Wall Street Journal*, October 1, 2014.

99. Barrick Suspends Zambian Output After Royalty Rise," *Financial Times* (UK), December 18, 2014; "Chinese Mining Firms Will Not Halt Operations in Zambia: Ambassador," *Xinhua*, January 4, 2015.

100. "'You'll Be Fired if You Refuse': Labor Abuses in Zambia's Chinese State-Owned Copper Mines," Human Rights Watch, November 3, 2011, 24,www.hrw.org/reports/2011/11/03/you-ll-be-fired-if-you-refuse.

101. Interview, Prof. John Lungu, Copperbelt University, Kitwe, August 15, 2011.

102. "中国赞比亚罢工事件" (The Strike Incident at Zambia's NFCA), 新世纪，November 7, 2011,http://magazine.caixin. cn/ 2011-11-05/100322640.html.

103. Interview, Gao Xiang, Beijing, October 20, 2011.

104. Barry Sautman and Yan Hairong, *The Chinese Are the Worst?: Human Rights and Labor Practices in Zambian Mining* (Baltimore: University of Maryland, 2012).

105. Interview, Venus Seti, Assistant Labor Commissioner, Lusaka, August 12, 2011; Counter Balance, "The Mopani Copper Mine, Zambia: How European Development Money Has Fed a Mining Scandal," December 2010, 17,http://www.counter-balance.org/wp-content/uploads/2011/03/Mopani-Report-English-Web.pdf; "100 KCM Miners Protest Against Their Employers' Defiance on Minimum Wage," LT, May 8, 2014.

106. Lee, "The Spectre of Global China," 48–49.

107. "China's Exportation of Labor Practices to Africa," ITUC/GUF Hong Kong Liaison Office, 2007; Thomas Lansner, "After a Democratic Power Transfer, Zambia Must Tackle Chinese Investment Issues and Human Rights Reforms," Freedom House, November 15, 2011,https://freedomhouse.org/blog/after-democratic-power-transfer-zambia-must-tackle-chinese-investment-issues-and-human-rights -.VUu9UtNVhBc.

108. "Mining Salaries," Technomine, August 2014,http://technology.infomine.com/reviews/miningsalaries/welcome.asp?view=full.

109. Yan Hairong and Barry Sautman, "'Beginning of a World Empire'?: Contesting the Discourse of Chinese Copper Mining in Zambia," *Modern China* 39, no. 2 (2013): 131–64 (139).

110. "Mining Industry Safety Record from the Year 2000 to April, 2014," Zambia Mine Safety Department chart, Kitwe, June 2014.

111. Prudence Michelo et al., "Occupation Injuries and Fatalities in Copper Mining in Zambia." *Occupational Medicine* 59, no. 3 (2009): 191–94 (192).

112. Interview, Wilford Besa, Mine Safety Department officer, Kitwe, August 14, 2012.

113. "Why President Sata's Death May Breathe Life into Foreign Investments in Zambia," Ventures Africa, October 30, 2014.

114. "King Cobra and the Dragon," Al Jazeera, January 2012; Zumani Katasefa, Mwila Chansa, and Mutuna Chanda, "Unions Welcome ZCCM-IH Takeover of LCM," TP, January 28, 2009.

115. China Nonferrous Mining Corp. Ltd., "2012 Interim Report," 25,http://www.cnmcl.net/Managed/Resources/docs/reports/0206440121142671_e.pdf.

116. Interview, Gabriel Maseko, Head of Industrial Relations, NFCA, August 13, 2012.

117. Interview, Teng Yan, NFCA Human Resources officer, Chambishi, June 16, 2014.

118. Interview, Elliot Sichone, Mineworkers Union of Zambia chairman, Chibuluma Mine, Kitwe, July 6, 2013.

119. John Sutton and Gillian Langmead, "An Enterprise Map of Zambia," London, International Growth Centre, 2013, 107,112,http://personal.lse.ac.uk/sutton/sutton_zambia_press.pdf.

120. David Blair, "Rioters Attack Chinese after Zambian Poll," *Daily Telegraph* (UK), March 10, 2006.

121. "Workers Complain of China Jiangsu's Importing of Labor," ZR, June 19, 2014.

122. Charles Sakala, "No Jobs for Locals on Choma Road Project," ZR, July 8, 2014; "Chinese Still Pushing Wheelbarrows Under PF Reign," *Zambian Eye*, June 20, 2014,http://zambianeye.com/archives/21720.

123. Tendai Musakwa, "Chinese People Are Not More Civilized Than Africans," ChinaAfrica Project, August 10, 2013,http://www.chinaafricaproject.com/chinese-people-are-not-more-civilized-than-africans-translation/.

124. Dambisa Moyo, "Beijing a Boon for Africa," *New York Times*, June 27, 2012.

125. Dambisa Moyo, *Winner Take All: China's Race for Resources and What It Means for the World* (New York: Basic Books, 2012), 159.

126. Jessica L. Belk, "China's Role in the Zambian Presidential Elections: Africa's Friend or Foe?" *China Elections and Governance*, October 28, 2011.

127. Shen and Han, "China's Harsh Squeeze"; "Wage Riots Spread to Lusaka; Chinese Fear for Safety," *ZR*, August 7, 2012.

128. "Ambassador Yang Youming Pays Tribute to President Sata," Chinese Foreign Ministry, November 5, 2014,http://www.fmprc.gov.cn/mfa_eng/wjb_663304/zwjg_665342/zwbd_665378/t1207610.shtml.

129. McNamee, "Africa in Their Words," 19.

130. Shih Chih-yu, *Sinicizing International Relations: Self, Civilization, and Intellectual Politics in Subaltern East Asia* (New York: Palgrave Macmillan, 2013), 39.

131. Stephen Chan, "Guy Scott's Whiteness Is Not the Issue in Zambia," The Conversation, October 31, 2014,http://theconversation.com/guy-scotts-whiteness-is-not-the-issue-in-zambia-33690.

132. George Schoneveld et al., "The Developmental Implications of Sino-African Economic and Political Relations: A Preliminary Assessment for the Case of Zambia," CIFOR, 2014,http://www.cifor.org/library/4486/the-developmental-implications-of-sino-african-economic-and-political-relations-a-preliminary-assessment-for-the-case-of-zambia/.

133. "China Plans Continued Exchange Programmes with Zambia," *Lusaka Voice*, December 19, 2014.

134. Barry Sautman and Yan Hairong, "Localization of Chinese Enterprises and African Agency," *African-East Asian Affairs* (June 2015): 1.

Chapter Eight

#MadeinAfrica

How China-Africa Relations Take on New Meaning Thanks to Digital Communication

Mark Kaigwa and Yu-Shan Wu

While China is a known contender in debates about political values and economic growth in sub-Saharan Africa,[1] there is today mounting interest in its establishment of African media bases across the continent and its provision of content via outlets like CCTV, *Xinhua*, and *China Daily*. As Iginio Gagliardone (in this volume) notes, Chinese telecommunications firms increasingly assist African governments with commercial media infrastructure projects, and journalists on both sides of the Indian Ocean participate in joint training exchanges. While the intentions of China's foray into African media spaces are to some extent unclear, its entrance into this sector has raised concern over its likely implications in both African and Western policy circles.[2]

China's engagement in African media has so far been haphazard. It takes place alongside many competing trends that today shape the continent—population growth; economic development; technological innovation; and especially innovation in communication technology. Such trends stand to influence Chinese engagement in Africa as much as, if not more so than, China stands to influence them. Prominent among these is the latter point—communication technology—advances in which have given rise to an increasingly active African social media. While still in early days, the ways in which Africans are using social media points to a potential new platform for political activism, citizen journalism,[3] and the expression of African agency alongside, and beyond, the realm of the state.

This chapter focuses on South Africa and Kenya. However, similar patterns can be discerned in other regions of the continent. This chapter begins by mapping some of the defining features of African media innovation, paying especial attention to the interface between social media and civil society activism. This analysis is by definition incomplete: social media has yet to penetrate all African regions and socioeconomic groups. Still, social media commentary sheds insight into general public sentiments—here, sentiments toward China. The chapter then moves from an analysis of what is being said about China to why. Here we see the salience of the contextual embeddedness of social media users in informing their views and opinions. Finally, the chapter argues that in near-paradoxical fashion Chinese communications infrastructure investments help to construct the mediums via which African agency is asserted. Social media and similar platforms have the long-term potential to affect future engagements between Kenyan and South African policymakers and foreign actors like China.

TECHNOLOGICAL LEAPFROGGING AND THE EMERGENCE OF AFRICAN SOCIAL MEDIA

The African growth story is in many ways a story about the triumph of technology—about the move away from labor-intensive industries and toward ones that largely rest on telecommunications. There are today around ninety tech hubs across the continent; more than half of African countries have at least one.[4] Application developers, hackers, and entrepreneurs are part of a large-scale African technological renaissance. What is especially unique is that the innovation driving the renaissance is homegrown. In other sectors of the African economy, like mining or agriculture, much of the know-how is imported and wealth exported. With few exceptions, the technology propelling Africa's growth and development is being developed and used locally. Although the African growth story is far from homogenous, the prospects for its future largely rest on investments in its technology, and on a so far remarkable technological transformation.

The term most generously used to describe this phenomenon is *leapfrogging*, by which is meant an accelerated development in which inferior, less efficient, more expensive, or more polluting technologies and industries are bypassed and more advanced versions adopted. In most of the developed world, the initial uptake of the Internet was the first step toward a mobile-first society: consumers adopted the Internet first, then gradually moved toward greater mobile device usage, including social networking. In Africa, the process has been reversed: Africa became a "mobile only"[5] market first, in which handsets became widely available and more often relied upon as sources of information and communication tools than traditional outlets; Africa surpassed the mainstream communications development trajectory by essentially democratizing mobile over fixed-line communications.

Since 2012, Africa has been the world's fastest growing mobile market. As of November 2013, 720 million out of roughly 1.1 billion Africans have mobile phones[6] compared to the 297.8 million Africans who use the Internet (June 2014).[7] It is projected that by 2016 there will be one billion mobile devices across the continent.[8] According to the GSM Association, too, mobile telecommunications in sub-Saharan Africa contributes 6.2 percent to the region's GDP—more than in any other region in the world. Still, the continent is the least penetrated mobile region, globally.[9] With 60 percent[10] of the continent's population living in rural areas, it is not too difficult to understand why.

The rapid expansion of mobile technology has allowed for uses beyond communications—many with positive knock-on growth and development effects. A well-known example is M-Pesa; M for *mobile*, and *Pesa* the Swahili word for "money." M-Pesa facilitates money transfers through the Kenyan telecommunications network, Safaricom, using SMS technology. Users register for the service at any of the various eighty thousand dealers countrywide,[11] where they deposit funds for the transactions; funds are stored on mobile SIM cards. Via PIN-secured SMS text messages, users can then send the funds to other mobile users, including sellers of goods, services, and utilities, and redeem deposits for cash. Upon depositing as little as ten cents, users can transfer as much as $777.00 in a single transaction. Since it first emerged on the Kenyan market in 2007, this simple interface has seen a 67 percent adoption rate, with a reported 43 percent of Kenya's GDP transferred through it.[12]

Digital platforms like M-Pesa are creating new opportunities for African corporations and individuals. In so doing, they are often disrupting longstanding industries. African cinematography is one example. Noted South African multimedium filmmaker Sibs Shongwe-La Mer produces "independent, self-financed liberal pieces of cinema" that are "made for virtually nothing,"[13] and which, still, receive international recognition. Shot on mobile phones and low-cost camcorders, La Mer's films explore the experiences of first-generation South Africans born after the demise of apartheid. Creative entrepreneurs like Sibs are emerging all over the continent thanks to the connectivity and availability afforded by advances in mobile technology. Bozza, an online community of African musicians, poets, and artists, is another example. Established in 2011 and funded by Hasso Plattner Ventures Africa in South Africa, Bozza is a social networking service targeted at township users across the continent.[14] By uploading media from their mobile devices, users can share local music, photos, videos, and the m-commerce platform, *Myhood*, with their communities.[15] As La Mer notes, "[Africa's] mass [and online] media consciousness is alive and well."[16]

Mapping African Social Media

African social media emerged within this context of communications and technological innovation. For example, Mxit, a Stellenbosch-based social networking and instant messaging platform, was established in 2003. As one of the continent's largest homegrown social networks, Mxit had roughly thirty million registered users in 2012.[17] Since then, its user base has declined to an estimated 1.6 million in 2014 as many users have switched to global sites like Facebook, WhatsApp, and the Chinese-created WeChat.[18] In Nigeria, leading local networking sites like Eskimi and 2go, a South African-based mobile social network, compete with the US instant messaging client, WhatsApp; global competitors are phasing out many local platforms. As of early 2015, Facebook, Twitter, and LinkedIn are the three most popular social networking sites across Africa. An estimated one hundred million Africans are subscribed to Facebook,[19] which remains the foremost social site in Kenya and South Africa, respectively.[20]

Despite their inherently "social" design, platforms like Facebook and Twitter are increasingly seen as outlets for political expression and information. The "Baba Jukwa" Facebook account, for example, gained in popularity around the 2013 Zimbabwean elections. The account—an anonymous icon depicting a cartoon of an elderly man—served as an informant on domestic political affairs and as a platform for public opinion.[21] Baba Jukwa's three hundred thousand followers were provided with up-to-date leaks on government activities and practical information about polling stations and voting procedures. The account also became an important resource for the Zimbabwean diaspora to stay informed about events back home. Because of its implied anonymity, the account gained prominence as something of a "safe" space in which citizens could express their political sentiments and connect with others with similar experiences and opinions. The political potential of African social media largely rests in its intangibility.

Kenyan social media played a similarly important role after the 2013 Westgate Mall attack by the militant Islamist militant group, Al-Shabaab. On one hand, via platforms like Twitter, Kenyans were able to voice criticism of the September 22 cover of the *Daily Nation*, Kenya's leading newspaper, which graphically displayed one of the suffering victims. While causation is difficult to determine, it is generally accepted that this criticism at minimum played a role in the firing of the *Nation*'s then-managing editor, Eric Obino. At the same time, the Twitter hashtag #WeAreOne enabled Kenyans to unite in an expression of solidarity. The hashtag found its way into political speeches, including a speech given by President Kenyatta in which he said, "I salute national leaders of every stripe who stood together to reassure the nation that deep inside, where it counts, we are one, indivisible national family."[22] The May 2013 hashtag, #OccupyParliament, similarly served as a rallying point for the two hundred civil society activists who on May 13 protested outside of Nairobi's Parliament in opposition to the alleged public-sector pay raises after having organized together online.[23] The moments that spark African ingenuity online usually exist when other avenues of communication are perceived to be absent.

In his 2011 *Foreign Policy* piece, Clay Shirky aptly argues that "the potential of social media lies mainly in their support of civil society and the public sphere"[24]—this, rather than the "power of mass protests to topple governments." While African social media has been used for the latter purpose—as seen in the mass protests that shaped the 2011 ouster of former Tunisian president Zine El Abidine Ben Ali, and the Arab Spring more broadly[25]—its potential indeed lies in the former. Yet the gradual emergence of African social media as a platform for African agency does not negate the influence of other media outlets. In this respect, the confusion of Sino-African ties is met by the confusion of African media development. Many traditional media outlets, including Western outlets such as *The New York Times*, have moved their content online where they dominate African digital spaces; what might be called "citizen journalism" via sites like Facebook and Twitters lags far behind.[26] "Citizen journalists," too, often cross over to more traditional outlets, blurring the line between social network agents and members of the mainstream (often state-owned) press. While the lack of central authority in social media provides greater space for sharing ideas and accessing information, it at the same time constrains widespread and organized expressions of agency. Any such expressions are likely to be ad-hoc for the foreseeable future.

The value of social media also depends on the context in which it emerges. Social media platforms do not "arrive" but rather unlock certain critical masses in a country. This "unlocking" often comes down to a convergence of several factors, including the availability and affordability of smartphones and sophisticated telecommunications technology (EDGE, 3G, and 4G connectivity); the means and desire of citizens to participate in social media in politically active ways; and the ability to finance the cost of the required airtime and data when the activism occurs via handheld devices, as is often the case. The potential of social media varies across cases, as societies and users shape how the platforms are used.[27]

Much of this chapter focuses on Kenya, for example, because, as we will see, the ways in which social media is used in South Africa—even in the context of South African ties with China—is, indeed, social. Data from AFKInsider,[28] an African business news website, shows that the ten most followed Kenyan Twitter accounts in 2014 included those of former prime minister Raila Odinga (@RailaOdinga); the former prime minister's wife, Ida Odinga (@IdaOdinga); former Kenyan minister of justice, Martha Karua (@MarthaKarua); the Kenyan Red Cross (@KenyaRedCross); Equity Bank

(@KeEquityBank); the government-led initiative "Kenya Vision 2030" (@KenyaVision2030); and the Kenyan Premier League (@KenyaPremierLg). The most followed South African accounts during the same time were largely those of celebrities,[29] including the shock-jock radio personality Gareth Cliff (@GarethCliff), and sports icons including South African cricketer and former captain of the South African cricket team, Graeme Smith (@GraemeSmith), and fellow South African cricketer, Hashim Amla (@amlahash). This divergence in Twitter followers is reflected in the way in which Chinese engagement is presented and addressed by social media users in both countries.

READING THE SUBTLE SPACES: ONLINE PUBLIC SENTIMENT TOWARD "CHINA-IN-AFRICA"

Although expressions of African agency via social media are still in early days and the scale of their influence uncertain, social media platforms like Facebook and Twitter are already being used in creative and meaningful ways. The ways in which average Africans today use such platforms sheds light on overarching trends and popular discourses, and points to how and why they may—or may not—be used in the longer term.

Our scoping of social media relies primarily on comments on Twitter; platforms like Facebook and LinkedIn generally operate on the premise of increasing social capital and maintaining contact with friends and acquaintances that users likely know offline, and with whom they have willingly chosen to connect.[30] Twitter, on the other hand, is akin to something of a "global town square"[31] where a focus on real-time breaking news, trending topics, and anonymous as well as friendly interactions makes it a more apt reflection of public sentiment. Here, too, the dominant currency is public broadcast rather than amassing social capital per se.

Of course, the fluid and real-time nature of these interactions makes commentary bound to specific timelines and occurrences; as a social media platform, Twitter generates sentiment and reaction toward individual developments in China-Africa relations rather than revealing overarching perceptions of the ties. Still, it points to factors that underpin public sentiment and interests—and reveals, too, the ways in which this sentiment shapes the reactions of, and in some cases, actions taken by, Kenyan and South African leaders vis-à-vis China's growing domestic presence.

For this chapter, lexical analyses of Twitter were undertaken by the Kenyan data science startup *Odipo Dev*[32] between January 15, 2014, and February 15, 2014. During this time, Kenya generated more political comments about China than South Africa (see figure 8.1). The dominant theme in Kenya was the issue of Chinese involvement in the illegal ivory trade and its impact on the country's wildlife, which, as part of the tourism sector, is the largest foreign exchange earner contributing roughly 10 percent of the country's GDP.[33] In South Africa, most comments were neutral and based around South African business engagements with China. While from this limited time frame it is difficult to assess whether Kenyans generally comment on China more than South Africans, several trends do emerge. The analysis also points to the salience of context in shaping how and why Africans take to social media as a platform on which to be vocal about China.

Kenya: From Connected to Conversing

In September 2007, mobile subscription in Kenya stood 10.7 million with 28.7 percent mobile penetration.[34] Eight years later, and with increased connectivity brought by three fiber-optic cables (SEACOM, The East African Marine System [TEAMS] and the East Africa Submarine Cable System [EASSY]), 32.2 million Kenyans subscribe to mobile services with penetration at an impressive 79.2 percent. Additionally, 22.3 million Kenyans subscribe to the Internet, with 99 percent of subscriptions based on mobile devices.[35] Seventy-six percent of Internet users are active on social media.[36] Perhaps unsurprisingly, Facebook is the most frequented social networking site and the second most visited site in the country. Twitter is the seventh most visited website overall, and the second most popular social networking site. The popularity of sites reflects the country's demographics: over 60 percent of Kenya's population is under the age of twenty-four.[37]

Over the January to February 2014 period, much online concern centered on the issue of illegal ivory trade. Kenya is one of the main export hubs for poaching across all of Africa; it has recently been facing an escalating poaching threat tied to domestic corruption, organized crime, and local poverty.[38]

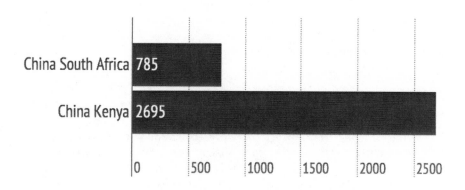

Figure 8.1.   China-related comments on Twitter, January - February 2014
(Source: Odipo Dev.)

An estimated 85 percent of Kenya's elephant population has been killed since 1970, many in the past five years.[39] In January, Kenyan authorities arrested a Chinese national, Xue, on suspicion of his involvement in an ivory-smuggling ring. Xue is the first Chinese national to be arrested overseas in relation to ivory smuggling; his two accomplices, Zheng and Li, were arrested when trying to enter China.[40] This incident came on the heels of the case of Tang Yong Jian, a Chinese national who pleaded guilty to illegal possession of ivory after attempting to transport a 3.4 kilogram (7.5 pound) elephant ivory tusk in his suitcase. Jian was ordered to pay twenty million shillings ($230,000) or face a seven-year jail sentence in accordance with Kenya's recent Wildlife Conservation and Management Act.

Kenyan social media has generally been active on the subject of illegal ivory trade. In April 2013, an online petition by a rights group, Kenyans United Against Poaching, called on the government and industry leaders to declare poaching a national disaster. On April 22, 2013, the petition had reached Kenya's State House with six thousand signatures.[41] The Art Directors and Copywriters Club of Kenya, a Facebook group of creative professionals, in 2013 also launched "Save our Heritage KE"—an online campaign aimed at raising awareness about poaching. Such activism has increased in line with the expansion of China-Africa trade. The online #HandsOffOurElephants campaign, for example, was spearheaded by Wildlife Direct, one of the leading wildlife blogging sites in Africa,[42] and was launched in 2013 by Kenyan first lady Margaret Kenyatta with the aim of ending elephant poaching. Since its launch, over ten thousand users have signed a petition calling on President Kenyatta to initiate talks with leading countries in the ivory trade, including China. Many #HandsOffOurElephants tweets have targeted China, specifically:

@DennisOkari: How can Uhuru tell the Chinese to keep their hands off our elephants when we are borrowing from them. No upper hand.

@Profesy: To save elephants, should we shoot: a) poachers; b) Chinese ivory buyers?

@serahmutethya: *Rolls eyes* Of course . . . "@CapitalFM_kenya: Another Chinese ivory smuggler nabbed at JKIA

The online campaigns have unfolded against a backdrop of mainstream media attention to the issue. Editorial cartoonist for *The Daily Nation*, Godfrey "Gado" Mwampembwa, has established a reputation for satirizing China-Kenya relations. In August 2013 he published a cartoon depicting Xi Jinping and Kenyatta in a handshake atop a carcass of a dead elephant stripped of its tusks. That same month, he illustrated Kenyatta and an aide in the State House in which the aide says, "Your Excellency, the report says a cabinet minister, a governor, two MPs and four influential businessmen are involved in poaching and ivory smuggling." The president replies: "Ah! Include them in my entourage for my coming trip to China."[43] Some of the cartoons are published exclusively on Gado's personal website; users turn to them as discussion points or disseminate them via Facebook and Twitter profiles.

When Chinese premier Li Keqiang visited Kenya in August 2014, he was quick to emphasize China's commitment to wildlife protection, pointing to environmental cooperation as a key area of future China-Africa cooperation. He pledged $10 million for wildlife conservation and inaugurated the Nairobi-based China-Africa Joint Research Centre for the study of biodiversity, technology, and environmental protection. Li's remarks came during a ceremony in which Chinese antipoaching equipment was donated to the Kenya Wildlife Service.[44] In late 2014, the Chinese Embassy in Kenya together with the State Forestry Administration of China hosted a workshop on wildlife protection in Nairobi to educate the local Chinese community about the harms of poaching and illegal trade. A group of students from Tsinghua University and the University of Nairobi launched volunteer efforts with a similar objective.[45] The Chinese leadership and its public are waking up to the reality that their ventures are being held in check by an increasingly vocal Kenyan civil society. Kenyan reliance on social media and digital platforms makes this oversight more immediate and the need for a Chinese response more essential.

Popular opposition to construction of the East African Railway, for example, has been aired on social media outlets; social media was instrumental in organizing local protests that kicked off alongside construction in October 2014. In May 2014 China Road and Bridge Company (CRBC) was awarded a contract for the construction of the railway. Financing is provided by the Export-Import Bank of China through a $1.6 billion commercial loan and a $1.63 billion concessional facility for the Mombasa to Nairobi section. Yet even before the contract was awarded, questions began to emerge over the transparency of the tender process and its benefit to local communities. In Parliament, members raised red flags over cost inflation and under-the-table dealings. On social media, public sentiment teetered between sarcastic and critical:

@Ben_Kitilli: @kacungira @KTNKenya Not yet! There seems 2be a lot of dirt being swept under the carpet. The ghosts will come haunting 1 day.

@johngithongo: Why do so many Kenyans seem to believe the standard gauge railway project is corrupt?

@msaladus: @johngithongo It is real! Check modus operandi of the tendering process and disgruntled would be beneficiaries have let the cat of the bag.

Parliamentary committees formed to investigate the tender process drew on comments and questions that were posted on Twitter and Facebook and directed at members of Parliament and political leaders.[46] Government officials are more and more aware of Kenyans' civic engagement on virtual platforms and have likewise begun to engage them to bridge the government–civil society divide. In the end, the efforts changed little. Fearing damaged relations with China, the Kenyatta government shied from further probing the CRBC. Karanja Kibicho, principal secretary in Kenya's Ministry of Foreign Affairs and International Trade, warned, "It is of the opinion of this ministry that summoning and questioning China Road and Bridge Corporation on this matter would be tantamount to summoning the Government of China. Such a measure is likely to have serious and irrevocable negative consequences to Kenya's national interests and relations with China."[47] The issue was swiftly tabled with no irregularities cited.

Days after construction began, in October 2014, protests erupted in the Kenyan town of Voi;[48] CRBC had days prior disclosed that five thousand foreigners—mostly Chinese—would be airlifted to Kenya to work on the project as part of its total thirty thousand workforce. The protestors, who blocked highways with burning tires, accused CRBC of denying them jobs in favor of Chinese expatriates. In Lamu, along the Kenyan coast, citizens staged protests over land compensation. While in some cases spontaneous, many of the protestors first organized themselves via social networking sites on their mobile devices—the time, location, and protest strategies were all agreed upon by individuals with a phone in their back pocket.

South African: From Trade to Temperament

South African social media also plays an increasing role in shaping relations with China, albeit with less tenacity than in Kenya. Most social media interactions on the topic of China involve the posting of anecdotes, practical information, and news developments; most are posted by thought leaders or journalists, among the most prominent social media actors.[49] The kind of issue-based social media advocacy seen in Kenya has not yet taken hold in South Africa.

A 2013 survey conducted among 3,500 South Africans found that 26 percent are interested in learning about poverty alleviation from China; 53 percent perceive China as the country's most important trading partner, followed by the United States and Europe.[50] This is not surprising. Just eight years after official diplomatic ties were established, in 2008, China was South Africa's primary trade partner. Since 2008, the volume of trade has grown from R121 billion ($10.5 billion) to R271 billion ($24 billion) in 2013.[51] Investment remains modest. In 2012 total Chinese foreign direct investment in South Africa stood at $5.1 million, compared to $124 million from the EU and $11.7 million from the United States.[52] Results from the same survey reveal that 51 percent of the sampled population believes that trade with China should not be obstructed by human rights considerations. Overall, 44 percent of respondents prioritize "promoting economic growth in South Africa"—only 16 percent stress "promoting human rights."[53] Social media commentary tends to reflect this economic bias:

@IRR_SouthAfrica: China is South Africa's single biggest trading partner although trade with the European Union as whole is larger. #IRRTrade
@SanushaNaidu: Latest Emerging Powers newsletter frm @FahamuEP: Zuma in China, Chinese railways in Africa, East African Oil money
@PolityZA: Chinese investment improves—Zuma: At the end of last year, bilateral trade between South Africa and China . . .

The mainstream South African media likewise reports on China through an economic and high-politics prism.[54] When President Zuma visited China in December 2014, the press was quick to point out that the objective of the trip was economic and aimed at furthering South Africa's industrialization policies.[55] His visit coincided with the South Africa-China Business Forum, underscoring the importance that both sides ascribe to economic considerations.

Still, South Africans remain suspicious of such extensive economic interactions. A 2013 online survey of African perceptions of Chinese business practices conducted by the Ethics Institute of South Africa found that out of 1,056 respondents across fifteen African countries, South Africans were among the least enthusiastic about doing business with Chinese firms; Kenyans were the most enthusiastic.[56] This highlights a discrepancy noted by Eisenman (in this volume): while most South Africans readily acknowledge the economic benefits of increased trade and investment, they become more skeptical when interactions with China become more immediate. Concerns over job losses due to Chinese manufacturing imports and direct competition from labor-intensive Chinese industries in Africa lead to more negative perceptions overall. While these concerns are not so openly articulated on social media platforms, kernels of cynicism can be found:

@Sacorrupt: @EricJWest @Appietrader I think they must check Zuma —may be a tag saying: MADE IN CHINA !
@Awotzo: @ZeldalaGrangeSA those unions supporting Zuma are compromised. He claims to create jobs, yet ANC buys elections T-shirts in China . . . fool me!!"
@EsethuHasane: MY President, his Excellency President Zuma has been honoured with a Professorship by a University in China. KEEP MOVING NXAMALALA!!

@Kafflut: Africa not China 's poor cousin Zuma http://www. city-press.co.za/news/africa-ch inas-poor-cousin-zuma/ . . . Tell me, Prof, does China have some noble reason for its involvement in Africa?

What is interesting about much South African China-Africa social media commentary is that the comments implicate South Africa's political leadership more than they do the Chinese, per se; South Africa's relationship with China forms the backdrop to government-citizen interactions. On the one hand, South Africans tend to be more active on social media when they feel that they are not "receiving the full story,"[57] either from mainstream outlets or from their leadership. On the other hand, South Africans generally perceive the China-Africa narrative not as its own story, but as one narrative within a broader story of local unemployment and government corruption.[58] Unlike in Kenya, however, comments on South African social media have so far remained reactive rather than proactive to the point that they would influence government decisions or outcomes.

Popular suspicion of the ruling African National Congress' close alliance with Beijing was apparent when the Dalai Lama—perceived as a separatist by the Chinese leadership—was denied a South African visa ahead of Desmond Tutu's birthday in August 2011,[59] and again in October 2014 ahead of Nobel Peace summit in which the late Nelson Mandela was to be honored:

@poplak: South Africa, hang your head in shame over Dalai Lama, lost ideals and dreams forever deferred

@ferialhaffajee: How can we not give a visa to the Dalai Lama? Mandela's South Africa? Tutu's South Africa? Maybe we aren't that anymore . . . make a noise!

@Mzukisi_Qobo: Revealing interview between Chris Barron and Dalai Lama rep in South Africa #SundayTime DIRCO cast as a Chinese sub-imperial outpost

@ImranGarda: As South Africa readies the red carpet for Justin Bieber— worth noting we denied a visa to the Dalai Lama. We sure are going places.

@safmpmlive: @PatriciaDeLille has accused government of being disingenuous about @DalaiLama Lama's visa application in India for entry to SA #SABCNEWS

Even here, the reactions remained muted and high-level; few engaged with the issue in a substantial way. Most either reported on it or proffered generalized statements of displeasure. When social media commentary regarding China does become meaningful, this is often when it is incited by "thought leaders," either on platforms like Twitter or Facebook or via online media outlets. For example, the *Daily Maverick*, a South African online newspaper, frequently produces articles that analyze the China-Africa relationship. In

November 2014 the *Maverick* published a piece, "Tencent, WeChat and Chinese Censorship: Does Naspers Have a Free Speech Problem?"[60] The piece examined Naspers, a South African independent media outlet and among the largest independent media players in Africa. Naspers holds a majority stake in Chinese social media giant, Tencent, and is regarded as largely complicit in China's strict media regulations. The article spurred a flurry of online commentary over profit, capitalism, and freedom of speech. Other *Daily Maverick* headlines have prompted similar debates.

Besides such occasional concerned social media exchanges, however, much of the conversation about South Africa's relations with China remains confined to the mainstream press, think tanks, and policy circles.[61] For most South Africans, social media is a platform for content sharing and general commentary, rather than an avenue for political enterprise. A 2013 study conducted by Portland Communications on "How Africa Tweets" found that while South Africans are active on Twitter—indeed, Johannesburg is the most active African city on Twitter[62]—football and popular culture–related commentary has tended to dominate the platform. This, even over issues like the death of Nelson Mandela. In general, political hashtags are limited compared to others. Where politically relevant hashtags have in recent years been prominent was when the National Union of Metalworkers of South Africa (#NUMSA)—the "core of the urban African working class"[63]—in December 2013 announced that it would not support Zuma and his ruling ANC in the 2014 general election:

@TheMercurySA: TOP STORY: Zuma must go, says Numsa's new boss. http:// iol.io/b61cs #Numsa is the top trending topic on @Twitter in SA

Overall, however, when it comes to political commentary, most South Africans opt to engage in avenues where gains have historically been successful. The country's strong tradition of labor unions is in this respect important; South Africa's strong labor unions remain prominent platforms leveraged by nearly one-quarter of the formal workforce. Labor unions remain powerful players in the negotiation of industrial relations and wage disputes, education, and awareness of issues like HIV/AIDS, human rights, and environmental issues, among others. The influence of platforms like Facebook, Twitter, or other homegrown networking sites is exceptionally limited in comparison. Unlike in Kenya, too, where prominent political figures have become active social media users, a similar uptake has not yet transpired in South Africa.[64] The extent to which citizens are able to reach their leaders through communications platforms is still limited.

This paradigm is, however, gradually starting to change. In the May 2014 elections the ANC provided free Wi-Fi access at the FNB Stadium during its #Siyanqoba rally, the party's final mass campaign before the polls.[65] The main opposition party, the Democratic Alliance, as well as the newly formed Economic Freedom Fighters—a revolutionary Socialist Party started in 2013 by expelled former African National Congress Youth League president Julius Malema—relied on social media outlets, conducting live chats with the public via Facebook and Twitter. South Africa's Independent Electoral Commission (@IECSouthAfrica) also engaged voters on Twitter, urging them to provide updates about procedural bottlenecks and anecdotal stories from the polls. Such developments reveal the growing political use of social media in South Africa. Still, its potential is not yet fully realized; whether this will transpire is unclear.

Why social media commentary does or does not exist is difficult to account for. Equally, "measurements" of social media commentary are methodologically complex.[66] However, what social media commentary in South Africa, as in Kenya, does show is the direction of public trends, and the sentiments and reactions of average Africans regarding a relationship that is often perceived as high level, elite, and abstract. A scoping of social media commentary also points to the emergence of new channels of grassroots African agency—or, as in South Africa, continued reliance on tried and tested methods. The gradual emergence of social media outlets like Twitter and Facebook and their sometimes political usage also underscores the complexity and messiness of China-Africa relations; Chinese engagement is met by an increasingly engaged and virtually connected African public.

NEGOTIATING RELATIONS IN PHYSICAL SPACES

As Iginio Gagliardone (in this volume) points out, what is interesting about China-Africa engagement in the media sector is that China ultimately builds the platforms on which African content, including social media content, is conveyed. Ironically and imperfectly, China's finance of African communications technology is expanding the multiplicity of platforms for, and opportunities for expression by, African civil society.

Already in 2010 Chinese telecommunication companies Huawei and ZTE Corporation were active in fifty out of Africa's fifty-four countries, providing communications services for over three hundred million users.[67] In comparison, the South African communications giant, MTN—the largest African-owned telecommunications provider—is present in twenty-one African states with a market capitalization of roughly $31 billion.[68] As of 2011, Huawei's IDEOS mobile phone is a leading product on the Kenyan market. An IDEOS device can be purchased for around $80 as part of a bundled offer through Safaricom. As of 2011, an estimated 350,000 Kenyans own IDEOS cell phones.[69] As of May 2014, Huawei is Safaricom's leading partner active, among other things, in the upgrade and migration of M-Pesa servers from Germany to Kenya.

The African market is predominantly a "mobile-first" market: over 96 percent of Africans use a variety of top-up scratch-cards, airtime credit services, and mobile money to stay connected.[70] China's media engagement in the continent has therefore started to shift beyond content and telecommunications to include instant messaging and social networking. WeChat, the Chinese-based instant messaging application, launched the English version of the application in 2012 and by 2013 had already entered the South African market. This has brought it in direct competition with other instant messaging applications like the American WhatsApp, which has tended to dominate African markets.[71] WeChat is owned by China's Tencent Holdings in which South Africa's Naspers holds a one-third share. While WhatsApp is a pure instant messaging mobile application, WeChat entails additional social features like real-time location sharing or "friends radar"; unique animated stickers; voice and video calls; and an interface with official company accounts. WeChat is thus a de facto mobile social network with advanced instant messaging features. As of 2014, WeChat still falls behind WhatsApp (the most popular app) in South Africa, ranking sixth and eighth for iPhone and Android phones, respectively.[72] As a newcomer to the African market, however, its market penetration is still modest.[73]

Since 2013, WeChat has been engaged in a rigorous advertising campaign in South Africa.[74] One advertisement, for example, depicts a lookalike of Facebook founder Mark Zuckerberg as a patient visiting his therapist due to a case of "friendphobia" caused by him being "unfriended" by his Facebook followers.[75] Local radio stations also promote WeChat by running advertisements and competitions that require listeners to download the application. The website of the well-known broadcast personality, Gareth Cliff, previously of South Africa's 5FM, for example, offers free streaming of his new morning show, *Cliff Central*, on WeChat. If listeners also have a mobile subscription with MTN, all data consumed when interacting with the show— voice and video clips, daily polls, vouchers, and group chats—is free of charge. On the other hand, South African mobile provider Cell-C has been seeking to grow its subscriber base by offering WhatsApp for "free"—that is, with no data charges. The commercial success of Chinese mobile and social networking platforms in Africa is largely contingent on the extent to which they are promoted by local individuals and corporations—and by the consumers who purchase and use them.

China's involvement in the African mobile technology space has been met with some criticism—locally, as well as globally. Western companies, for example, find it difficult to compete with the Chinese telecommunications firms that provide such services owing to the latter's low-interest vendor-guaranteed loan agreements underwritten by Chinese intergovernmental financiers. A January 2014 exposé by the *Wall Street Journal* found that firms like ZTE and Huawei often overcharge, violate procurement regulations, and engage in corrupt practices when securing tenders.[76] Locally, Africans are more concerned with the use of such technologies for mass surveillance, and what the Chinese connection might mean for freedom of speech. African disquiet echoes that of many in Western policy circles. Former US Department of Homeland Security secretary Michael Chertoff noted, "There's a great deal of concern about Huawei acting to advance the interests of the Chinese government in a strategic sense, which includes not only traditional espionage but as a vehicle for economic espionage. If you build the network on which all the data flows, you're in a perfect position to populate it with backdoors and vulnerabilities that only you know about."[77] While the build-up of Chinese communications technology and social networking platforms on the one hand gives voice to segments of African civil society, it on the other hand gives Beijing more political oversight and African leaders more civil society control.

CONCLUSION

At face value, online platforms appear insignificant when thinking about China's engagement with Africa. In reality, however, they are emerging as important tools for African expression and, in some cases, civil society activism.

The ways and purposes in which they are used vary. In Kenya, social media commentary on platforms like Facebook and Twitter often runs parallel to mainstream media discussions; users are engaged with their political leadership and see social media as a way of raising issues or attempting to influence decisions. In South Africa, social media commentary remains more neutral; platforms are used to share information rather than incite political dialogue or activity. Comments on South Africa's relations with China, too, ultimately end up being comments about relations between the South African people and their government in which the China-Africa narrative is one piece in a much bigger puzzle. The availability of other channels of influence also makes it unlikely that South African social media will over time come to play a role similar to that which it does in Kenya, although it is still too soon to tell.

Ultimately, social media becomes what its users will it to be; dialogues about "China-in-Africa" on platforms like Twitter and Facebook are in the end conversations about the users themselves. With the rise of a young African population, the continent's demographics are changing; social media may also change. A 2012 study conducted by the South African Network Society Project at the University of the Witwatersrand, for example, found that a new group of Internet and mobile communication users has emerged in South Africa: they are black, low-income youths—almost half are women.[78] So far, this demographic leverages mobile communications to retrieve information and socialize online. Yet gradually, too, it has begun to use communications technology and social media platforms to assert itself. The more that this demographic realizes the political and commercial potential of such platforms, the more that policymakers will be compelled to engage in these spaces. Issues like that of China-Africa ties will increasingly engage the key—and so far largely overlooked—stakeholders: average Africans. Citizen demands on their governments will increase. In this way, too, heightened citizen participation will determine the contours of the continent's relations with China. Yet we are still some time away from such a reality. Still today Africa's socioeconomic challenges prevent certain segments of the continent's population from coming online. Social media is not yet a fully democratic or representative platform. Yet it is one of the leading spaces where various playing fields can be leveled, with wider implications for government policies and government-citizen relations.

It is important to recall, too, that social media platforms are not the only online platforms. Many mainstream media outlets have also moved their operations and content online. For example, what is now the online newspaper the *Daily Maverick* was until 2005 a print magazine titled *Maverick*.[79] Kenya's *The Nation Group* offers a digital version of its daily newspaper, which is a replica of its print version. The African media and communication landscape is in the midst of an evolution rather than a revolution. Social media platforms are part of this expansion, not necessarily a counter to it.

With the availability of the many online platforms, ideas, information, and opinions are today readily shared between Africans within and across states. This is made possible by the construction of communications infrastructure and the expansion of digital platforms. In this, China plays a critical role: Chinese firms are engaged in the construction and provision of the very platforms upon which African civil society engages, and via which it holds Beijing—as well as its governments—accountable. Chinese telecommunications companies partner with African multinationals; Chinese-owned social networking tools like WeChat, too, are gaining in prominence and competing with foreign, often Western, look-alikes. Here, concerns about transparency and personal freedoms emerge. Yet the multiplicity of platforms across Africa means that Africans still have a choice; the success of Chinese platforms ultimately depends on African perceptions of them. As Howard French notes, "grassroots activism and vibrant independent media"[80] are important checks on ties between African governments and Beijing; included in this, too, is communication technology. The greater the number of devices and affordable connection fees available, the more sophisticated will be African interactions and responses.

Engagements between "China" and "Africa" are slowly moving from boardrooms and into the hands of average Africans and their smartphones. As the relations increase, so, too, will the need to creatively address the gaps in the relationship.

NOTES

1. Daniel Large, "Beyond 'Dragon in the Bush': The Study of China-Africa Relations," *African Affairs* 107, no. 426 (2008): 52–54; Barry Sautman and Yan Hairong, "Friends and Interests: China's Distinctive Links with Africa," *African Studies Review* 50, no. 3 (2007): 77–85.

2. Germany's Federal Commissioner for Culture and the Media, Bernd Neumann, explicitly noted in his ceremonial address at the 2013 Global Media Forum the increase in international English-speaking channels to include China, Russia, and Iran.

3. Fackson Banda, *Citizen Journalism and Democracy in Africa: An Exploratory Study* (Grahamstown: Highway Africa, 2010), 43.

4. Tim Kelly, "The Hubs across Africa: Which Will Be the Legacy-Makers?" *World Bank Information and Communications for Development* Blog, April 30, 2014, http://blogs.worldbank.org/ic4d/tech-hubs-across-africa-which-will-be-legacy-makers?cid=EXT_WBBlogSocialShare_D_EXT&utm_content=buffer7bbfd&utm_medium=social&utm_source=twitter.com&utm_campaign=buffer.

5. Toby Shapshak, "Africa Not Just a Mobile-First Continent—It's Mobile Only," October 4, 2012, http://www.cnn.com/2012/10/04/tech/mobile/africa-mobile-opinion.

6. McKinsey & Company, "Lions Go Digital: The Internet's Transformative Potential in Africa," McKinsey & Company, November 2013, http://www.mckinsey.com/insights/high_tech_telecoms_Internet/lions_go_digital_the_Internets_transformative_potential_in_africa.

7. Miniwatts Marketing Group, June 2014, http://www.Internetworldstats.com/stats1.htm.

8. Mark Casey, Director for Technology, Media and Telecoms at Deloitte South Africa; Jonathan Kalan, "African Youth Hungry for Connectivity," *Africa Renewal Magazine* Online, May 2013, http://www.un.org/africarenewal/magazine/may-2013/african-youth-hungry-connectivity.

9. GSMA, *New GSMA Report Forecasts Half a Billion Mobile Subscribers in Sub-Saharan Africa by 2020*, November 6, 2014, http://www.gsma.com/newsroom/press-release/gsma-report-forecasts-half-a-billion-mobile-subscribers-ssa-2020/.

10. United Nations Department for Economic and Social Affairs (Population Division), *World Urbanization Trends Prospects, The 2014 Revision, Highlights*, http://esa.un.org/unpd/wup/Highlights/WUP2014-Highlights.pdf.

11. Communications Authority of Kenya, *Q4 Sector Statistics Report*, http://ca.go.ke/images/downloads/STATISTICS/Q4SectorStatisticsReport2014-2013FINAL.pdf.

12. FinAccess 2013 report, October 2013, http://www.fsdkenya.org/finaccess/documents/13-10-31_FinAccess_2013_Report.pdf.

13. FinAccess 2013 report.

14. Steven Norris. "Bozza: A Mobile Startup Aimed at Township Mobihoods," September 21, 2011, http://ventureburn.com/2011/09/bozza-a-mobile-startup-aimed-at-township-mobihoods/.

15. Norris, "Bozza."

16. Shongwe-La Mer, "I Just Killed the Movie Executive," in Norris, "Bozza."

17. Gerrit Beger and Akshay Sinha, "South African Mobile Generation: A Study on South African Young People on Mobiles," *UNICEF*, 2012, 16–17.

18. Gareth van Zyl, "Shrinking SA User Numbers for Mxit," June 27, 2014, http://www.itwebafrica.com/mobile/320-south-africa/233126-shrinking-sa-user-numbers-for-mxit.

19. Josh Constine, "Facebook Hits 100M Users in Africa, Half the Continent's Internet-Connected Population," September 8, 2014, http://techcrunch.com/2014/09/08/facebook-africa/.

20. Regardt van der Berg, SA Social Media by the Numbers, September 16, 2014, http://www.techcentral.co.za/sa-social-media-by-the-numbers/51047/.

21. For more information see: Y. Wu, and C. Grant-Makokera, "Baba Jukwa, Social Media and Zimbabwe's Future," July 31, 2013, http://www.saiia.org.za/opinion-analysis/baba-jukwa-social-media-and-zimbabwes-future.

22. Brand Kenya Board, "The President's Speech on the Westgate Attack," September 2013, http://www.brandkenya.go.ke/news-and-events2/149-president-s-speech-on-the-westgate-attack.

23. Mark Kaigwa, "Kenya at 50: How Social Media Has Increased the Pace of Change," *The Guardian*, December 2013, http://www.theguardian.com/global-development-professionals-network/2013/dec/13/kenya-social-media-mark-kaigwa.

24. Clay Shirky, "The Political Power of Social Media: Technology, the Public Sphere, and Political Change," *Foreign Affairs*, January/February 2011, http://www.foreignaffairs.com/articles/67038/clay-shirky/the-political-power-of-social-media.

25. N. Bohler-Muller, and C. van der Merwe, "The Potential of Social Media to Influence Socio-Political Change on the African Continent," in *Africa Institute of South Africa*, Briefing No. 46, March 2011, 5.

26. Sharon Meraz, "Is There an Elite Hold? Traditional Media to Social Media Agenda Setting Influence in Blog Networks," *Journal of Computer-Mediated Communication*, 14 (2009): 701–2.

27. Banda, *Citizen Journalism and Democracy in Africa*, 40.

28. Becca Blond, "10 Most-Followed Kenyans on Twitter," AFK Insider, May 2014, http://afkinsider.com/54949/10-followed-kenyans-on-twitter/11/.

29. Becca Blond, "10 Most-Followed South Africans on Twitter," AFK Insider, April 29, 2014, http://afkinsider.com/53559/10-most-followed-south-africans-on-twitter.

30. Weiwu Zhang, Thomas J. Johnson, Trent Seltzer, and Shannon L. Bichard, "The Revolution Will Be Networked: The Influence of Social Networking Sites on Political Attitudes and Behavior," *Social Science Computer Review* 28, 1 (2010): 80.

31. Greg Otto, "Twitter CEO Dick Costolo: We Are the 'Global Town Square,'" June 26, 2013, http://www.usnews.com/news/articles/2013/06/26/twitter-ceo-dick-costolo-we-are-the-global-town-square.

32. Scoping survey undertaken by Odipo Dev, especially for the purpose of this chapter.

33. Paul Udoto, *The George Wright Forum* 29, no. 1 (2012), 51–58, http://www.georgewright.org/291udoto.pdf.

34. Communications Commission of Kenya, Quarterly Statistics Report, Q2 (FY 2008/2009), http://ca.go.ke/images/downloads/STATISTICS/Sector percent20Statistics percent20Report percent20Q2 percent202008.pdf;

35. 35 Communication Authority of Kenya, Quarterly Sector Statistics, Q4 (FY 2013–2014), http://ca.go.ke/images/downloads/STATISTICS/Q4SectorStatisticsReport2014-2013FINAL.pdf

36. Pew Internet Research, Spring 2013 Global Attitudes Survey, February 2014, http://www.pewglobal.org/2014/02/13/emerging-nations-embrace-Internet-mobile-technology/.

37. CIA World Factbook, https://www.cia.gov/library/publications/the-world-factbook/geos/ke.html.

38. Vira Varun, Thomas Ewing, and Jackson Miller, "Out of Africa: Mapping the Global Trade in Illicit Elephant Ivory," August 2014, http://www.bornfreeusa.org/a9_out_of_africa.php.

39. Varun, Ewing, and Miller, "Out of Africa."

40. *Xinhua*, "China, Africa Arrest Cross-Border Ivory Smuggler," http://news.xinhuanet.com/english/africa/2014-02/10/c_126104674.htm; Richard L. Cassin, "Kenya, China Team Up Against Illegal Ivory Trade," February 14, 2014, http://www.fcpablog.com/blog/2014/2/14/kenya-china-team-up-against-illegal-ivory-trade.html.

41. Change.org Petition by Kenyans United Against Poaching. Update: Delivered to H. E. President Kenyatta, https://www.change.org/p/president-of-kenya-please-declare-poaching-a-national-disaster/u/3534450.

42. Christina Russo, "Using the Power of the Web to Protect Africa's Wildlife," *Yale Environment* 360, June 2011, http://e360.yale.edu/feature/using_the_power_of_blogs_to_protect_africas_wildlife/2413/.

43. Kenya China and Poaching, August 15, 2013, http://gadocartoons.com/kenya-china-and-poaching/.

44. Dr. Liu Xianfa, "China Is Committed to Wildlife Conservation," *Daily Nation*, August 18, 2014, http://www.nation.co.ke/oped/Opinion/Liu-Xianfa-China-poaching-ivory-Kenya-Li-Keqiang/-/440808/2423152/-/bwvpejz/-/index.html.

45. Xianfa, "China Is Committed to Wildlife Conservation."

46. Standard Digital News—Kenya: Edward Sifuna, "Social Media a Useful Tool for Pushing Leaders to Act," May 19, 2014, http://www.standardmedia.co.ke/?articleID=2000121502&story_title=Kenya-social-media-a-useful-tool-for-pushing-leaders-to-act.

47. John Ngirachu, "Probe 'Sparked' Diplomatic Tension," *Daily Nation*, May 1, 2014, http://www.nation.co.ke/news/Public-Investments-Committee-Standard-Gauge-Railway-China/-/1056/2300888/-/61wjciz/-/index.html.

48. Reuters, "Kenyans Protesting Over Jobs Blocks Highway from Mombasa Port, 3 October 2014.

49. According to Alastair Otter (editor of IOL the online publishing arm of Independent Newspapers Limited in South Africa), there are over five hundred South African journalists actively on Twitter (as of June 2014). See his personal project and list at: http://hacks.mediahack.co.za/.

50. Presentation by Karen Smith and Janis Van der Westhuizen on "The Foreign Policy Views of Ordinary South Africans: A Public Opinion Survey" at the Institute of Global Dialogue, Pretoria, July 29, 2013; Janis Van der Westhuizen and Karen Smith, "South Africa's Role in the World: A Public Opinion Survey," *SAFPI*, Policy Brief 55 (2013): 10.

51. Chris Alden and Yu-Shan Wu, "South Africa and China: The Making of a Partnership," *South African Institute of International Affairs* Occasional Paper 199 (2014): 14; South African Government, "Minister Rob Davies: Media Briefing on State Visit by President Jacob Zuma to the People's Republic of China," November 27, 2014, http://www.gov.za/statement-minister-trade-and-industry-dr-rob-davies-outgoing-state-visit-president-zuma-people   percentE2 percent80 percent99s.

52. UNCTAD, "Table 3. FDI Stock in the Host Economy, by Geographical Origin," http://unctad.org/Sections/dite_fdistat/docs/webdiaeia2014d3_ZAF.pdf.

53. Karen Smith and Janis Van der Westhuizen. "What South Africa's Citizens Think of Foreign Policy," July 19, 2013, http://www.bdlive.co.za/opinion/2013/07/19/what-south-africas-citizens-think-of-foreign-policy.

54. Herman Wasserman, "China in South Africa: Another BRIC in the Wall?" in *Africa Growth Report 2012*, edited by Mark Fuller, Marianne Nebbe, and Wadim Schreiner (Beirut, Boston, Pretoria, Tianjin and Zurich: Innovatio Publishing, 2012), 137–46.

55. South African Government, "Minister Maite Nkoana-Mashabane: Media Briefing on President Zuma's Outgoing Visit to the People's Republic of China," November 27, 2014, http://www.gov.za/minister-maite-nkoana-mashabane-media-briefing-president-zuma percentE2 percent80 percent99s-outgoing-visit-people percentE2 percent80 percent99s-republic.

56. L. Louw-Vaudran, "SA Leads Africa in Anti-Chinese Sentiment," in *Mail & Guardian*, February   21,   2014,   http://mg.co.za/article/2014-02-20-sa-leads-africa-in-anti-chinese-sentiment. For the full study see: Ethics Institute of South Africa, "Africans' Perception of Chinese Business in Africa: A Survey," February 2014, http://davidshinn.blogspot.com/2014/02/africans-perception-of-chinese-business.html.

57. Kelly Opdycke, Priscilla Segura, and Ana M. Vasquez, "The Effects of Political Cynicism, Political Information Efficacy and Media Consumption on Intended Voter Participation," *Colloquy* 9 (2013): 80–81.

58. *The Africa Report*, "Election Watch 2014: South Africa's Born Frees and Battlegrounds," Theafricareport.com, December 16, 2013, http://www.theafricareport.com/News-Analysis/election-watch-2014-south-africas-born-frees-and-battlegrounds.html.

59. David Smith, "Dalai Lama Forced to Pull Out of Desmond Tutu Birthday in Visa Dispute," October 4, 2011, http://www.theguardian.com/world/2011/oct/04/dalai-lama-desmond-tutu-visa; Ross Anthony, "China, South Africa and the Dalai Lama: Costs and Benefits," September 10, 2014, 2014, http://china-africa-reporting.co.za/2014/09/china-south-africa-and-the-dalai-lama-costs-and-benefits/.

60. Simon Allison, "Tencent, WeChat and Chinese Censorship: Does Naspers Have a Free Speech Problem?" November 20, 2014, http://www.dailymaverick.co.za/article/2014-11-20-tencent-wechat-and-chinese-censorship-does-naspers-have-a-free-speech-problem/#. VLJGOCdFLR2.

61. Janis Van der Westhuizen and Karen Smith, "South Africa's Role in the World: A Public Opinion Survey," *SAFPI* Policy Brief 55 (2013): 1.

62. For more of their analysis see: Portland Communications, "How Africa Tweets—2014," http://www.portland-communications.com/publications/how-africa-tweets-2014/.

63. "Numsa's ANC Boycott a Serious Blow—Analyst," News24, December 21, 2014, http://www.news24.com/SouthAfrica/Politics/Numsas-ANC-boycott-a-serious-blow-analyst-20131220.

64. Yu-Shan Wu, "The Role of Public Sentiment and Social Media in the Evolving China-Africa Relationship," *South African Institute of International Affairs* Occasional Paper 134 (2013): 15.

65. Glenda Nevill, "The Vote on South Africa's Social Media Elections," May 15, 2014, http://themediaonline.co.za/2014/05/the-vote-on-south-africas-social-media-elections/.

66. Wu, "The Role of Public Sentiment and Social Media in the Evolving China-Africa Relationship," 7–8.

67. Andrea Marshall, "China's Mighty Telecom Footprint in Africa," February 14, 2011, http://www.newsecuritylearning.com/index.php/archive/75-chinas-mighty-telecom-footprint-in-africa.

68. MSN Money, "MTN Group Ltd.," http://www.msn.com/en-us/money/stockdetails? symbol=US:MTNOY.

69. Jeremy Ford, "$80 Android Phone Sells Like Hotcakes in Kenya, the World Next?" Singularity Hub, August 16, 2011, http://singularityhub.com/2011/08/16/80-android-phone-sells-like-hotcakes-in-kenya-the-world-next/.

70. The Mobile Economy, GSMA/A. T. Kearney, http://www.gsmamobileeconomy.com/ GSMA percent20Mobile percent20Economy percent202013.pdf.

71. Joanne Carew, "WeChat Looks to Africa," July 2, 2013, http://www.itweb.co.za/?id= 65370:WeChat-looks-to-Africa.

72. Paul Mozur and Devon Maylie, "'Mark Zuckerberg' Sees a Therapist in WeChat Ad," April 24, 2014, http://blogs.wsj.com/chinarealtime/2014/04/24/mark-zuckerberg-sees-a-therapist-in-wechat-ad/.

73. Mike Wronski, of Fuseware, noted in September 2013 that WhatsApp had 53 percent of the South African mobile user market while WeChat had 5 percent. Even though WhatsApp does not give country-specific user numbers, they have previously stated that the South African market is in their top ten globally. Simnikiwe Mzekandaba, "WhatsApp Dominates South Africa's Instant Messaging Market," IT Web Africa, November 26, 2013, http://www.itwebafrica.com/mobile/320-south-africa/232050-whatsapp-dominates-south-africas-instant-messaging-market.

74. Quinton Bronkhorst, "Tencent's WeChat in Big Push for Africa," July 2, 2013, http:// businesstech.co.za/news/mobile/41038/tencents-wechat-in-big-push-for-africa/.

75. Suman Varandani, "WeChat Targets Mark Zuckerberg in New Ad Promoting Messaging Service in South Africa," April 25, 2014, http://www.ibtimes.com/wechat-targets-mark-zuckerberg-new-ad-promoting-messaging-service-south-africa-1576215.

76. Matthew Dalton, "Telecom Deal by China's ZTE, Huawei in Ethiopia Faces Criticism," *Wall Street Journal Online*, January 2014,http://online.wsj.com/news/articles/ SB10001424052702303653004579212092223818288.

77. John Reed, "Africa's Big Brother Lives in Beijing," *Foreign Policy*, July 30, 2013, http:/ /foreignpolicy.com/2013/07/30/africas-big-brother-lives-in-beijing/.

78. Indra de Lanerolle, "The New Wave: Who Connects to the Internet, How They Connect and What They Do When They Connect," 2012, 8, March 5, 2013, http://www.networksociety. co.za/Internet-report.php or http://www.scribd.com/doc/114640231/TheNewWave-Small.

79. Anton Harber, "'Best, Worst of Times for Online 'Maverick,'" July 11, 2013, http:// www.bdlive.co.za/opinion/columnists/2013/07/11/best-worst-of-times-for-online-maverick.

80. Howard W. French, "Into Africa: China's Wild Rush," May 16, 2014, http://www. nytimes.com/2014/05/17/opinion/into-africa-chinas-wild-rush.html?_r=0.

Chapter Nine

Afro-Chinese Cooperation

The Evolution of Diplomatic Agency

Calestous Juma

INTRODUCTION

The emerging relationship between Africa and China represents a unique diplomatic opportunity that is today receiving increasing popular and scholarly attention. Much of the attention so far has shown the degree to which past perceptions about Africa shape current interpretations of African trends—often in the face of countervailing evidence. In a move away from such narratives, this volume has brought together a rich collection of material on how Africa is gradually strengthening its agency in the global diplomatic arena. This is reflected in the way in which African state and nonstate actors are leveraging their cooperation with China in ways that appear to defy classical views about Africa's relative diplomatic strength.

Inspired by the preceding chapters and additional sources, this chapter outlines the key lessons arising from Afro-Chinese cooperation; it assumes from the outset the complex nature of the agency relationship and the coexistence between the economic and management aspects of agency.[1] The focus of the chapter is on the role of learning in the evolution of Africa's diplomatic agency. The chapter is divided into four sections: the first section examines how the convergence of interests between Africa and China created the diplomatic space that enabled Africa to identify agency niches through which to expand its influence. The second section analyzes the relationships between infrastructure and governance, with special reference to the role of the media. The third section explores the broader implications of the lessons learned from the engagement for future Afro-Chinese cooperation. The final section outlines future avenues for expanding Africa's diplomatic agency in light of the lessons learned from its engagement with China.

CONVERGENT INTERESTS AND AGENCY

To appreciate the strategic importance of Afro-Chinese cooperation, it is important to acknowledge the importance of timing and the convergence of interests. As noted by Mulugeta Berhe, "China's opening up and re-discovery of Africa coincided with Africa's deteriorating economic performance as a result of conflicts, mismanagement, as well as structural adjustment policies. China brought a viable alternative of social, political and economic development formulas to the uni-polar world of the 1990s. Frustrated by complex donor policies and the high overhead costs of multilateral development projects, African governments continue to appreciate the alternative presented by China in an increasingly multipolar world."[2] Africa's engagement with China has, in short, allowed African governments to diversify their foreign relations and to consider alternative pathways to development— or, indeed, to reinforce preconceived ideologies. It has also given currency to Africa's participation in the international arena: as African partnerships with China deepen, so, too, does global attention to Africa.

China's engagement with Africa has become a highly debated international diplomacy issue.[3] The intensity has been fuelled by the sheer scale and rate of growth of trade and investment cooperation between China and Africa. Much of this growth in cooperation has been done through the structure of the Forum on China-Africa Cooperation (FOCAC), which has created the political and diplomatic mechanisms through which official relations between the two are largely transacted. "China has consistently doubled its financing commitment to Africa during the past three FOCAC meetings— from $5 billion in 2006 to $10 billion in 2009 and $20 billion in 2012. Half of the $20 billion committed in 2012 had been disbursed by the end of 2013, leading to China increasing the credit line by another $10 billion in 2014."[4] It is expected that at the sixth Forum on China-Africa Cooperation, being held in South Africa in 2015, China will again boost its financing commitments and development priorities in Africa.

Equally dramatic has been China's trade cooperation with Africa (Eisenman in this volume). In 1980, Afro-Chinese trade volume stood at $1 billion. In 2000 it rose to $10 billion. By 2010 China surpassed the United States as Africa's largest trading partner with a total volume of $114 billion. In 2012, the total China-Africa trade volume reached $198.49 billion, an annual growth of 19.3 percent. Of this, China's export to Africa accounted for $85.319 billion while Africa's export was $113.171 billion.[5] By 2013, trade between the two stood at over $210 billion. For every $100 worth of goods

Africa exported in 2013, about $20 of them were sold to China. The figure was only $3 in 2000.

By 2013, too, China's foreign direct investment (FDI) in Africa was $25 billion; Africa's FDI in China was $15 billion that same year. African investments in China generally receive little attention and remain obfuscated by the persistent focus on China as the principal actor in China-Africa relations. Yet as the contributions to this volume show, the relations are a two-way dialectic rather than a one-way domination; they are most valuable when understood as interactive. African investment in China is also linked to the increase of Africans living in China; it is estimated that there are up to two hundred thousand Africans living in Guangzhou alone. This figure excludes the rapidly expanding number of African students in China, including a projected allocation of eighteen thousand full scholarships between 2013 and 2018.[6]

The immensity and diversity of China's engagements in Africa is largely the result of the convergence of at least four factors that have made the relations attractive for both sides. The first area of convergence relates to the foreign policy objectives of China and African states. China's engagement with Africa goes back to the early 1960s at the height of Africa's liberation movements.[7] As Yun Sun notes, "Beijing identified Africa's newly independent nations as a key group with which to unite." It "saw natural common ground and bore a sense of empathy with Africa as a result of their shared historical experiences: Africa and China were both victims of 'colonialization by the capitalists and imperialists' and faced the same task of national independence and liberation after World War II."[8] China's original foreign policy toward Africa was guided by its own historical experience, and it encompassed five principles: sovereignty, nonaggression, noninterference in domestic matters, mutual benefit, and peaceful coexistence. These principles over time became part of China's larger strategy of asserting itself as a global economic, political, and diplomatic force; their continued relevance makes Africa an important sphere of strategic engagement for Beijing.[9]

For example, the principle of noninterference is derived from China's experience with the former Soviet Union. China's postwar reconstruction was based on extensive technical assistance and credit from the Soviet Union; the implementation of the First Five Year Plan adopted in 1950 owed its success largely to Soviet support. Yet the existence of a large number of Soviet technical expertise, equipment, and joint state companies in fields such as energy, mining, transportation, and aviation also brought with it considerable ideological influence.[10] The divergence in China's economic policy from the Soviet approach—rooted as it was in a disparity in the interpretation of Marxist doctrine—led to a split between the nations in 1960.[11] Among the key lessons of this rift was that of the difficulties inherent

in close connections between technical assistance and ideological condition-
ality.

During the Cold War—and in light of its rivalry with the Soviet Union—
China sought to maintain foreign policy consistency toward Africa.[12] Seeking to impose conditions on Africa's internal affairs would have been inconsistent with its stance toward the Soviet Union prior to the split. This approach was largely welcomed by African leaders, who had historically been
denied much diplomatic space owing first to colonialism, and second to the
conditions attached to Western foreign assistance following independence.
This early convergence of interests would later play a key role in ascribing
agency to African leaders—or at least in helping them to build up the confidence to engage with China in full knowledge that their domestic affairs
would go untouched with no conditionalities imposed. As Barry Sautman (in
this volume) argues, China has historically more obviously recognized
African agency than have most Western powers.

Natural resources became the second area of convergence. China's increased demand for natural resources occurred at a time when Africa was
seeking new outlets for its resources.[13] Chinese demand for Africa's raw
materials has in many ways helped to bolster Africa as a source of valuable
commodities for the global market,[14] and has facilitated opportunities for
economic growth on the back of its natural endowments.[15] In the years
following independence, Africa's position in the global economy was dramatically affected by fluctuations in commodity markets, substitute sourcing,
and tariff escalations that prevented the continent from adding value to raw
materials. Finding new markets that would help to stabilize prices and guarantee long-term export opportunities was key. In this respect, the African
need for markets converged with China's resource demands. Yet as Taylor
(in this volume) points out, convergence around natural resources also poses
a risk to African states trying to diversify their economies, and often en-
trenches preexisting patterns of corruption. Convergent interests do not always imply mutual benefit.

The third area of convergence relates to trade relations. At the end of the
Cold War, Europe—Africa's major diplomatic partner—shifted its attention
to Eastern Europe. The primary effect of this shift was felt in the area of trade
cooperation: Africa's share in the European Union's foreign trade dropped
from 3.2 percent in 1989 to roughly 1.3 percent in 2009. Much of this drop
occurred among longstanding African partners like the United Kingdom and
France. Preferential trade cooperation between the EU and its former African
colonies was additionally affected by the creation of the World Trade Organization: many agreements were simply annulled. The emergence of China as
a diplomatic player in Africa helped to offset some of the associated economic risks, and gave rise to different expressions of African agency—unlike
with its European partners, Africa has no colonial relations with China.[16]

The fourth area of convergence includes several special cases like Sudan and Zimbabwe that are under Western sanctions; such countries have been able to find opportunities for trade and diplomatic engagement with China. Often controversial, the alliances reflect China's own process of international reengagement following decades of isolation. When in 1989—following the Tiananmen Square incident—Beijing faced significant Western sanctions, six African countries (Botswana, Lesotho, Zimbabwe, Angola, Zambia, and Mozambique) were the first to invite then Chinese Foreign Minister Qian Qichen to visit in August 1989. The first heads of state and foreign ministers to visit China after Tiananmen Square were also African. "In appreciation for this tremendous political favor," Yun Sun notes, "China has reciprocated by making Africa the first destination of Chinese foreign ministers in the new year every year since 1991."[17] In aligning itself with autocratic African regimes, however, China is accused of shielding governments from sanctions over their human rights violations and political misconduct. Whether or not China does so intentionally is unclear; at minimum it may be a reflection of China's domestic treatment of such issues. While shared autocracy is not a key driver behind Africa's relations with China, it is surely a piece of a much wider puzzle.

The elements of cooperation between Africa and China illustrate a general shift among African countries to seek cooperation with non-Western countries, either to offset Western influence or to diversify their foreign partners. Although complex and riddled with questions and concerns, the rise of China as Africa's economic and political partner has given African countries opportunities to expand their diplomatic and trade options with little concern over external interference in their internal affairs. But there is also a wider point to be made about the interests of African states to "look east" that has less to do with noninterference and economic advantage and more with the exercise of sovereignty. As argued by Corkin (in this volume), external recognition has been a key element in the ability of African states to assert their sovereignty. For a variety of internal political reasons, many African governments rely on external recognition as a way to articulate domestic influence. William Brown aptly notes, despite "the increased space created by tectonic shifts in the international arena, and the additional scope for action that this creates, the agency of African leaders, of Africa collectively, and even more of those excluded from the seats of power, is still operating in the tight corners bequeathed by these longer histories of state formation and incorporation into the international system."[18] The engagement of African states with China, as well as with other foreign powers, enables leaders to consolidate the instruments of state power and their application to the development process. Yet as both Corkin and Taylor (in this volume) point out, such consolidation is also often a means by which corrupt leaders amass power for themselves.

The timing of Afro-Chinese cooperation has created opportunities for African countries to articulate their interests and expand the scope of their influence on the international scene. But the same timing also raises important questions about the ability of African actors to fully exercise this agency and, when exercised by African state leaders, who benefits from it. This is a question of great relevance for public policy. It is one that has long been asked of relations between Africa and Western countries, especially in the context of foreign aid. It is an equally legitimate question in the case of Africa's relations with China. [19]

INFRASTRUCTURE, THE MEDIA, AND DEVELOPMENT

Understanding the role of China in Africa's governance requires more detailed knowledge of yet another convergent factor: infrastructure. There is a well-established debate over whether the arrow of causality flows from democracy to development or vice versa; equally, there is a deterministic view that it is the former and democracy is a prerequisite for economic development. This view is widely held and often with little consideration of the diverse ways by which national economies and political systems coevolve. Much of the confusion arises from the failure to appreciate the critical role that investments in fundamentals like infrastructure play in both economic transformation and democratic governance.

Infrastructure development has been a major feature of the evolution of the Chinese economy. [20] Research on regional growth differences in China shows that "transport facilities are a key differentiating factor in explaining the growth gap (between the interior and the periphery), and point to the role of telecommunication in reducing the burden of isolation." [21] The investments were a shift from earlier efforts to socialize production through agrarian revolution. [22] The focus on infrastructure entailed significant investment in the creation of engineering capacity as well as engineering-oriented state-owned enterprises (SOEs). This capacity would later become important in China's relations with Africa. Unlike other foreign actors that require a longer lead time on their infrastructure investments, China has a standing capacity that it deploys on short notice to respond to Africa's needs. Put differently, Africa can articulate its infrastructure needs because China is able to respond.

At face value, China's infrastructure investments evoke the specter of nineteenth-century European investments designed to serve colonial interests: China is building roads and railways that connect the continent's major cities to ports and export hubs. Where they differ, however, is in the fact that China's presence is supplemented by a diversity of other domestic and foreign investors, including "states, multinational corporations and regional development funds. The broader market economic system in which *China* and *Africa* engage today entails that Chinese unfettered access to projects is complicated by the interests of multiple stakeholders. The Chinese presence has been exaggerated at the expense of other actors and thus, in any future conflict, it cannot be assumed that *China* will be able to mobilize this infrastructure in its interests."[23] The tendency to emphasize China in Africa's foreign relations has not only obfuscated African agency, but also that of other foreign powers.

An essential part of economic growth is the broadening of individual liberties. Yet this is often discussed in abstract terms and with little reference to foundational issues like infrastructure development: the ability to harness the creativity that arises from such liberties largely depends on the existence of critical economic infrastructure such as transportation, energy, irrigation, and telecommunications. In this regard, China's media engagement in Africa represents an interesting aspect of its cooperation with the continent. As explained by Gagliardone (in this volume), China's media cooperation has adapted to the priorities advanced by individual African governments, offering greater space for African agency to find expression in ways that are less constrained by conditionalities and template approaches.

Chinese media engagement in Africa is part of its larger infrastructure investments. China has become a leading investor in African telecommunications infrastructure, laying backbone fiber optic cables and providing telecommunications facilities. In a way, it is not possible to separate such investments—investments needed to stimulate economic transformation—from the support needed to expand personal liberties; freedoms like the freedom of expression remain circumscribed without the requisite infrastructure upon which they can be articulated. China's investment in telecommunications infrastructure is therefore proving to be a vital aspect in the creation of democratic space in Africa. Kaigwa and Yu's contribution offers a vivid example of just how much this is the case. Kaigwa and Yu argue that social media has become an important force in discussing diplomatic issues like cooperation between Africa and China. Social media is also becoming an important tool for public education across the continent; for engendering direct activism, of which the Arab Spring represents one of the most lasting examples; and for the articulation of specific demands, some of which end up being misrepresented in mainstream outlets. The example of social media shows how Chinese investments in infrastructure help to give effect to democratic liberties that would otherwise stay dormant.

At the same time, China's support to government actors in the shaping of national information societies may risk skewing the balance of power in the long run, marginalizing other important players in the private sector, the civil society, and the media. The relationship between infrastructure, freedom, and development is anything but linear. Corruption and other forms of mismanagement often hinder African leaders from leveraging infrastructure investments in ways that may genuinely contribute to economic and democratic development. The question of whether Afro-Chinese media cooperation benefits the wider population therefore needs to be addressed at a different level of analysis: the extent to which governments widen access to infrastructure, and the degree to which it supports the population's ability to use that infrastructure for their personal and entrepreneurial ends. Ultimately, it is the role of governments to design strategies that expand the opportunities arising from the investments. In other words, the burden of responsibility lies with African governments and not with China.

AGENCY AND PRAGMATISM

One of the most important features of contemporary relations between Africa and China is the extent to which African countries are turning to China as a role model for their economic programs.[24] This is partly due to China's recent emergence as a major actor on the global industrial and technological scene, and also partly due to the fact that China's recent history includes lessons that resonate with many current African realities. Gadzala (in this volume) suggests there is in some cases a protracted ideological affinity between China and African states in which the evolution of political thought in the former informs similar evolutions in the latter; Ethiopian ideals of revolutionary democracy are founded upon key Maoist precepts. Beyond this are lessons for Africa to leverage its natural resources for industrial development. In fact, some of the features of Africa's relations with China mirror previous cooperation between China and Japan.

The rise of China as an industrial power owes a great deal to Japan as a source of technology. Following the Sino-Soviet split in the early 1960s, Japan emerged as a source of technology for a then developing China. By the 1970s Japan accounted for nearly 70 percent of China's technological imports. The imports also included strategic know-how as well as management practices. In a way, Japan served as an industrial role model for China at a time when the country was isolated from much of the world. Technological cooperation between China and Japan entailed at least four aspects. First, the two countries developed a supplier-buyer relationship at a time when the United States and European powers were, for ideological reasons, reluctant to sell technology to China. Second, trade patterns centered on the transfer of entire manufacturing clusters from Japan to China, with Japan an active participant in the construction of China's large industrial systems. The Baoshan Iron and Steel Complex in Shanghai, the Qilu Petrochemical Complex in Shandong province, and the Daqing Petrochemical Complex in Heilongjiang province are telling examples. Third, although the boundary between state and society remained blurred, much of the transferred technology was intended for civilian use. With this buildup of local technological capacity, China was able to transition from importing plants to acquiring technology through licensing. This cooperation also directed global attention to the existence of a viable technology market in China; this later played a role in improving Sino-American relations in the late 1970s.

Finally, and importantly, Chinese and Japanese scientists and engineers strengthened their cooperation through the creation of organizations like the Association of the Chinese Scientists and Engineers in Japan, formed in 1993, and the Chinese Association of Scientists and Engineers in Japan, formed in 1996. Subsequent cooperation in the 1990s involved research projects on scientific frontiers in fields including photonics, informatics, and environmental technologies.

In recent years, African countries have entered into resource-for-infrastructure swaps with China. According to some, the "swaps offer access to low-cost, large-scale financing for infrastructure development at times when governments are faced with a large infrastructure gap and limited availability of external finance. Infrastructure improvements will lower the cost of doing business and, in turn, will improve international competitiveness."[25] Yet if improperly managed, the swaps can also lead to inflated project prices, diminished quality, and greater government indebtedness.

On their own, infrastructure investments are insufficient to trigger sustained economic growth unless they are accompanied by complementary strategies that leverage their potential. This also requires long-term commitment to development objectives and consistency in their implementation. Nigeria, for example, attempted to leverage its natural resources to secure support for infrastructure projects. Under President Olusegun Obasanjo, Nigeria and China signed oil-for-infrastructure agreements despite China's initial hesitation to enter into such arrangements. When President Obasanjo left office, his successor, Umaru Musa Yar'Ardua, suspended the deal and replaced it with oil-for-cash arrangements. The termination of the arrangement exposed the "incompatibility between this model and the Nigerian electoral cycle, which is designed to alternate rule every ten years between northern Muslim and southern Christian elites."[26] The case of Nigeria points to how political systems and cultures can undermine the ability of a country to exercise diplomatic agency in ways that could be beneficial in the long run. This is particularly the case when strategic infrastructure investments are needed to build the foundations for long-term growth. The issue often is whether a state has the capacity to distribute the means of long-term development such as infrastructure and higher technical education, or whether the focus is on meeting short-term revenue-sharing arrangements or patronage promises. The Nigerian example also reinforces the view, advanced in this volume by Ian Taylor, that political systems and culture are the stages upon which Chinese agents act, and which either enable or constrain their activities.

From the perspective of infrastructure investments, the key lesson that Africa can learn from China is that the onus to make the arrangements work for Africa lies with African governments, not with China. The structure of state institutions also matters. For example, from a Chinese standpoint, "the extension of infrastructure-for-oil loans seems to perform best in institutional contexts where the executive wields a high degree of control over the oil sector (like Angola), and worst in more liberalized contexts."[27] China's elite-based approach is most successful in states that share similar institutional arrangements; corporate strategies, in turn, are more effective when the field of actors is diversified. African states, too, must discover the arrangements and strategies that work to their respective advantages. In some cases these may align with those of their Chinese counterparts, yet in others they might not.

LESSONS LEARNED

Indeed, Africa's cooperation with China has yielded a number of lessons that illustrate the role of learning for future expressions of African agency. Among the most salient are the evolution of state capacity for development management; growing diplomatic influence; and governance performance, especially with regard to corruption.

State Capacity

One of the key lessons from China's contemporary history is the triumph of pragmatism over ideology in economic policy. The central element of this approach is China's emphasis on building a strong technical foundation for economic growth. This is evident in the emphasis placed on training individuals in the fields of science, technology, engineering, and mathematics. But also important and less obvious are efforts to raise the technical literacy of the general population. These efforts focus on defining development as problem-solving processes that require greater human competence. For example, China's mission-driven Spark Programme under the Ministry of Science and Technology was created to popularize the use of modern technology in rural areas; it played a key role in raising agricultural productivity by upgrading the technical skills of China's rural population. The program established a nationwide distance education network and supported rural enterprises in becoming globally competitive.

The shift to pragmatism was associated with the rise of the engineering community to top political positions.[28] This is a basic lesson that has so far eluded African countries. Agency is not just a rhetorical expression but a process that entails the continuous improvement and upgrading of leadership capabilities. In China, such upgrades were the products of an active national policy. In Africa, such improvements tend to occur absent a specific policy focus and are often passive outcomes rather than consequences of a concerted effort to improve state capacity. It is notable, for example, that in 2012 six African countries (Angola, Egypt, Ethiopia, Senegal, Somalia, and Tunisia) elected engineers as heads of state and government. But this was not necessarily a result of conscious efforts to bring technocrats to positions of influence. In fact, this would be difficult to achieve in most African states: long-term development is not normally the basis upon which succession in leadership is based. It is also not clear if and how the duration of presidential term limits may affect a country's ability to sustain investments in long-term programs such infrastructure projects. While regime change in Nigeria reversed progress in infrastructure construction, countries like Burkina Faso or Zimbabwe have had little regime change—and little progress in infrastructure.

There are two other aspects of state capacity that are generally deficient in African countries. The first is the capacity for strategic thinking; this is normally carried out through think tanks. Thus far, South Africa is the only African country with think tanks devoted to analyzing Chinese trends. Yet even here, the few research facilities that do exist have tended to limit their analyses to narrow aspects of Sino-Africa cooperation. A broader understanding of developments in China, as well as of China's foreign policy—in Africa and elsewhere—can help African states to shape their own strategies and positions, which are today largely lacking. Lack of African strategies is reflected in the fact that China essentially sets the agenda for all FOCAC meetings. Some of this thinking could benefit from the input of independent African think tanks. But they would still struggle to get the ear of government officials responsible for shaping cooperation with China. In contrast, China is expanding its global think tank capacity, an increasing portion of which is devoted to African affairs. The African Union could also benefit from advice provided through high-level panels comprised of leading experts on Afro-Chinese relations, although it is unclear how constructive a pan-African China policy would actually be.

The second and interrelated aspect of state capacity in Africa is high-level policy advice to government leaders. Elsewhere, much of this is done through scientific and technological academies. In Africa, such academies are still in the early stages of development; scientific and technological academies are present in sixteen of Africa's fifty-four countries. Still, their effectiveness is limited by the absence of chief scientists in executive offices; China and other countries have pledged to increase their scientific and technological cooperation with Africa, with the aim of leveraging existing and emerging technologies for development. Yet the capacity needed to effectively translate such cooperation to Africa's advantage is so far absent across much of the continent.

Diplomatic Influence

One of the most lasting impacts of Afro-Chinese cooperation has been the confidence it has given African leaders on the global stage. The fact that China regularly meets with African presidents under the auspices of FOCAC has given leaders a place on the global stage that they have so far not been accorded elsewhere. This confidence is not limited to cooperation with China. China's recognition of African agency offers Africa "the bargaining power to renegotiate the terms of its relationships with the West. Most importantly, China–Africa relations will enable Africa to tap into global value chains made possible by globalization. Africa needs to seize the opportunity offered by its partnership with China to reconstruct a new architecture of mutually beneficial relationships."[29]

An interesting example of African trade and diplomatic agency is the growing role of Angola as an investor in Portugal, its former colonizing power. Over time, Angola has used the economic strength arising from oil revenue from China to invest in Portugal.[30] The Eurozone crisis provided Angola with the opportunity to extend its support to Portugal. In 2011, Angolan president Eduardo dos Santos announced that he would be prepared to invest in Portugal after the International Monetary Fund ordered the country to privatize its state-owned enterprises under a €80 billion bailout plan. Anbessa Shoes, described in this book's introductory chapter, similarly points to the growth in African trade agency. Faced with competition from Chinese footwear imports, Anbessa honed its strategic advantage and remade itself into a global market competitor.

The collections in this volume aptly argue that relations between African states and China must, ultimately, proceed bilaterally. The disparate political and economic makeup and needs of African states are such that it is in the interest of each country to negotiate the terms of the relations to its own advantage. Nevertheless, there is something to be said of collective African agency. Though African leaders do not usually have advance preparatory meetings to formulate a common position on their relations with China, they have tried to assert a collective stance in various other international forums. One example of this is the collective position assumed during the 2009 meeting of the United Nations Framework Convention on Climate Change in Copenhagen. While their stance was unlikely to have been inspired by their collective appearances at FOCAC meetings, shared interactions with China are nevertheless an important source of heuristics for participation in global forums.

An obvious entry point for collective African negotiations with China is interstate infrastructure investment. This has two important elements. First, such projects would be large enough to give African countries greater power in negotiations with China. Second, they would go a long way in addressing Africa's own deficiencies in promoting regional integration and trade through larger markets. One of the most critical aspects of the creation of larger markets is the growth in the potential for product development and economic diversification. The regional nature of industrial development has been observed across the world, but its significance is only starting to be empirically demonstrated. For example, it has been shown that "on average, the probability that a product is added to a country's export basket is 65 percent larger if a neighboring country is a successful exporter of that same product. For existing products, growth of exports in a country is 1.5 percent higher per annum if it has a neighbor with comparative advantage in these products."[31]

African countries in June 2015 launched the Tripartite Free Trade Area that encompasses twenty-six members and partners from the Common Market for Eastern and Southern Africa (COMESA), the East African Community (EAC), and the Southern African Development Community (SADC). This trading bloc has a combined population of 625 million people and a GDP of $1.3 trillion. It represents half of the membership of the African Union and 58 percent of the continent's GDP. But signing the agreement is only the start. Realizing its objectives will require considerable investment in infrastructure projects and manufacturing capacity.

Such a large infrastructure market provides a major opportunity for Africa to exercise its diplomatic agency, not only with China but also with other international partners. The potential for diplomatic influence goes beyond the construction of transportation, energy, telecommunications, and other related public works projects. It also involves training people to design, build, and maintain the infrastructure. One possible way to ramp up the needed capacity would be to create "education free zones" along the lines of special economic zones that would attract technical universities from around the world to locate their campuses in Africa. Such a large market, too, demands an upgrade of Africa's manufacturing capabilities. This requires the creation of competence in key fields like product design and manufacturing. The buildup of such competencies demands a long-term focus on African industrial development that would mirror China's recent economic history. This necessitates considerable policy discipline on levels that have not been seen in the past.

An important opportunity for Africa to exercise agency in industrial development—multilaterally and bilaterally—lies in the nature of African FDI in China, which covers technology-intensive fields such as "petrochemical engineering, machinery and electronics, transportation and telecommunications, light industry and household appliances, garments and textiles, biopharmaceuticals, agricultural development, entertainment and catering."[32] Africans investing in China could become important sources of industrial development in their respective countries and across the continent by transferring their know-how. Such investment flows would also help to strengthen Afro-Chinese industrial cooperation, as it would involve investors from both sides.

Governance

One of the key features of Afro-Chinese relations has been its implications for governance in Africa. As argued by Lampert and Mohan (in this volume), China is not a monolithic political entity that is engaging with Africa in a rational and structured way. On the contrary, Chinese engagement is mediated through a variety of channels with commerce as the primary driving force; while the main actors are state-owned enterprises, they are not necessarily controlled by the central government. SOEs operate through public and private contractors that are not always under the control of the central government.[33] In fact, many of the Chinese enterprises operating in Africa are provincial.[34] The composition of provincial actors is equally complex, often involving a mix of state and nonstate actors and driven largely by commercial interests. The diversity of actors and interests provides a number of lessons that could inform future cooperation between Africa and China on governance. These include the strengthening of state capacity, the implications of the relations on government corruption, and the future role of civil society.

The most visible feature of China-Africa partnerships is the relations between state leaders. Here, African leaders are often portrayed as incapable of managing their respective national affairs, and the relations as ones consisting entirely of backdoor deals and clandestine handshakes. While in many respects true, this is not the whole story. The case of Angola, for example, shows how relations with China have gone some way in helping to enhance rather than undermine the country's governance. In the early 2000s, many internationally accepted measures of governance, including Transparency International's Corruption Perception Index, ranked Angola poorly, signaling a marked lack of state capacity. But as its financial base expanded with the advance of Chinese credit lines (described by Corkin, in this volume) so, too, did its ability to improve transparency; this in part included disclosing accounts of its management of China's ExIm Bank loan. Institutions like Transparency International, the Mo Ibrahim Foundation, and the IMF later acknowledged the improvements in Angola's public management. An expanding revenue base, provided in part by oil exports to China, signaled to Angola's elites that improved transparency would likely lead to additional foreign finance. But the key was not only Angola's increased funding base but that its leadership, too, had the political will to strengthen state capacity.

The case of Angola, however, does not diminish concerns over corruption. This is not to say that China's engagement with Africa on its own drives African corruption; the nature of Africa's political systems and the relative weak development of governance capacities are the major drivers of corruption. Yet that the state in Africa is in many cases a tool for wealth capture raises fundamental questions about China's emphasis on forging partnerships with African governments. Indeed, China's own experiences with high-level corruption illustrate the risks of corruption in African states with even less capacity for oversight.

Addressing the issue of corruption entails identifying ways by which African governments can be held accountable to their own populations. This is partly a function of the openness of the state to public accountability and the capacity of nonstate actors to hold them to account. But the level of advocacy needed to hold China and African governments accountable will need to be based on a deeper understanding of the issues. New alliances between research institutions and civil society organizations will need to be forged. China's own efforts to provide language lessons to young Africans though the Confucius Institutes being built across Africa may provide a basis for such understanding. But more will need to be done on the African side to deepen its knowledge of China. The purpose of any such efforts should be mutual understanding and awareness of both shared and divergent national interests as an essential element of a balanced and equitable relationship. Much of this should take into account the growing use of online platforms in shaping perceptions of Africa in China and vice versa. But even on such platforms, more will need to be done to deepen the knowledge base on either side.[35]

It is commendable that some African diplomatic missions in China are actively seeking new opportunities for deepening bilateral cooperation. For example, South African diplomats in Beijing "are regularly lauded by Chinese officials as being the most active of delegates among the African ambassadors based in Beijing. Over the years, this activism has translated into the incorporation of measures calling for beneficiation as a feature of Chinese investments in the resource sector, improved terms of trade, and greater adherence by Chinese companies to environmental and labor standards."[36] However, some of the ideas championed by African leaders must also take into account the extent to which they are likely to be influenced by emerging global trends. For example, Africa is unlikely to become a major destination of industrial outsourcing, despite the fact that China has started to locate its industrial operations in various African countries. It is therefore important for African leaders to pay more attention to industrial development both for

regional and international markets rather than to stress the large-scale relocation of Chinese industrial clusters to Africa.

Much of the thinking on industrialization, however, is strongly influenced
by the view that adding value to natural resources should be the starting
point. Yet there is little evidence to support this notion; a causal look at
recent economic trends indeed tells a different story. Taiwan was once a
leading exporter of mushrooms and shrimps. But it did not become a world
leader in semiconductor exports by adding value to mushrooms and shrimps.
After its separation from North Korea, South Korea's first exports were false
teeth and wigs. In a few decades, South Korea became an industrial power-
house, but not by adding value to rice. Kenya is a leading exporter of tea, but
its money transfer industry was not a result of adding value to these commodities. Neither did Finland become a world leader in mobile technology
by adding value to wood, its top raw material. Nevertheless, African countries continue to adhere to this line of reasoning, partly because of their tacit
acceptance of their roles as sources of raw materials for the global economy.

What the above examples illustrate, however, is that industrial development and economic diversification are consequences of strategic acquisition
and the buildup of technological capabilities that can easily be leveraged for
product diversification. To add value to raw materials presupposes the existence of these generic or platform technologies. But to build them requires a
different industrial logic that is decoupled from working within the limits of
low-knowledge natural resources. Platform or generic fields covering electronics, chemicals, mechanics, transportation, and biology provide a broad
basis for the creation of new product combinations that can benefit from
natural resources as inputs but are not limited to raw materials as a starting
point. By clinging to natural resources, Africa is not only failing to understand the dynamics of industrial development but is in fact hobbling its own
potential.

Of course, adding value to natural resources deserves attention within its
limits. But pursing it as a means for rapid industrialization and economic
diversification is as ineffectual as it is misguided. Focusing on building generic technological capabilities is not an argument against making new products from raw materials. It is a case against inverted logic. Industrial policy
should be the priority and the adding of value to natural resources one among
many industry-sector activities, but surely not the focus. A robust industrial
policy requires countries to focus on searching for available and emerging
technologies that have broad product development and combination potential. The search for such technologies has the potential to inform an important
function of Africa's diplomatic missions in China and globally.

CONCLUSION

This book has documented how Africa is using the rise of China to exert unexpected influence not only on China itself, but also on the international arena in general. It is a tentative story that explores how emerging nations can leverage new opportunities in the international arena, especially where there are convergent interests. It is a checkered story that shows a certain degree of diplomatic entrepreneurship but also one that raises fundamental questions about the extent to which the benefits from the relations spread to the general population or are captured by elites in leadership. It is also a promising story that suggests the potential for average Africans to dictate their realities.

How this story will unfold remains to be answered. What is important, however, is that the story would not exist, and the questions would not be asked, in the absence of present-day interactions between Africa and China. It is evident, however, that the "extent to which *Africa* is able to take advantage of opportunities opened up by *China* to move to a new, more inclusive growth path will largely be determined by political developments in *Africa*."[37] Inasmuch as China's economic and political African footprint stands to shape African realities, the burden of proof ultimately rests with African governments and African peoples; African agency is key.

Afro-Chinese cooperation is also opening up opportunities for new forms of international development partnerships that build on convergence of interests. There were early concerns that Africa's engagement with China would come at the expense of its traditional partners such as the United States. However, this has so far been limited. A study of Angola, Ghana, and Kenya by the United States Government Accountability Office has acknowledged that "the United States and China have emphasized different policies and approaches for their engagement with sub-Saharan Africa. US goals have included strengthening democratic institutions, supporting human rights, using development assistance to improve health and education, and helping sub-Saharan African countries build global trade. The Chinese government, in contrast, has stated the goal of establishing closer ties with African countries by seeking mutual benefit for China and African nations and by following a policy of noninterference in countries' domestic affairs."[38] The key point here is not that of competition for influence in Africa, but rather that Afro-Chinese cooperation has yielded a number of lessons that can be used to construct new forms of international development cooperation based on common interests. In this respect, Africa may yet come to play a role as a global locus for peaceful engagement. This is particularly important when one considers the rise of new economic actors in Africa such as Brazil, Turkey, and Malaysia. Africa's role as a theater for peaceful international cooperation would further strengthen its diplomatic agency.

It is hoped that this book will provide a basis for deeper analysis of the issues raised in its chapters. But even more importantly, this book serves as a collection of signposts on new intellectual terrains worthy of exploration. For example, much has been said about the extent to which China's policy of noninterference has shaped the conduct of internal policy among African states. Yet there is emerging evidence that Africa is in fact forcing China to participate in diplomatic negotiations and peacekeeping in places like South Sudan—activities that would have otherwise been considered interference. Similarly, while much is said of poor labor conditions in Chinese-operated factories and mines, pressure from African civil society groups is slowly leading China to reform its ways. In this respect, Africa is changing China in ways that are different from the ways in which China is changing Africa.[39]

Whether Africa can negotiate better terms with China will largely depend on the ability of Africans to define their needs. It will take a different kind of state with considerable entrepreneurial capabilities that focus on creating new economic structures,[40] and that are responsive to the demands of its citizens. We are still some time away from such an African state, although, still, we are closer today than yesterday. Through their engagements with China, African governments and populations are pushing back against narratives of a passive continent. They are, slowly, too, taking charge of their circumstances and finding in their relations with China lessons for their own advancement. But what will be the outcomes of these assertions of African agency remains to be seen. Whether they will open the door to further empowerment, and ultimately to economic development, will depend, as we have seen in many different instances, on the ways and ends for which they are expressed. The story of Africa's relations with China is ultimately an African story. It is up to Africa to write the plot.

NOTES

1. Peter Wright, Ananda Mukherji, and Mark Kroll, "A Reexamination of Agency Theory Assumptions: Extensions and Extrapolations," *Journal of Socio-Economics* 30 (2001): 413–29.

2. Mulugeta G. Berhe, "Introduction," in *China-Africa Relations Governance, Peace and Security*, edited by Mulugeta G. Berhe and Liu Hongwu, 1 (Addis Ababa: Institute for Peace and Security Studies, University of Addis Ababa, 2013).

3. Deborah Bräutigam, *The Dragon's Gift: The Real Story of China in Africa* (New York: Oxford University Press, 2009); Howard French, *China's Second Continent: How a Million Migrants Are Building a New Empire in Africa* (New York: Alfred A. Knopf, 2014).

4. Yun Sun, *The Sixth Forum on China-Africa Cooperation: New Agenda and New Approach?* (Washington, DC: Brookings Institution, 2014).

5. People's Republic of China, *China-Africa Economic and Trade Cooperation (2013)* (Beijing: Information Office of the State Council, People's Republic of China, 2013).

6. Changsong Niu, "China's Educational Cooperation with Africa: Toward New Strategic Partnerships," *Asian Education and Development Studies* 3 (2014): 31–45.

7. Daniel Large, "Beyond 'Dragon in the Bush': The Study of China-Africa Relations," *African Affairs* 107 (2008): 45–61.

8. Yun Sun, *Africa in China's Foreign Policy* (Washington, DC: Brookings Institution, April 2014).

9. Jianwei Wang and Jing Zou, "China Goes to Africa: A Strategic Move?" *Journal of Contemporary China* 23, no. 90 (2014): 1113–32.

10. Central Intelligence Agency, *Soviet Economic Assistance to the Sino-Soviet Bloc Countries* (United States Central Intelligence Agency, 1955), 59.

11. Zhihua Shen and Yafeng Xia, "The Great Leap Forward, the People's Commune and the Sino-Soviet Split," *Journal of Contemporary China* 20, no. 72 (2011): 861–80.

12. Robert Scalapino, "Sino-Soviet Competition in Africa," *Foreign Affairs* 42, no. 4 (1964): 640–54.

13. Ruben Gonzalez-Vicente, "China's Engagement in South America and Africa's Extractive Sectors: New Perspectives for Resource Curse Theories," *Pacific Review* 24 (2011): 65–87.

14. Raphael Kaplinsky and Masuma Farooki, *How China Disrupted Global Commodities: The Reshaping of the World's Resource Sector* (London: Routledge, 2011).

15. Raphael Kaplinsky and Mike Morris, "Chinese FDI in Sub-Saharan Africa: Engaging with Large Dragons," *European Journal of Development Research* 21 (2009): 551–69.

16. Maurizio Carbone, "The European Union and China's Rise in Africa: Competing Visions, External Coherence and Trilateral Cooperation," *Journal of Contemporary African Studies* 29 (2014): 203–21.

17. Yun Sun, *Africa in China's Foreign Policy*, 4–5.

18. William Brown, "A Question of Agency: Africa in International Politics," *Third World Quarterly* 33 (2012): 1904.

19. Zhang Chun, *China–Zimbabwe Relations: A Model of China–Africa Relations?* (Johannesburg: South African Institute of International Affairs, 2014); Abiodun Alao, *China and Zimbabwe: The Context and Contents of a Complex Relationship* (Johannesburg: South African Institute of International Affairs, 2014).

20. Chong-En Bai and Yingyi Qian, "Infrastructure Development in China: The Cases of Electricity, Highways, and Railways," *Journal of Comparative Economics* 38 (2001): 34–51.

21. Sylvie Démurger, "Infrastructure Development and Economic Growth: An Explanation for Regional Disparities in China?" *Journal of Comparative Economics* 29 (2001): 95.

22. Calestous Juma, *The New Harvest: Agricultural Innovation in Africa* (New York: Oxford University Press, 2011).

23. Ross Anthony, "Infrastructure and Influence: China's Presence on the Coast of East Africa," *Journal of the Indian Ocean Region* 9, no. 2 (2013): 134.

24. John Anyanwu, "Factors Affecting Economic Growth in Africa: Are There Any Lessons from China?" *African Development Review* 26, no. 3 (2014): 468–93.

25. Peter Konijn, *Chinese Resources-for-Infrastructure (R4I) Swaps: An Escape from the Resource Curse?* (Johannesburg: South African Institute of International Affairs, 2014), 24.

26. Gregory Mthembu-Salter, *Elephants, Ants and Superpowers: Nigeria's Relations with China* (Johannesburg: South African Institute of International Affairs, 2009).

27. Ana Cristina Alves, "Chinese Economic Statecraft: A Comparative Study of China's Oil-Backed Loans in Angola and Brazil," *Journal of Current Chinese Affairs* 42 (2013): 124.

28. Cheng Li, *China's Leaders: The Next Generation* (Lanham, MD: Rowman & Littlefield, 2001).

29. Felix Edoho, "Globalization and Marginalization of Africa: Contextualization of China–Africa Relations," *Africa Today* 58 (2011): 121.

30. Pedro Seabra and Paulo Gorjão, *Intertwined Paths: Portugal and Rising Angola* (Johannesburg: South African Institute of International Affairs, 2011).

31. Dany Bahar, Ricardo Hausmann, and Cesar Hidalgo, "Neighbors and the Evolution of the Comparative Advantage of Nations: Evidence of International Knowledge Diffusion?" *Journal of International Economics* 92 (2014): 111.

32. People's Republic of China, *China-Africa Economic and Trade Cooperation* (Beijing: Information Office of the State Council, People's Republic of China, 2010).

33. Xu Yi-Chong, "Chinese State-Owned Enterprises in Africa: Ambassadors or Freebooters?" *Journal of Contemporary China* 23 (2014): 822–40.

34.   Chen Zhimin and Jian Junbo, *Chinese Provinces as Foreign Policy Actors in Africa* (Johannesburg: South African Institute of International Affairs, 2009).

35.   Simon Shen, "A Constructed (Un)reality on China's Re-Entry into Africa: The Chinese Online Community Perception of Africa (2006–2008)," *Journal of Modern African Studies* 47 (2009): 425–48.

36.   Chris Alden and Yu-Shan Wu, *South Africa and China: The Making of a Partnership* (Johannesburg: South African Institute of International Affairs, 2014), 13.

37.   Raphael Kaplinky, "What Contribution Can China Make to Inclusive Growth in Sub-Saharan Africa?" *Development & Change* 44, no. 6 (2013): 1295.

38.   GAO, *Sub-Saharan Africa: Trends in US and Chinese Economic Engagement* (Washington, DC: United States Government Accountability Office, 2013), i.

39.   Harry Verhoeven, "Is Beijing's Non-Interference Policy History? How Africa Is Changing China," *Washington Quarterly* 37 (2014): 55–70.

40.   Mariana Mazzucato, *The Entrepreneurial State: Debunking Public vs. Private Sector Myths* (London: Anthem Press, 2013).

Bibliography

Abbink, Jon. "Breaking and Making the State: The Dynamics of Ethnic Democracy in Ethiopia." *Journal of Contemporary African Studies* 13, no. 2 (1995): 149–63.

Abbink, Jon. "Ethnicity and Constitutionalism in Contemporary Ethiopia." *Journal of African Law* 41, no. 2 (1997): 159–74.

Adam, Lishan. Ethiopia ICT Sector Performance Review 2009/2010: Towards Evidence-Based ICT Policy and Regulation. Edited by Research ICT Africa (2010).

Adesoji, Abimbola. "The Boko Haram Uprising and Islamic Revivalism in Nigeria." *Africa Spectrum* 45, no. 2 (2010).

Africa Confidential. "Blood and Money in the Streets: China''s Business Ties to the Loathed Câmara Junta Could Quickly Backfire." October 20, 2009. http://www.africa-confidential. com/article-preview/id/10301/Blood_and_money_in_the_streets.

Agence France Presse. "Angola Wins New Billion Dollar Loan from China." March 12, 2009.

Alao, Abiodun. *China and Zimbabwe: The Context and Contents of a Complex Relationship* (Johannesburg: South African Institute of International Affairs, 2014).

Alden, Chris. *China in Africa*. London: Zed Books, 2007.

Alden, Chris, and Ana Alves. "China and Africa's Natural Resources: The Challenges and Implications for Development and Governance." *South African Institute of International Affairs (SAIIA)*, Occasional Paper no. 41 (September 2009), 1–26.

Alden, Chris, and Yu-Shan Wu. "South Africa and China: The Making of a Partnership." *South African Institute of International Affairs (SAIIA)*, Occasional Paper no. 199 (August 2014).

Allison, Graham, and Philip Zelikow. *Essence of Decision: Explaining the Cuban Missile Crisis*, 2nd ed. New York: Longman, 1999 [1971].

Allison, Simon. "Tencent, WeChat and Chinese Censorship: Does Naspers Have a Free Speech Problem?" November 20, 2014.http://www.dailymaverick.co.za/article/2014-11-20-tencent-wechat-and-chinese-censorship-does-naspers-have-a-free-speech-problem/#. VLJGOCdFLR2.

Althusser, Louis. *Lenin and Philosophy and Other Essays*. New York: Monthly Review Press, 1971.

Alves, Ana Cristina. "Chinese Economic Statecraft: A Comparative Study of China's Oil-Backed Loans in Angola and Brazil." *Journal of Current Chinese Affairs* 42 (2013): 124.

Alves, Ana Cristina. "The Oil Factor in Sino-Angolan Relations at the Start of the 21st Century." *South African Institute for International Affairs*, Occasional Paper no. 55 (February 2010).

Andreas, Eshete. "The Protagonists in Constitution-Making in Ethiopia." Symposium of the African Institute, "The Experience of Constitution-Making in Africa: Ethiopia, Uganda and South Africa," Pretoria, May 26–28, 1997.

Angola Government. "Regulamento do Processo de Preparação, Aprovação, Execução, Acompanhamento e Avaliação do Programa de Investimento Público." *Diário da Republica*, April 12, 2010.

Angola Press. "Angola e China Rubricam Acordos de Cooperação." November 19, 2010. http://www.portalangop.co.ao/angola/pt_pt/noticias/politica/2010/10/46/Angola-China-rubricam-acordos-cooperacao,00047b9c-b809-48a8-ae71-fd280c46b116.html.

Angola Press. "Country and Spain Sign Investment Protection Accord." November 21, 2007. http://allafrica.com/stories/200711220031.html.

Anthony, Ross. "Infrastructure and Influence: China's Presence on the Coast of East Africa." *Journal of the Indian Ocean Region* 9, no. 2 (2013): 134–49.

Anyanwu, John. "Factors Affecting Economic Growth in Africa: Are There Any Lessons from China?" *African Development Review* 26, no. 3 (2014): 468–93.

Avuru, Austin. *Politics, Economics and the Nigerian Petroleum Industry*. Lagos: Festac Books, 2005.

Axelrod, Robert. *The Complexity of Cooperation: Agent-Based Models of Competition and Collaboration*. Princeton: Princeton University Press, 1997.

Axelsson, L. *Making Borders: Engaging the Threat of Chinese Textiles in Ghana*. Stockholm: Acta Universitatis Stockholmiensis, 2012.

Baah, A. Y., and H. Jauch, eds. *Chinese Investments in Africa: A Labour Perspective*. Windhoek, African Labour Research Network, 2009.

Bach, D. "Patrimonialism and Neopatrimonialism: Comparative Receptions and Transcriptions." In *Neopatrimonialism in Africa and Beyond*, edited by D. Bach and M. Gazibo. London: Routledge, 2012, 25–45.

Bach, Jean-Nicolas. "*Abyotawi* Democracy: Neither Revolutionary nor Democratic, a Critical Review of EPRDF's Conception of Revolutionary Democracy in Post-1991 Ethiopia." *Journal of Eastern African Studies* 5, no. 4 (2011): 641–63.

Bahar, Dany, Ricardo Hausmann, and Cesar Hidalgo. "Neighbors and the Evolution of the Comparative Advantage of Nations: Evidence of International Knowledge Diffusion?" *Journal of International Economics* 92 (2014): 111.

Bai, Chong-En, and Yingyi Qian. "Infrastructure Development in China: The Cases of Electricity, Highways, and Railways." *Journal of Comparative Economics* 38 (2001): 34–51.

Banda, Fackson. *Citizen Journalism and Democracy in Africa: An Exploratory Study*. Grahamstown: Highway Africa, 2010.

Barboza, David. "In Roaring China, Sweaters Are West of Socks City." *New York Times*, December 24, 2004.

Barma, Naazneen, and Ely Ratner. "China's Illiberal Challenge." *Democracy: A Journal of Ideas* 2 (Fall 2006): 57.

Barma, Naazneen, Ely Ratner, and Steven Weber. "A World without the West." *The National Interest* 90 (July/August 2007): 25.

Bassil, Noah. "The Roots of Afropessimism: The British Invention of the 'Dark Continent.'" *Critical Arts* 25, no. 3 (2011): 377–96.

Bayart, Jean-Francois. "Africa in the World: A History of Extraversion." *African Affairs* 99 (2000): 217–67.

Bayart, Jean-François et al. "From Kleptocracy to the Felonious State?" In *The Criminalisation of the State in Africa*, edited by Jean-François Bayart et al. Oxford: James Curry, 1999), 1–31.

Bayart, Jean-François. *The State in Africa: The Politics of the Belly*. London: Longman Group UK Limited, 1993.

Beger, Gerrit, and Akshay Sinha. "South African Mobile Generation: A Study on South African Young People on Mobiles." *UNICEF*, May 29, 2012.

Belk, Jessica L. "China's Role in the Zambian Presidential Elections: Africa's Friend or Foe?" *China Elections and Governance*, October 28, 2011.http://chinaelectionsblog.net/?p=18228.

Bergsten, C. Fred et al. *China's Rise: Challenges and Opportunities*. Washington: United Book Press, 2008.

Bergstrand, Jeffrey H. "The Gravity Equation in International Trade: Some Microeconomic Foundations and Empirical Evidence." *The Review of Economics and Statistics* 67, no. 3 (August 1985): 474–81.

Berhe, Aregawi. "Ethiopia: Success Story or State of Chaos?" In *Postmodern Insurgencies: Political Violence, Identity Formation and Peace-Making in Comparative Perspective*, edited by Ronaldo Munck and Purnaka de Silva, 96–124. New York: Palgrave MacMillan, 2000.

Berhe, Aregawi. "The Origins of the Tigray People's Liberation Front." *African Affairs* 103, no. 413 (2004): 569–92.

Berhe, Aregawi. "A Political History of the Tigray People's Liberation Front (1975–1991): Revolt, Ideology and Mobilisation in Ethiopia." Doctor of Philosophy, Faculty of Social Sciences, University of Amsterdam, 2008.

Berhe, Mulugeta G., and Liu Hongwu, eds. *China-Africa Relations: Governance, Peace and Security*. Addis Ababa: Institute for Peace and Security Studies, University of Addis Ababa, 2013.

Betzold, Carola. "'Borrowing Power' to Influence International Negotiations: AOSIS in the Climate Change Regime, 1990–1997." *Politics* 30, no. 3 (2010): 131–48.

Bliss, Harry, and Bruce Russett. "Democratic Trading Partners: The Liberal Connection, 1962–1989." *The Journal of Politics* 60, no. 4 (November 1998): 1127.

Blond, Becca. "10 Most-Followed Kenyans on Twitter." *AFK Insider*, May 2014.http://afkinsider.com/54949/10-followed-kenyans-on-twitter/11/.

Blond, Becca. "10 Most-Followed South Africans on Twitter." *AFK Insider*. April 29, 2014.http://afkinsider.com/53559/10-most-followed-south-africans-on-twitter/.

Bodomo, Adams. "Africa-China Relations: Strengthening Symmetry with Soft Power." *Pambazuka News* 440 (July 2, 2009),www.pambazuka.net/en/category/africa_china/57385.

Bohler-Muller, Narnia, and Charl van der Merwe. "The Potential of Social Media to Influence Socio-Political Change on the African Continent." *African Institute of South Africa*, Policy Brief 46 (2011).

Bonacich, E. "A Theory of Middleman Minorities." *American Sociological Review* 38, no. 5 (1973): 583–94.

Boone, C. "Trade, Taxes, and Tribute: Market Liberalizations and the New Importers in West Africa." *World Development* 22, no. 3 (1994): 453–67.

Bratton, Michael, and Nicholas van de Walle. *Democratic Experiments in Africa*. Cambridge: Cambridge University Press, 1997.

Bratton, Michael, and Nicholas van de Walle. "Neopatrimonial Regimes and Political Transitions in Africa." *World Politics* 46, no. 4 (1994): 453–89.

Bräutigam, Deborah. "Aid 'with Chinese Characteristics': Chinese Foreign Aid and Development Finance Meet the OECD-DAC Aid Regime." *Journal of International Development* 23, no. 5 (2011): 752–64.

Bräutigam, Deborah. "China's Resource-Backed Weapons Exports: Norinco." *China in Africa: The Real Story*, December 27, 2010.

Bräutigam, Deborah. "Close Encounters: Chinese Business Networks as Industrial Catalysts in Sub-Saharan Africa." *African Affairs* 102, no. 408 (2003): 447–67.

Bräutigam, Deborah. *The Dragon's Gift: The Real Story of China in Africa*. New York: Oxford University Press, 2009.

Bräutigam, Deborah, and Haisen Zhang. "Green Dreams: Myth and Reality in China's Agricultural Investment in Africa." *Third World Quarterly* 34, no. 9 (2013): 1676–96.

Bronkhorst, Quinton. "Tencent's WeChat in Big Push for Africa." July 2, 2013.http://businesstech.co.za/news/mobile/41038/tencents-wechat-in-big-push-for-africa/.

Brookes, Peter, and Ji Hye Shin. "China's Influence in Africa: Implications for the United States, Backgrounder #1916." The Heritage Foundation, February 22, 2006.

Brooks, A. "Spinning and Weaving Discontent: Labour Relations and the Production of Meaning at Zambia-China Mulungushi Textiles." *Journal of Southern African Studies* 36, no. 1 (2010): 113–32.

Brown, William. "A Question of Agency: Africa in International Politics." *Third World Quarterly* 33, no. 10 (2012): 1904.

Brown, William, and Sophie Harman, eds. *African Agency in International Politics*. London: Routledge, 2013.

Burke, Christopher, Lucy Corkin, and Nastasya Tay. "China's Engagement of Africa: Preliminary Scoping of African Case Studies: A Scoping Exercise Evaluating China's Engagement of Six African Case Studies," prepared for the Rockefeller Foundation. Stellenbosch: Centre for Chinese Studies, Stellenbosch University, November 2007.

Caporaso, James A. "Dependence, Dependency, and Power in the Global System: A Structural and Behavioral Analysis." *International Organization* 32, no. 1 (1978).

Carbone, Maurizio. "The European Union and China's Rise in Africa: Competing Visions, External Coherence and Trilateral Cooperation." *Journal of Contemporary African Studies* 29 (2014): 203–21.

Carew, Joanne. "WeChat Looks to Africa." July 2, 2013.http://www.itweb.co.za/?id= 65370:WeChat-looks-to-Africa.

Cargill, Thomas. "Our Common Strategic Interests: Africa's Role in a Post-G8 World." *Chatham House* (June 2010): 1–48.

Carmody, P., and I. Taylor. "Flexigemony and Force in China's Geoeconomic Strategy in Africa: Sudan and Zambia Compared." *Geopolitics* 15, no. 3 (2010): 495–515.

Cassin, Richard L. "Kenya, China Team Up against Illegal Ivory Trade." February 14, 2014.http://www.fcpablog.com/blog/2014/2/14/kenya-china-team-up-against-illegal-ivory-trade.html.

Central Intelligence Agency. *Soviet Economic Assistance to the Sino-Soviet Bloc Countries*. Washington, United States Central Intelligence Agency, 1955, 59.

Chabal, Patrick, and J. P. Daloz. *Africa Works: Disorder as Political Instrument*. London: James Currey, 1999.

Chabal, Patrick, and Nuno Vidal. "E Pluribus Unum: Transitions in Angola." In *Angola: The Weight of History*. London: Hurst Publishers Ltd., 2007.

Chalfin, B. "Cars, the Customs Service and Sumptuary Rule in Contemporary Ghana." *Comparative Studies in Society and History* 50, no. 2 (2008): 424–53.

Chama, Brian. "Economic Development at the Cost of Human Rights: China Nonferrous Metal Industry in Zambia." *Human Rights Brief* 17, no. 2 (2010): 1–6.

Chan, Stephen. "Guy Scott's Whiteness Is Not the Issue in Zambia," *The Conversation*, October 31, 2014.http://theconversation.com/guy-scotts-whiteness-is-not-the-issue-in-zambia-33690.

Chan, Stephen. "Ten Caveats and One Sunrise in Our Contemplation of China and Africa." In *China Returns to Africa: A Rising Power and a Continent Embrace*. Edited by Chris Alden, Daniel Large, and Ricardo Soares de Oliveira, 339–48. London: Hurst & Company, 2008.

Chanie, Paulos. "Clientelism and Ethiopia's Post-1991 Decentralisation." *Journal of Modern African Studies* 45, no. 3 (2007): 355–84.

Chen, Shaofeng. "Motivations behind China's Foreign Oil Quest: A Perspective from the Chinese Government and the Oil Companies." *Journal of Chinese Political Science* 13, no. 1 (2008): 79–104.

Chen, Te-Ping. "China in Africa Podcast: Understanding the 'Negative Narrative.'" *China Talking Points*, June 12, 2010.www.chinatalkingpoints.com/china-in-africa-podcast-the-negative-narrative/.

China Daily. "*China Daily* Launches *Africa Weekly* Edition." *China Daily*, December 14, 2012. http://www.chinadaily.com.cn/china/2012-12/14/content_16016334.htm.

China Nonferrous Mining Corporation, Ltd. "2012 Interim Report."http://m.todayir.com/todayirattachment_hk/chinanonferrous/attachment/20120914170201001503963_en.pdf.

Cho. "Mining Reflections: A People Betrayed." *Zambian Economist*, November 22, 2009.

Chun, Zhang. *China–Zimbabwe Relations: A Model of China–Africa Relations?* Johannesburg: South African Institute of International Affairs, 2014.

Cilliers, Jakkie. "Resource Wars—A New Type of Insurgency." In *Angola's War Economy: The Role of Oil and Diamonds*, edited by Jakkie Cilliers and Christian Dietrich, 1–15. Pretoria: Institute for Security Studies, 2000.

Clapham, Christopher. *Africa and the International System: The Politics of Survival*. Cambridge: Cambridge University Press, 1996.

Clapham, Christopher. "Discerning the New Africa." *International Affairs* 74, no. 2 (1998): 263–70.

Clapham, Christopher. "Fitting China In." In *China Returns to Africa: A Rising Power and a Continent Embrace*, edited by Chris Alden, Daniel Large and Ricardo Soares de Oliveira, 361–70. London: Hurst and Company, 2008.

Clapham, Christopher. "Sovereignty and the Third World State." *Political Studies* XLVII (1999): 522–37.

Clapham, Christopher. *Third World Politics: An Introduction*. London: Croom and Helm, 1985.

Constine, Josh. "Facebook Hits 100M Users in Africa, Half the Continent's Internet-Connected Population." Tech Crunch, September 8, 2014.http://techcrunch.com/2014/09/08/facebook-africa/.

Corkin, Lucy. *Uncovering African Agency: Angola's Management of China's Credit Lines*. Farnham: Ashgate, 2013.

Counter Balance. "The Mopani Copper Mine, Zambia: How European Development Money Has Fed a Mining Scandal," December 2010. www.counterbalance-eib.org/?p=347.

Cunliffe-Jones, Peter. *My Nigeria: Five Decades of Independence*. New York: Palgrave, 2010.

Dalton, Matthew. "Telecom Deal by China's ZTE, Huawei in Ethiopia Faces Criticism." *Wall Street Journal*, January 7, 2014. http://online.wsj.com/news/articles/SB10001424052702303653004579212092223818288.

De Beer, Hannelie, and Virginia Gamba. "The Arms Dilemma: Resources for Arms or Arms for Resources." In *Angola's War Economy: The Role of Oil and Diamonds*, edited by Jakkie Cilliers and Christian Dietrich. Pretoria: Institute for Security Studies, 2000.

De Bruijn, M., R. van Dijk, and J. B. Gewald. "Social and Historical Trajectories of Agency in Africa." In *African Alternatives*, edited by P. Chabal, U. Engel, and L. de Haan, 9–20. Leiden: Brill, 2007.

De Comarmond, Cecile. "China Lends Angola $15 bn, But Few Jobs Are Created," *Mail and Guardian*, March 6, 2001. http://mg.co.za/article/2011-03-06-china-lends-angola-15bn-but-few-jobs-are-created.

De Lanerolle, Indra. "The New Wave: Who Connects to the Internet, How They Connect and What They Do When They Connect?" South African Network Society Project.http://www.networksociety.co.za/internet-report.phporhttp://www.scribd.com/doc/114640231/TheNewWave-Small.

Démurger, Sylvie. "Infrastructure Development and Economic Growth: An Explanation for Regional Disparities in China?" *Journal of Comparative Economics* 29 (2001): 95.

De Waal, Alexander. *Evil Days: Thirty Years of War and Famine in Ethiopia*. New York: Human Rights Watch, 1991.

Dobler, G. "Chinese Shops and the Formation of a Chinese Expatriate Community in Namibia." *China Quarterly* 199 (2009): 707–27.

Dobler, G. "Solidarity, Xenophobia and the Regulation of Chinese Businesses in Namibia." In *China Returns to Africa: A Rising Power and a Continent Embrace*, edited by C. Alden, D. Large, and R. S. de Oliveira, 237–55. London: Hurst, 2008.

Dolan, Michael B., and Brian W. Tomlin. "First World–Third World Linkages: External Relations and Economic Development." *International Organization* 34, no. 1 (Winter 1980).

Downs, Erica. "The Fact and Fiction of Sino-African Energy Relations." *China Security* 3, no. 3 (Summer 2007): 42–68.

Durkheim, Emile. *Suicide: A Study in Sociology*. London: Routledge, 2002.

Economist. "China International Fund: The Queensway Syndicate and the Africa Trade." April 13, 2011. http://www.economist.com/node/21525847.

Edoho, Felix. "Globalization and Marginalization of Africa: Contextualization of China–Africa Relations." *Africa Today* 58 (2011): 121.

Eisenstadt, S. N., and L. Roniger. "Patron-Client Relations as a Model of Structuring Social Exchange." *Comparative Studies in Society and History* 22, no. 1 (1980): 42–77.

Ekaney, Nkwelle. "Scramble for Africa." *The Diplomat*, September 2012.

Ekeh, Peter. "Colonialism and the Two Publics: A Theoretical Statement." *Comparative Studies in Society and History* 17, no. 1 (1975).

Ellis, R. "The Politics of the Middle: Re-Centring Class in the Postcolonial." *ACME* 10, no. 1 (2011): 69–81.

Emeagwali, Gloria M. "Intersections between Indigenous Knowledge and Economic Development in Africa." In *Indigenous Discourses of Knowledge and Development in Africa*, edited by Edward Shizha and Ali Abdi, 31–45. London: Routledge, 2013.

Emirbayer, Mustafa, and Ann Mische. "What Is Agency?" *American Journal of Sociology* 103, no. 4 (1998): 962–1023.

Engels, Frederick. *Ludwig Feuerbach and the End of Classical German Philosophy*. Honolulu, HI: University Press of the Pacific, 2005.

Erdmann, G., and U. Engel. "Neopatrimonialism Reconsidered: Critical Review and Elaboration of an Elusive Concept." *Commonwealth and Comparative Politics* 45, no. 1 (2007): 95–119.

Escobar, A. "Culture Sits in Places: Reflections on Globalism and Subaltern Strategies of Localization." *Political Geography* 20 (2001): 139–74.

Etabohen, Bisong. "Cameroon Looks to Fix Chinese Employment Blues." *Africa Review* (Nairobi), January 15, 2012.

Evans, Peter. "Building an Integrative Approach to International and Domestic Politics: Reflections and Projections." In *Double-Edged Diplomacy: International Bargaining and Domestic Politics*, edited by Peter Evans et al., 397–430. Berkeley: University of California Press, 1993.

Executive Research Associates (ERA). "China in Africa: A Strategic Overview." Report prepared for the Institute of Developing Economies, Japan External Trade Organisation (IDE-JETRO), October. http://www.ide.go.jp/English/Data/Africa_file/Manualreport/pdf/china_all.pdf.

Farah, Douglas, and Andy Mosher. "Winds from the East: How the People's Republic of China Seeks to Influence the Media in Africa, Latin America, and Southeast Asia." ChinaFile.com. http://www.chinafile.com/winds-east-how-peoples-republic-china-seeks-influence-media-africa-latin-america-and-southeast-asia.

Faucon, Benoit, and Spencer Swartz. "African Pressures China's Oil Deals." *Wall Street Journal*, September 30, 2009. http://online.wsj.com/article/SB125425680269850381.html.

Ferreira, Manuel Ennes. China in Angola: Just a Passion for Oil?" In *China Returns to Africa: A Rising Power and a Continent Embrace*, edited by C. Alden, D. Large, and R. Soares de Oliveira, 274–94. London: Hurst, 2008.

Ferreira, Manuel Ennes. "Nacionalização e confisco do capital português na indústria transformadora de Angola (1975–1990)." *Análise Social* 162, no. 37 (Spring 2002): 47–90.

Financial Express. "Sinopec Beats ONGC, Gets Angola Block," July 15, 2006. http://www.financialexpress.com/news/Sinopec-beats-ONGC,-gets-Angola-block-/171139/.

Ford, Jeremy. "$80 Android Phone Sells Like Hotcakes in Kenya, the World Next?" *Singularity Hub*, August 16, 2011.http://singularityhub.com/2011/08/16/80-android-phone-sells-like-hotcakes-in-kenya-the-world-next/.

Foster, Vivien, et al. *Building Bridges: China's Growing Role as an Infrastructure Financier in Sub-Saharan Africa*. Washington: World Bank, 2008.

Foucault, Michel. "Afterward: The Subject and Power." In Michel Foucault: Beyond Structuralism and Hermeneutics, edited by Hubert Dreyfus and Paul Rabinow, 208–26. Chicago: University of Chicago Press, 1982.

Foucault, Michel. "Body/Power" and "Truth and Power." In *Michel Foucault: Power/Knowledge*, edited by C. Gordon, 142.London: Harvester, 1980).

Foucault, Michel. *The History of Sexuality: The Will to Knowledge*. London, Penguin: 2008.

Foucault, Michel. *Michel Foucault: The Essential Works, Power, Volume 3*, edited by Colin Gordon. London: Penguin, 2002.

Fraser, Alastair. "Conference Report: Minewatch Zambia," September 19–20, 2008.http://orenga.politics.ox.ac.uk/materials/funding_reports/Fraser_Conf_Report.pdf.

Freeden, Michael. *Ideologies and Political Theory: A Conceptual Approach*. Oxford: Clarendon Press, 1996.

French, Howard W. "China and Africa." *African Affairs* 106, no. 422 (2006): 127–32.

French, Howard W. *China's Second Continent: How a Million Migrants Are Building a New Empire in Africa.* New York: Alfred A. Knopf, 2014.

French, Howard W. "In Africa, an Election Reveals Skepticism of Chinese Involvement." *The Atlantic*, September 29, 2011.

French, Howard W. "The Next Empire." *The Atlantic* 305, no. 4 (May 2010): 59–69.

Frynas, Jedrzej, and Manuel Paulo. "A New Scramble for African Oil? Historical, Political, and Business Perspectives." *African Affairs* 106, no. 423 (2007).

Fu, Xiaolan. "Foreign Direct Investment, Absorptive Capacity and Regional Innovation Capabilities: Evidence from China." *Oxford Development Studies* 36, no. 1 (2008): 89–110.

Fu, Xiaolan, Carlo Pietrobelli, and Luc Soete. "The Role of Foreign Technology and Indigenous Innovation in the Emerging Economies: Technological Change and Catching-Up." *World Development* 39, no. 7 (2011): 1204–12.

Gabinet de Apoio Técnico (GAT). "Linha de Crédito com o Eximbank da China: Relatório das actividades desenvolvidas II trimestre de 2008." http://www.minfin.gv.ao/fsys/China-Relatorio_do_II_trim_2008SitedoMINFIN2.pdf.

Gadzala, Aleksandra. "The Silliness of 'China-in-Africa.'" *National Interest*, November 19, 2013.http://nationalinterest.org/commentary/the-silliness-china-africa-9422.

Gagliardone, Iginio. "China as a Persuader: CCTV Africa's First Steps in the African Mediasphere." *Ecquid Novi: African Journalism Studies* 34, no 3 (2013).

Gagliardone, Iginio. "New Media and the Developmental State in Ethiopia." *African Affairs* 113, no. 451 (2014): 279–99.

Gagliardone, Iginio. "The Socialization of ICTs in Ethiopia." *International Journal of Sociotechnology and Knowledge Development* 1, no. 4 (2009): 13–28. doi:10.4018/jskd.2009062602.

Gagliardone, Iginio, and Nicole Stremlau. *Digital Media, Conflict and Diasporas in the Horn of Africa.* Open Society Foundations, 2011. http://www.alnap.org/pool/files/sf-media-report-handbook-digital-media-conflict-and-diaspora-in-the-horn-of-africa-02-20-2012-final-web.pdf.

Gagliardone, Iginio, Nicole Stremlau, and Daniel Nkrumah. "Partner, Prototype or Persuader? China's Renewed Media Engagement with Ghana." *Communication, Politics & Culture* 45, no. 2 (2012). http://mams.rmit.edu.au/xbo3w37se3t8z.pdf.

Gambari, Ibrahim. "From Balewa to Obasanjo: The Theory and Practice of Nigeria's Foreign Policy." In *Gulliver's Troubles: Nigeria's Foreign Policy After the Cold War*, edited by Adekeye Adebajo and Abdul Mustapha, 61. Scottsville: University of KwaZulu-Natal Press, 2008.

Gao, Ping, and Kalle Lyytinen. "Transformation of China's Telecommunications Sector: A Macro Perspective." *Telecommunications Policy* 24, no. 8 (2000): 719–30.

Gazel, Ricardo. "Macro-Brief: Angola." World Bank (February 2010): 1–3.

Giddens, Anthony. *New Rules of Sociological Method: A Positive Critique of Interpretive Sociologies.* London: Hutchinson, 1976.

Giese, K. "Same-Same But Different: Chinese Traders' Perspectives on African Labor." *China Journal* 69 (2013): 134–53.

Giese, K., and A. Thiel. "The Vulnerable Other: Distorted Equity in Chinese Ghanaian Employment Relations." *Ethnic and Racial Studies*, 2012. doi: 10.1080/01419870.2012.681676

Gill, Bates, et al. *China's Expanding Role in Africa: Implications for the United States.* Washington: Center for Strategic and International Studies, 2007.

Gillies, Alexandra. "Obasanjo, the Donor Community and Reform Implementation in Nigeria." *Round Table* 96, no. 392 (2007).

Global Witness. "Oil Revenues in Angola: Much More Information, but Not Enough Transparency." London, February 2011, 1–50.

Goel, Ran. "A Bargain Born of Paradox: The Oil Industry's Role in American Domestic and Foreign Policy." *New Political Economy* 9, no. 4 (2004): 482.

Gonzalez-Vicente, Ruben. "China's Engagement in South America and Africa's Extractive Sectors: New Perspectives for Resource Curse Theories." *Pacific Review* 24 (2011): 65–87.

Green, Duncan. "A Copper-Bottomed Crisis? The Impact of the Global Economic Meltdown on Zambia." Oxfam GB, March 2009.www.oxfam.org.uk/resources/policy/economic_crisis/ impact_on_zambia.html.

Greenhalgh, S. "De-Orientalizing the Chinese Family Firm." *American Ethnologist* 21, no. 4 (1994): 742–71.

GSMA Association. "New GSMA Report Forecasts Half a Billion Mobile Subscribers in Sub-Saharan Africa by 2020," November 6, 2014.http://www.gsma.com/newsroom/press-release/gsma-report-forecasts-half-a-billion-mobile-subscribers-ssa-2020/.

Gu, J. "China's Private Enterprises in Africa and the Implications for African Development." *European Journal of Development Research* 21, no. 4 (2009): 570–87.

Habeeb, William. *Power and Tactics in International Negotiation: How Weak Nations Bargain with Strong Nations.* Baltimore: Johns Hopkins University Press, 1988.

Haglund, D. "In It for the Long Term? Governance and Learning among Chinese Investors in Zambia's Copper Sector." *The China Quarterly* 199 (2009): 627–46.

Haglund, D. "Regulating FDI in Weak African States: A Case Study of Chinese Copper Mining in Zambia." *Journal of Modern African Studies* 46, no. 4 (2008): 5487–5575.

Hagmann, T., and D. Péclard, "Negotiating Statehood: Dynamics of Power and Domination in Africa." *Development and Change* 41, no. 4 (2010): 539–62.

Hairong, Yan, and Barry Sautman. "'The Beginning of a World Empire?' Contesting the Discourse of Chinese Copper Mining in Zambia." *Modern China* 39, no. 2 (2013): 131–64.

Han Wei, and Shen Hu, "China's Harsh Squeeze in Zambia's Copperbelt." *Caixin*, November 10, 2011.

Handel, Michael. *Weak States in the International System.* London: Frank Cass, 1981.

Hanson, Stephanie, "China, Africa, and Oil, Backgrounder." Council on Foreign Relations 6 (June 2008).

Hart, G. "Global Connections: The Rise and Fall of Taiwanese Production Network on the South African Periphery." Working Paper No. 6, University of California, California, Institute of International Studies, 1996.

Herbst, Jeffrey, and Greg Mills. "Commodities, Africa and China." S. Rajaratnam School of International Studies (RSIS) *Commentaries* (Singapore: Nanyang Technological University, January 9, 2009).

Hess, Steven, and Richard Aidoo. "Charting the Roots of Anti-Chinese Populism in Africa: A Comparison of Zambia and Ghana." *Journal of Asian and African Studies* 49, no. 2 (2013): 129–47.

Hevi, Emmanuel. *The Dragon's Embrace: The Chinese Communists and Africa.* London: Pall Mall Press, 1967.

Hibou, B. (1999) "The 'Social Capital' of the State as an Agent of Deception." In *The Criminalization of the State in Africa*, edited by J. Bayart, S. Ellis, and B. Hibou, 69–133. Oxford: James Currey, 1999.

Hicken, A. "Clientelism." *Annual Review of Political Science* 14 (2011): 289–310.

Hirschman, Albert. "Beyond Asymmetry: Critical Notes on Myself as a Young Man and on Some Other Old Friends." *International Organization* 32, no. 1 (1978): 45–50.

Hirschman, Albert. *National Power and the Structure of Foreign Trade.* Berkeley: University of California Press, 1981.

Hodges, Tony. *Angola: Anatomy of an Oil State.* London: James Curry, 2004.

Holslag, J. "China and the Coups: Coping with Political Instability in Africa." *African Affairs* 110, no. 440 (2011): 367–86.

Hughes, Lilian. "The Real Housewives of Post-Feminism: False Agency and the Internalization of Patriarchy on Reality TV." MA thesis, Georgetown University, 2012.https://repository. library.georgetown.edu/bitstream/handle/10822/557535/Hughes_georgetown_0076M_ 11826.pdf?sequence=1.

Human Rights Watch. "'You'll Be Fired if You Refuse': Labor Abuses in Zambia's Chinese State-Owned Copper Mines," November 3, 2011.www.hrw.org/reports/2011/11/03/you-ll-be-fired-if-you-refuse.

Hyden, G. *No Shortcuts to Progress: African Development Management in Perspective.* London: Heinemann, 1983.

Ifidon, E. A. "Citizenship, Statehood and the Problem of Democratization in Nigeria." *Africa Development* 21, no. 4 (1996).

Iliffe, John. *Obasanjo: Nigeria and the World*. Oxford: James Currey, 2011.

IMF. "Angola: Letter of Intent, Memorandum of Economic and Financial Policies, and Technical Memorandum of Understanding," November 3, 2009.

ITUC/GUF Hong Kong Liaison Office. "China's Exportation of Labor Practices to Africa," 2007.

Jackson, Robert H., and Carl G. Rosberg. "Why Africa's Weak States Persist: The Empirical and the Juridical in Statehood." *World Politics* 35, no. 1 (October 1982): 1–24.

Jackson, Steven F. "China's Third World Foreign Policy: The Case of Angola and Mozambique, 1961–93." *The China Quarterly* 142 (June 1995): 388–422.

Jenkins, Rhys, and Chris Edwards. "The Effect of China and India's Growth and Trade Liberalisation on Poverty in Africa, DCP 70." Department for International Development of the United Kingdom, May 2005, 18.

Jessop, B. *State Theory: Putting the Capitalist State in Its Place*. Cambridge: Polity Press, 1990.

Jones, Mark T. "Somaliland President Stops Over in Addis Ababa en Route to China." *Somaliland Press*, August 9, 2011.

Joseph, Richard A. *Democracy and Prebendal Politics in Nigeria: The Rise and Fall of the Second Republic*. Cambridge: Cambridge University Press, 1987.

Kahler, Miles. "Bargaining with the IMF: Two-Level Strategies and Developing Countries." In *Double-Edged Diplomacy: International Bargaining and Domestic Politics*, edited by Peter Evans et al., 363–94. Berkeley: University of California Press, 1993.

Kahneman, Daniel. *Thinking, Fast and Slow*. New York: Farrar, Straus and Giroux, 2011.

Kaigwa, Mark. "Kenya at 50: How Social Media Has Increased the Pace of Change." *The Guardian*, December 2013.http://www.theguardian.com/global-development-professionals-network/2013/dec/13/kenya-social-media-mark-kaigwa.

Kaira, Thula. "The Chinese and Unfair Competition: Part 2." *The Post* (Zambia), March 8, 2010.

Kalan, Jonathan. "African Youth Hungry for Connectivity." *Africa Renewal Magazine* Online, May 2013.http://www.un.org/africarenewal/magazine/may-2013/african-youth-hungry-connectivity.

Kaplinky, Raphael. "What Contribution Can China Make to Inclusive Growth in Sub-Saharan Africa?" *Development & Change* 44 (2013): 1295–1316.

Kaplinsky, Raphael, and Masuma Farooki. *How China Disrupted Global Commodities: The Reshaping of the World's Resource Sector*. London: Routledge, 2011.

Kaplinsky, Raphael, and Mike Morris. "Chinese FDI in Sub-Saharan Africa: Engaging with Large Dragons." *European Journal of Development Research* 21 (2009): 551–69.

Kapwmbwa, John. "Jury Out on How Zambia's New Leader Will Deliver on Promises." *Sunday Independent* (South Africa), September 25, 2011.

Katsouris, Christina. "Angola: China's Complex Connections." *Energy Compass*, 2009. http://www.energyintel.com/documentdetail.asp?document_id=633690.

Kelly, Tim. "Tech Hubs across Africa: Which Will Be the Legacy-Makers?" World Bank Information and Communications for Development Blog, April 30, 2014.http://blogs.worldbank.org/ic4d/tech-hubs-across-africa-which-will-be-legacy-makers?cid=EXT_WBBlogSocialShare_D_EXT&utm_content=buffer7bbfd&utm_medium=social&utm_source=twitter.com&utm_campaign=buffer.

Khan, Mushtaq H. "Patron-Client Networks and the Economic Effect of Corruption in Asia." *The European Journal of Development Research* 10, no. 1 (1998): 15–39.

Kiala, Carine. (2010) "China-Angola Aid Relations: Strategic Cooperation for Development?" *South African Journal of International Affairs* 17, no. 3 (2010): 313–31.

Kiss, Eric, and Kate Zhou. "China's New Burden in Africa." In *Dancing with the Dragon: China's Emergence in the Developing World*, edited by Dennis Hickey and Baogang Guo, 156. Lanham, MD: Rowman & Littlefield Publishers, Inc., 2010, 156.

Kong, Bo. *China's International Petroleum Policy*. Santa Barbara: Praeger Security International, 2010.

Konijn, Peter. *Chinese Resources-for-Infrastructure (R4I) Swaps: An Escape from the Resource Curse?* Johannesburg: South African Institute of International Affairs, 2014, 24.

Kremenyuk, Victor A. "The Emerging System of International Negotiation." In *International Negotiation*, edited by Victor Kremenyuk, 22–39. Oxford: Jossey-Bass Publishers, 1991.

Krugman, Paul. "Was It All in Ohlin?" Massachusetts Institute of Technology website, October 1999.

Lansner, Thomas. "After a Democratic Power Transfer, Zambia Must Tackle Chinese Investment Issues and Human Rights Reforms." Freedom House, November 15, 2011.https://freedomhouse.org/blog/after-democratic-power-transfer-zambia-must-tackle-chinese-investment-issues-and-human-rights -.VUkwjdNVhBc.

Large, Daniel. "Beyond 'Dragon in the Bush': The Study of China-Africa Relations." *African Affairs* 107 (2008): 45–61.

Large, Daniel. "China's Sudan Engagement: Changing Northern and Southern Political Trajectories in Peace and War." *The China Quarterly* 199 (2009): 610–26.

Lauder Institute, The Wharton School. "Huawei Technologies: A Chinese Trail Blazer in Africa." In *Lauder Global Business Insight Report 2009: Firsthand Perspectives on the Global Economy*. Philadelphia: University of Pennsylvania, 2009.

Leamer, Edward E. *Sources of International Comparative Advantage: Theory and Evidence.* Cambridge, MA: Massachusetts Institute of Technology, 1984.

Lee, C. "Raw Encounters: Chinese Managers, African Workers and the Politics of Casualization in Africa's Chinese Enclaves." *The China Quarterly* 199 (2009): 647–66.

Lee, M. "Uganda and China: Unleashing the Power of the Dragon." In *China in Africa*, edited by Ching Kwan Lee, 29–65. "The Spectre of Global China." *New Left Review* 89 (2014).

LeFort, René. "The Great Ethiopian Land-Grab: Feudalism, Leninism, Neo-Liberalism . . . Plus Ça Change." *openDemocracy.net*, December 2011.

Levkowitz, Lee, Marta McLellan Ross, and J. R. Warner. "The 88 Queensway Group: A Case Study in Chinese Investors' Operations in Angola and Beyond." *US-China Economic and Security Review Commission*, July 10, 2009.

Lewis, Peter. "From Prebendalism to Predation: The Political Economy of Decline in Nigeria." *Journal of Modern African Studies* 34, no. 1 (1996).

Leys, C. *The Rise and Fall of Development Theory, EAEP.* London: Indiana University Press and James Currey, 1996.

Li, Cheng. *China's Leaders: The Next Generation.* Lanham, Maryland: Rowman & Littlefield, 2001.

Lin, Justin Yifu. *New Structural Economics: A Framework for Rethinking Development and Policy.* Policy Research Working Paper, The World Bank, February 2010, 28.

Lin, Justin Yifu, and Yan Wang. *China-Africa Co-Operation in Structural Transformation: Ideas, Opportunities, and Finances.* Helsinki: United Nations University World Institute for Development Economics Research, 2014.

Long, N. "Exploring Local/Global Transformations: A View from Anthropology." In *Anthropology, Development and Modernities: Exploring Discourses, Counter-Tendencies and Violence*, edited by A. Arce and N. Long, 184–201. Routledge: London, 2000.

Long, N., and J. D. van der Ploeg. "Heterogeneity, Actor and Structure: Towards a Reconstitution of the Concept of Structure." In *Rethinking Social Development: Theory, Research and Practice*, edited by D. Booth, 62–89. London: Longman, 1994.

Long, N., and M. Villarreal. "Exploring Development Interfaces: From the Transfer of Knowledge to the Transformation of Meaning." In *Beyond the Impasse: New Directions in Development Theory*, edited by F. J. Schuurman, 140–68. London: Zed Books, 1993.

Lonsdale, John, and Bruce Berman. "Coping with the Contradictions: The Development of the Colonial State in Kenya, 1895–1914." *The Journal of African History* 20 (1979): 487–505.

Lorenz, Andreas, and Thilo Thielke. "Age of the Dragon: China's Conquest of Africa." Spiegel Online International, May 30, 2007.www.spiegel.de/international/world/the-age-of-the-dragon-china-s-conquest-of-africa-a-484603.html.

Louw-Vaudran, L. "SA Leads Africa in Anti-Chinese Sentiment." *Mail & Guardian*, February 21, 2014.http://mg.co.za/article/2014-02-20-sa-leads-africa-in-anti-chinese-sentiment.

Lungu, John. "Contextualizing Mining in Zambia." *ZIPPA Journal*, January–March 2011, 1–3.www.scribd.com/doc/46873541/ZIPPA-Journal-Jan-March-2011-Taxing-the-Mines.

Maasho, Aaron. "Ethiopia Charges Nine Bloggers, Journalists with Inciting Violence." *Reuters*, April 28, 2014. http://www.reuters.com/article/2014/04/28/us-ethiopia-politics-idUSBREA3R0YC20140428.

Macauhub. 2009. "Angolan Government Approves Credit Line Provided by Portugal." June 12, 2009. http://www.macauhub.com.mo/en/2009/06/12/7223/.

Macdonald, Kate, and Stephen Woolcock. "State Actors in Economic Diplomacy." In *The New Economic Diplomacy: Decision-Making and Negotiation in International Economic Relations*, edited Nicholas Bayne and Stephen Woolcock, 63–76. Aldershot: Ashgate, 2007.

Madebo, Ephrem. "Autocracy: China's Unsolicited Export." *The Addis Voice*, August 12, 2010.

Maier, Karl. *This House Has Fallen: Nigeria in Crisis*. London: Penguin, 2000.

Mallet, Victor. "The Chinese in Africa: Beijing Offers a New Deal." *The Financial Times*, January 23, 2007.

Mangena, Zoli. "Mugabe Left Out in the Cold." *Zimbabwe Mail*, April 10, 2011.

Mansfield, Edward D., Helen V. Milner, and B. Peter Rosendorff. "Free to Trade: Democracies, Autocracies, and International Trade." *The American Political Science Review* 94, no. 2 (June 2000): 312.

Marques, Helena. "The 'New' Economic Theories." FEP Working Papers 104 (Universidade do Porto, Faculdade de Economia do Porto), 8.

Marsh, Vivien. "Chinese State Television's 'Going Out' Strategy—a True Global News Contraflow? A Comparison of News on CCTV's Africa Live and BBC World News TV's Focus on Africa." In *Conference: China's Soft Power in Africa: Emerging Media and Cultural Relations between China and Africa*. Nottingham University's Ningbo Campus, China, 2014.

Martins, Vasco. "Keeping Business In and Politics Out: Angola's Multi-Vector Foreign Policy." *Portuguese Institute of International Relations and Security (IPRIS)* (October 2010): 1–2.

Marx, Karl. "Critique of Hegel's Philosophy in General." In *Economic and Philosophical Manuscripts of 1844*. Moscow: Progress Publishers, 1959.

Marx, Karl. "The Eighteenth Brumaire of Louis Bonaparte (selections)." In *Karl Marx: Selected Writings*, edited by Lawrence H. Simon. Indianapolis: Hackett Publishing, 1994 [1852].

Marx, Karl. *Grundrisse: Foundations of the Critique of Political Economy*. London: Penguin, 1993.

Marx, Karl, and Frederick Engels. *The Holy Family or Critique of Critical Critique*. London: Lawrence and Wishart, 1956.

Mazzucato, Mariana. *The Entrepreneurial State: Debunking Public vs. Private Sector Myths*. London: Anthem Press, 2013.

McCracken, Matthew J. "Abusing Self-Determination and Democracy: How the TPLF Is Looting Ethiopia." *Case Western Reserve Journal of International Law* 36 (2004): 183–222.

McGowan, Patrick J. "Economic Dependence and Economic Performance in Black Africa." *The Journal of Modern African Studies* 14, no. 1 (March 1976).

McKinsey Global Institute. "Lions Go Digital: The Internet's Transformative Potential in Africa." McKinsey & Company, November 2013.http://www.mckinsey.com/insights/high_tech_telecoms_internet/lions_go_digital_the_internets_transformative_potential_in_africa.

McNamee, Terence. "Africa in Their Words: A Study of Chinese Traders in South Africa, Lesotho, Botswana, Zambia and Angola." Brenthurst Foundation, Discussion Paper 2012/03, March 2012.http://www.thebrenthurstfoundation.org/a_sndmsg/news_view.asp?I=124294&PG=288.

Meagher, K. *Identity Economics: Social Networks and the Informal Economy in Nigeria*. Suffolk: James Currey, 2010.

Meagher, K. "Weber Meets Godzilla: Social Networks and the Spirit of Capitalism in East Asia and Africa." *Review of African Political Economy* 39, no. 132 (2012): 261–78.

Médard, J. F. "The Underdeveloped State in Tropical Africa: Political Clientelism or Neo-Patrimonialism." In *Private Patronage and Public Power: Political Clientelism in the Modern State*, edited by C. Clapham, 162–92. London: Frances Pinter, 1982.

Meraz, Sharon. "Is There an Elite Hold? Traditional Media to Social Media Agenda Setting Influence in Blog Networks." *Journal of Computer-Mediated Communication* 14 (2009): 701–2.

Messiant, Christine. *L'Angola postcolonial: Guerre et paix sans democratisation*. Paris: Karthala, 2008.

Messiant, Christine. "The Mutation of Hegemonic Domination." In *Angola: The Weight of History*, edited by Patrick Chabal and Nuno Vidal, 93–123. London: Hurst and Company, 2007.

Michelo, Prudence et al. "Occupation Injuries and Fatalities in Copper Mining in Zambia." *Occupational Medicine* 59, no. 3 (2009): 191–94.

Migdal, Joel S. *Strong Societies and Weak States*. Princeton: Princeton University Press, 1988.

Milkias, Paulos. 2003. "Ethiopia, the TPLF, and the Roots of the 2001 Political Tremor." *Northeast African Studies* 10, no. 2 (2003): 13–66.

Milkias, Paulos. "The Great Purge and Ideological Paradox in Contemporary Ethiopian Politics." *Horn of Africa* 19 (2001): 1–99.

Mine Safety Department, Zambia. "Mining Industry Safety Record from the Year 2000 to April, 2014." Chart in author's possession, June 2014.

Mobbs, Philip M. "The Mineral Industry of Zimbabwe." In *U.S. Geological Survey Minerals Yearbook 2006*, 42.1–42.7.

Mohan, Giles. "Beyond the Enclave: Towards a Critical Political Economy of China and Africa." *Development and Change* 44, no. 6 (2013): 1255–72.

Mohan, Giles, and Ben Lampert. "Negotiating China: Reinserting African Agency into China-Africa Relations." *African Affairs* 112, no. 446 (2013): 92–110.

Mohan, Giles, B. Lampert, D. Chang, and M. Tan-Mullins. *Chinese Migrants and Africa's Development: New Imperialists or Agents of Change?* London: Zed Books, 2014.

Moravcsik, Andrew. "Introduction: Integrating International and Domestic Theories of International Bargaining." In *Double-Edged Diplomacy: International Bargaining and Domestic Politics*, edited by Peter Evans et al., 3–42. Berkeley: University of California Press, 1993.

Morrissey, Beth et al. "China-Based Corporate Web behind Troubled Africa Resource Deals." *Center for Public Integrity*, iwatchnews, November 9, 2011. http://www.publicintegrity.org/2011/11/09/7108/china-based-corporate-web-behind-troubled-africa-resource-deals.

Moyo, Dambisa. "Beijing a Boon for Africa." *New York Times*, June 27, 2012.

Moyo, Dambisa. *Winner Take All: China's Race for Resources and What It Means for the World*. New York: Basic Books, 2012.

Mthembu-Salter, Gregory. *Elephants, Ants and Superpowers: Nigeria's Relations with China*. Johannesburg, South Africa Institute of International Affairs, 2009.

Mueller, Milton. *China in the Information Age: Telecommunications and the Dilemmas of Reform*. New York: Greenwood Publishing Group, 1997.

Munalula, Themba. "China's Special Preferential Tariff Africa." Statistical Brief Issue No. 3, Statistics Unit, Regional Integration Support Programme, Division of Trade, Customs and Monetary Affairs COMESA Secretariat, July 2007.

Murray, Laura et al. "African Safari: CIF's Grab for Oil and Minerals." *Caixin*, October 17, 2011. http://english.caixin.cn/2011-10-17/100314766.html.

Mzekandaba, Simnikiwe. "WhatsApp Dominates South Africa's Instant Messaging Market." IT Web Africa, November 26, 2013.http://www.itwebafrica.com/mobile/320-south-africa/232050-whatsapp-dominates-south-africas-instant-messaging-market.

Nabine, Djeri-Wake. *The Impact of Chinese Investment and Trade on Nigeria's Economic Growth*. Addis Ababa: Economic Commission for Africa, 2009.

Ndubuisi, Francis. "FG, China Exim Bank Seal $600m Deal on Abuja Light Rail, Galaxy Backbone." *This Day Live*, September 13, 2012. http://www.thisdaylive.com/articles/ fg-china-exim-bank-seal-600m-deal-on-abuja-light-railgalaxy-backbone/124857.

Negi, Rohit. "Beyond the 'Chinese Scramble': The Political Economy of Anti-China Sentiment in Zambia." *African Geographical Review* 27, no. 1 (2008): 41–63.

Newitt, Marlyn. "Angola in Historical Context." In *Angola: The Weight of History*, edited by Patrick Chabal and Nuno Vidal, 19–92. London: Hurst and Company, 2007.

Ngirachu, John. "Probe 'Sparked' Diplomatic Tension." *Daily Nation*, May 1, 2014.http://www.nation.co.ke/news/Public-Investments-Committee-Standard-Gauge-Railway-China/-/1056/2300888/-/61wjciz/-/index.html.

Nigerian National Petroleum Corporation. "Development of Nigeria's Oil Industry." http://www.nnpcgroup.com.

Nnatuanya, Linus Marvelos. *The Frozen Democracy: Godfatherism and Elite Corruption in Nigeria*. Enugu: Triumphant Creations, 2006.

Nnoli, Okwudiba. *Ethnic Politics in Nigeria*. Enugu, Nigeria: Fourth Dimension, 1980.

Nugent, P. "States and Social Contracts in Africa." *New Left Review* 63 (May–June 2010): 35–68.

"Numsa's ANC Boycott a Serious Blow—Analyst." News24, December 21, 2014.http://www.news24.com/SouthAfrica/Politics/Numsas-ANC-boycott-a-serious-blow-analyst-20131220.

Nwankwo, Agwuncha. *Nigeria: The Stolen Billions*. Enugu, Nigeria: Fourth Dimension, 2002.

Nyíri, P. "Chinese Entrepreneurs in Poor Countries: A Transnational 'Middleman Minority' and Its Futures." *Inter-Asia Cultural Studies* 12, no. 1 (2011): 145–53.

Nyíri, P. "Global Modernisers or Local Subalterns? Parallel Perceptions of Chinese Transnationals in Hungary." *Journal of Ethnic and Migration Studies* 31, no. 4 (2005): 659–74.

Oakland Institute. "Unheard Voices: The Human Rights Impact of Land Investments on Indigenous Communities in Gambella." Oakland, CA: The Oakland Institute, 2013.

Oarhe, Osumah, and Iro Aghedo. "The Open Sore of a Nation: Corruption Complex and Internal Security in Nigeria." *African Security* 3, no. 3 (2010).

Obadare, E., and W. Adebanwi. "Introduction—Democracy and Prebendalism: Emphases, Provocations, and Elongations." In *Democracy and Prebendalism in Nigeria: Critical Interpretations*, edited by W. Adebanwi and E. Obadare, 1–22. Basingstoke: Palgrave Macmillan, 2013.

Obama, Barack. "Remarks by Pres. Obama at Young African Leaders Initiative Town Hall." White House Press Release, June 29, 2013.

Obama, Barack, and Jakaya Kikwete. "Remarks by President Obama and President Kikwete of Tanzania at Joint Press Conference." White House Documents and Publications, July 1, 2013.

Odularu, Gbadebo Olusegun. "Crude Oil and the Nigerian Economic Performance." Unpublished paper, 2008.

Ogundiya, Ilufoye Sarafa. "Political Corruption in Nigeria: Theoretical Perspectives and Some Explanations." *Anthropologist* 11, no. 4 (2009).

Ojakorutu, Victor, and Ayo Wheto. "Sino-African Relation: The Cold War Years and After." *Asia Journal of Global Studies* 2, no. 2 (2008): 35–43.

Okonta, Ike. *When Citizens Revolt: Nigerian Elites, Big Oil and the Ogoni Struggle for Self-Determination*. Trenton, NJ: Africa World Press, 2008.

Okuttah, Mark. "Safaricom Loosens China's Grip on Local Contracts with Sh14bn Tender." *Business Daily*, December 6, 2012. http://www.businessdailyafrica.com/Corporate-News/Safaricom-loosens-China-grip-on-local-contracts/-/539550/1638364/-/11xotu6z/-/index.html.

Olivier de Sardan, Jean-Pierre. "A Moral Economy of Corruption in Africa?" *Journal of Modern African Studies* 37, no. 1 (1999).

Omobowale, Ayokunle. "Disorder and Democratic Development: The Political Instrumentalization of Patronage and Violence in Nigeria." *African Journal of Political Science and International Relations* 5, no. 6 (2011).

Opdycke, Kelly, Priscilla Segura, and Ana M. Vasquez. "The Effects of Political Cynicism, Political Information Efficacy and Media Consumption on Intended Voter Participation." *Colloquy* 9 (2013): 75–97.

Open Society Institute of Southern Africa (OSISA), et al. "Breaking the Curse: How Transparent Taxation and Fair Taxes Can Turn Africa's Mineral Wealth into Development," 2009.http://news.bbc.co.uk/2/shared/bsp/hi/pdfs/25_03_09_breaking_the_curse.pdf.

Orre, Aslak. "Who's to Challenge the Party-State in Angola? Political Space & Opposition in Parties and Civil Society." Paper presented at CMI and IESE Conference, "Election Processes, Liberation Movements and Democratic Change in Africa", Maputo, April 8–11, 2010, 1–20.

Osaghae, Eghosa. *Crippled Giant: Nigeria Since Independence*. London: Hurst and Company, 1998, 21.

Otto, Greg. "Twitter CEO Dick Costolo: We Are the 'Global Town Square.'" *USA News and World Report*, June 26, 2013.http://www.usnews.com/news/articles/2013/06/26/twitter-ceo-dick-costolo-we-are-the-global-town-square.

Palley, Thomas I. "Institutionalism and New Trade Theory: Rethinking Comparative Advantage and Trade Policy." *Journal of Economic Issues* 17, no. 1 (March 2008): 199.

Pawson, Lara. "The Angolan Elections: Politics of No Change." *Open Democracy*, September 25, 2008. http://www.isn.ethz.ch/Digital-Library/Articles/Detail//?ots591=4888CAA0-B3DB-1461-98B9-E20E7B9C13D4&lng=en&id=91981.

Peel, Michael. *A Swamp Full of Dollars: Pipelines and Paramilitaries at Nigeria's Oil Frontier*. London: IB Tauris, 2009.

Penubarti, Mohan, and Michael D. Ward. "Commerce and Democracy." Conference paper presented at the Development and Application of Spatial Analysis for Political Methodology, at the University of Colorado, Boulder, March 10–12, 2000.

People's Republic of China. *China-Africa Economic and Trade Cooperation*. Beijing: Information Office of the State Council, People's Republic of China, 2010.

People's Republic of China. *China-Africa Economic and Trade Cooperation (2013)*. Beijing: Information Office of the State Council, People's Republic of China, 2013.

Plummer, Janelle. 2012. *Diagnosing Corruption in Ethiopia: Perceptions, Realities, and the Way Forward for Key Sectors*. Washington: World Bank. http://econ.worldbank.org/external/default/main?pagePK=64165259&theSitePK=469372&piPK=64165421&menuPK=64166093&entityID=000386194_20120615035122.

Portes, A., and J. Sensenbrenner. "Embeddedness and Immigration: Notes on the Social Determinants of Economic Action." *American Journal of Sociology* 98, no. 6 (1993): 1320–50.

Portland Communications. "How Africa Tweets—2014."http://www.portland-communications.com/publications/how-africa-tweets-2014/.

Protalinski, Emil. "Former Pentagon Analyst: China Has Backdoors to 80% of Telecoms." *ZDNet*, July 14, 2012. http://www.zdnet.com/former-pentagon-analyst-china-has-backdoors-to-80-of-telecoms-7000000908/.

Putnam, Robert. "Diplomacy and Domestic Politics: The Logic of Two-Level Games." *International Organization* 42, no. 3 (1988): 427–60.

Rahmato, Dessalegn. "The Perils of Development from Above: Land Deals in Ethiopia." *African Identities* 12, no. 1 (2014).

Raine, Sarah. *China's African Challenges*. London: Routledge, 2013.

Ravallion, Martin. "Do Poorer Countries Have Less Capacity for Redistribution?" *Journal of Globalisation and Development* 1, no. 2 (2010): 1–29.

Reed, John. "Africa's Big Brother Lives in Beijing." *Foreign Policy*, July 30, 2013. http://foreignpolicy.com/2013/07/30/africas-big-brother-lives-in-beijing/.

Renard, Mary-Francoise. *China's Trade and FDI in Africa*. Tunis, Tunisia: African Development Bank, 2011.

Reno, William. "The (Real) War Economy in Angola." In *Angola's War Economy: The Role of Oil and Diamonds*, edited by Jackie Cilliers and Christian Dietrich, 219–38. Pretoria: Institute for Security Studies, 2000.

Rid, Thomas. 2014. "Snowden, 多谢 多谢 | Kings of War." http://kingsofwar.org.uk/2014/03/snowden-thanks-very-much/.

Rosendorff, B. Peter. "Do Democracies Trade More Freely?" Unpublished manuscript, dated September 29, 2005.

Rugonzibwa, Pius. "Tanzania: China Aid to Boost National Budget." *Tanzania Daily News*, March 27, 2013. http://allafrica.com/stories/201303270063.html.

Russell, Alec, and Michael Green. "Africa's Response: Big Push to Be More Assertive." *Financial Times*, January 23, 2008.

Russo, Christina. "Using the Power of the Web to Protect Africa's Wildlife." Yale Environment 360, June 2011.http://e360.yale.edu/feature/using_the_power_of_blogs_to_protect_africas_wildlife/2413/.

Sala-i-Martin, Xavier, and Arvind Subramanian. "Addressing the Natural Resource Curse: An Illustration from Nigeria." *IMF Working Paper WP/03/159*, 2003.

Sandiford, Keith. *Theorizing a Colonial Caribbean-Atlantic Imaginary: Sugar and Obeah.* London: Routledge, 2011.

Sasman, Catherine. "Chinese in Gobabis." *The Namibian* (Windhoek), January 12, 2012.

Sautman, Barry. "The Chinese Defilement Case: Racial Profiling in an African 'Model of Democracy.'" *Rutgers Race and the Law Review* 14, no. 1 (2014): 87–134.

Sautman, Barry, and Yan Hairong. "Bashing 'The Chinese': Contextualizing Zambia's Collum Coal Mine Shooting." *Journal of Contemporary China* 23, no. 90 (2014): 1073–92.

Sautman, Barry, and Yan Hairong. *The Chinese Are the Worst?: Human Rights and Labor Practices in Zambian Mining.* Baltimore: University of Maryland, 2012.

Sautman, Barry, and Yan Hairong. *East Mountain Tiger, West Mountain Tiger: China, Africa, the West and "Colonialism" in Africa.* Baltimore: University of Maryland, 2007.

Sautman, Barry, and Yan Hairong. "Localizing Chinese Enterprises in African." *African-East Asian Affairs*, April 2015.

Schatz, Sayre. "Pirate Capitalism and the Inert Economy of Nigeria." *Journal of Modern African Studies* 22 (1984).

Schneider, Christina J. "Weak States and Institutionalized Bargaining Power in International Organizations." *International Studies Quarterly* 55, no. 2 (2011): 331–55.

Schoneveld, George, et al. "The Developmental Implications of Sino-African Economic and Political Relations: A Preliminary Assessment for the Case of Zambia," CIFOR, 2014.www. cifor.org/library/4486/the-developmental-implications-of-sino-african-economic-and-political-relations-a-preliminary-assessment-for-the-case-of-zambia/.

Scott, J. "Patron-Client Politics and Political Change in Southeast Asia." *American Political Science Review* 66 (1972): 91–113.

Seabra, Pedro, and Paulo Gorjão. *Intertwined Paths: Portugal and Rising Angola.* Johannesburg: South African Institute of International Affairs, 2011.

Segers, Kaatje, Joost Dessein, Sten Hagberg, Patrick Develtere, Mitiku Haile, and Jozef Deckers. "Be Like Bees–The Politics of Mobilizing Farmers for Development in Tigray, Ethiopia." *African Affairs* 108, no. 430 (2008): 91–109.

Sewell, William. "A Theory of Structure: Duality, Agency, and Transformation." *American Journal of Sociology* 98, no. 1 (1992).

Shapshak, Toby. "Africa Not Just a Mobile-First Continent—It's Mobile Only." CNN.com, October 4, 2012,http://www.cnn.com/2012/10/04/tech/mobile/africa-mobile-opinion.

Shaxson, Nicholas. *Poisoned Wells: The Dirty Politics of African Oil.* New York: Palgrave Macmillan, 2007.

Shen, Gordon, and Victoria Fan. "China's Provincial Diplomacy to Africa: Applications to Health Cooperation," *Contemporary Politics* 20 (2014): 182–208.

Shen, Simon. "A Constructed (Un)reality on China's Re-Entry into Africa: The Chinese Online Community Perception of Africa (2006–2008)." *Journal of Modern African Studies* 47 (2009): 425–48.

Shen, Zhihua, and Yafeng Xia. "The Great Leap Forward, the People's Commune and the Sino-Soviet Split." *Journal of Contemporary China* 20 (2011): 861–80.

Shih Chih-yu. *Sinicizing International Relations: Self, Civilization, and Intellectual Politics in Subaltern East Asia.* New York: Palgrave Macmillan, 2013.

Shinn, David H., and Joshua Eisenman. *China and Africa: A Century of Engagement.* Pittsburgh: University of Pennsylvania Press, 2012.

Shirky, Clay. "The Political Power of Social Media: Technology, the Public Sphere, and Political Change." *Foreign Affairs*, January/February 2011.https://www.foreignaffairs.com/articles/2010-12-20/political-power-social-media.

Sifuna, Edward. "Social Media a Useful Tool for Pushing Leaders to Act." *Standard Digital News*, May 19, 2014.http://www.standardmedia.co.ke/?articleID=2000121502&story_title=Kenya-social-media-a-useful-tool-for-pushing-leaders-to-act.

Sikombe, Aaron. "Should Trade between Africa and China Be Regulated?" *Tumfweko*, April 20, 2012.http://tumfweko.com/2012/04/20/should-the-trade-between-africa-and-china-be-regulated/.

Simutanyi, Neo. "Why I Won't Vote for Sata." *The Post* (Zambia), September 25, 2006.

Skocpol, Theda. "Bringing the State Back In: Strategies for Analysis in Current Research." In *Bringing the State Back In*, edited by P. Evans, D. Rueschemeyer, and T. Skocpol, 3–43. New York: Cambridge University Press, 1985.

Smith, Daniel. *A Culture of Corruption: Everyday Deception and Popular Discontent in Nigeria*. Princeton, NJ: Princeton University Press, 2007.

Snyder, Glenn H. *Alliance Politics*. Ithaca, NY: Cornell University Press, 1997.

Soares de Oliveira, Ricardo. "Business Success, Angola-Style: Post-Colonial Politics and the Rise and Rise of Sonangol." *Journal of Modern African Studies* 45, no. 4 (2007a): 595–619.

Soares de Oliveira, Ricardo. *Oil and Politics in the Gulf of Guinea*. London: Hurst and Company, 2007b.

Sogge, David. "Angola: 'Failed' yet 'Successful.'" *Fundación par alas Relaciones Internacionales y el Diálogo Exterior (FRIDE)*, Working Paper 81 (April 2009): 1–28.

Soyinka, Wole. "Discounting the Electorate." *West Africa Review* 5 (2004).

Spilsbury, Laura. "Can Michael Sata Tame the Dragon and Channel Chinese Investment towards Development for Zambians?" *Journal of Politics & International Studies* 8 (2012–2013): 238–278.

Stien, Kari. "Kamwala Shopping World: Competition and Cooperation among Zambian and Chinese Trader in Lusaka." Master's Thesis, Norwegian University of Science & Technology, 2013.

Stream, The. "Kenyans Tell China: Hands Off Our Elephants." *Al Jazeera*, August 27, 2013.http://stream.aljazeera.com/story/201308271932-0023007.

Sun, Yun. *The Sixth Forum on China-Africa Cooperation: New Agenda and New Approach?* Washington, DC: Brookings Institution, 2014.

Sutton, John, and Gillian Langmead. "An Enterprise Map of Zambia." London: International Growth Centre, 2013.http://personal.lse.ac.uk/sutton/sutton_zambia_press.pdf.

Swire, Mary. "China's Shipping Sector Develops in Tianjin." *Tax-News.com* (Hong Kong), August 5, 2010.

Tan-Mullins, May, Giles Mohan, and Marcus Power. "Redefining 'Aid' in the China–Africa Context." *Development and Change* 41, no. 5 (2010): 857–81.

Taylor, Ian. "The 'All Weather Friend'? Sino–African Interaction in the 21st Century." In *Africa in International Politics: External Involvement on the Continent*, edited by Ian Taylor and Paul Williams. New York: Routledge, 2004.

Taylor, Ian. *China and Africa: Engagement and Compromise*. London: Routledge, 2006.

Taylor, Ian. "China's Relations with Nigeria." *Round Table: The Commonwealth Journal of International Affairs* 96, no. 392 (2007).

Tijani, Alou M. "Monitoring the Neopatrimonial State on a Day-to-Day Basis: Politicians, Customs Officials and Traders in Niger." In *Neopatrimonialism in Africa and Beyond*, edited by D. Bach and M. Gazibo. London: Routledge, 2012.

Tong, Nyuol. "Kony 2012: An African Perspective." *The Chronicle* (Duke University), March 16, 2012. http://www.dukechronicle.com/articles/2012/03/16/kony-2012-african-perspective.

Trade and Forfaiting. "Deals of the Year 2005." February 6, 2006. http://www.tfreview.com/awards/deals/deals-year-2005.

Tse-Tung, Mao. "Report on an Investigation of the Hunan Peasant Movement." In *Sources of Chinese Tradition*, edited by W. T. De Bary, Wing-Tsit Chan, and Burton Watson, 203–11. New York: Columbia University Press, 1960 [1927].

Tull, Denis M. "China's Engagement in Africa: Scope, Significance and Consequences." *Journal of Modern African Studies* 44, no. 3 (2006): 476.

Valentine, G. "Theorising and Researching Intersectionality: A Challenge for Feminist Geography." *Professional Geographer* 59 (2007): 10–21.

Van de Walle, Nicolas. *African Economies and the Politics of Permanent Crisis*. Cambridge: Cambridge University Press, 2001.

Van de Walle, Nicolas. "Meet the New Boss: Same as the Old Boss?: The Evolution of Political Clientelism in Africa." In *Patrons, Clients and Policies: Patterns of Democratic Accountability and Political Competition*, edited by Herbert Kitschelt and Steven Wilkinson. Cambridge: Cambridge University Press, 2007.

Van der Westhuizen, Janis, and Karen Smith. "South Africa's Role in the World: A Public Opinion Survey." *SAFPI*, Policy Brief 55 (2013).

Varun, Vira, Thomas Ewing, and Jackson Miller. "Out of Africa: Mapping the Global Trade in Illicit Elephant Ivory." Born Free USA, August 2014.http://www.bornfreeusa.org/a9_out_of_africa.php.

Vaughan, Sarah. "The Addis Ababa Transitional Conference of July 1991: Its Origins, History and Significance." Edinburgh: Centre of African Studies, Edinburgh University, 1994.

Vaughan, Sarah. "Ethnicity and Power in Ethiopia." PhD, The University of Edinburgh, 2003.

Vaughan, Sarah, and Kjetil Tronvoll. *The Culture of Power in Contemporary Ethiopian Political Life, SIDA Studies, No. 10* (2003).

Verhoeven, Harry. "Is Beijing's Non-Interference Policy History? How Africa Is Changing China." *Washington Quarterly* 37 (2014): 55–70.

Vines, Alex, Lillian Wong, Marcus Weimer, and Indira Campos. "Thirst for African Oil: Asian National Oil Companies in Nigeria and Angola," Chatham House, August 2009.

Wahito, Margaret. 2012. "Kenya: China to Fund Kenya's Fibre Optic Project." *Capital FM*, June 28, 2012. http://allafrica.com/stories/201206290024.html.

Wall Street Journal. "Sinopec to Acquire Angolan Oil Assets." March 29, 2011. http://www.chinamining.org/Investment/2010-03-29/1269828803d35006.html.

Wallis, William. "Chinese Investment Has Put Africans in the Driving Seat." *Financial Times*, January 26, 2010. http://www.ft.com/cms/s/0/85d10e8e-0945-11df-ba88-00144feabdc0.html.

Walther, O. "A Mobile Idea of Space: Traders, Patrons and the Cross-Border Economy in Sahelian Africa." *Journal of Borderlands Studies* 24, no. 1 (2009): 34–46.

Wang, Jianwei, and Jing Zou. "China Goes to Africa: A Strategic Move?" *Journal of Contemporary China* 23 (2014): 1113–32.

Wang, Jian-Ye. "What Drives China's Growing Role in Africa?" Working Paper No. 07/211. International Monetary Fund, August 2007, 22.

Wasserman, Herman. "China in South Africa: Another BRIC in the Wall?" in *Africa Growth Report 2012*, edited by Mark Fuller, Marianne Nebbe and Wadim Schreiner. Beirut, Boston, Pretoria, Tianjin, and Zurich: Innovatio Publishing, 2012, 137–47.

Weber, Max. *Economy and Society*. Berkeley, CA: University of California Press, 1978.

Weber, Max. *The Theory of Social and Economic Organization*. Edited by Talcott Parsons. New York: Free Press, 1964.

Weimar, Marcus. "Angola as a Global Player." Chatham House Conference Report, July 24, 2009 (August 12, 2009): 1–14.

White, Gregory, and Scott Taylor. "Well-Oiled Regimes: Oil and Uncertain Transitions in Algeria and Nigeria." *Review of African Political Economy* 28, no. 89 (2001).

Wight, Colin. "State Agency: Social Action without Human Activity?" *Review of International Studies* 30, no. 2 (2004): 269–80.

Wight, Colin. "They Shoot Dead Horses Don't They? Locating Agency in the Agent-Structure Problematique." *European Journal of International Relations* 5, no. 1 (1999): 109–42.

Winning, David, and Benoit Faucon. "Sinopec, CNOOC to Agree on $1.8B for Angola Asset." *Dow Jones Newswires*, 2008. http://www.rigzone.com/news/article.asp?a_id=67348.

Wright, Peter, Ananda Mukherji, and Mark Kroll. "A Reexamination of Agency Theory Assumptions: Extensions and Extrapolations," *Journal of Socio-Economics* 30 (2001): 413–29.

Wu, Yu-Shan. *The Rise of China's State-Led Media Dynasty in Africa*. South African Institute of International Affairs, 2012.

Wu, Yu-Shan. "The Role of Public Sentiment and Social Media in the Evolving China-Africa Relationship." *South African Institute of International Affairs*, Occasional Paper 134 (2013): 1–24.

Xin, Xin. 2009. "Xinhua News Agency in Africa." *Journal of African Media Studies* 1, no. 3 (2009): 363–77.

Yan, Hairong, and Barry Sautman. "'Beginning of a World Empire?': Contesting the Discourse of Chinese Copper Mining in Zambia." *Modern China* 39, no. 2 (2014): 131–64.

Yi-Chong, Xu. "Chinese State-Owned Enterprises in Africa: Ambassadors or Freebooters?" *Journal of Contemporary China* 23 (2014): 822–40.

Yo, Zushi. "Sympathy for the Devil Doctor." *New Statesman* (UK), November 28, 2014, 64–65.

York, Geoffrey. "Why China Is Making a Big Play to Control Africa's Media." *The Globe and Mail*, September 11, 2013. http://www.theglobeandmail.com/news/world/media-agenda-china-buys-newsrooms-influence-in-africa/article14269323/.

Young, John. *Peasant Revolution in Ethiopia: Tigray People's Liberation Front, 1975–1991.* Cambridge: Cambridge University Press, 1997.

Young, John. "The Tigray and Eritrean Peoples Liberation Fronts: A History of Tensions and Pragmatism." *The Journal of Modern African Studies* 34, no. 1 (1996): 105–20.

Yun, Sun. *Africa in China's Foreign Policy.* Washington, DC: Brookings Institution, April 2014.

Zartman, William. "Justice in Negotiation." In *International Negotiation: Actors, Structure/Process, Values*, edited by Peter Berton. London: Macmillan, 1999, 291–308.

Zhang, Bing. "Understanding China's Telecommunications Policymaking and Reforms: A Tale of Transition toward Liberalization." *Telematics and Informatics* 19, no. 4 (2002): 331–49.

Zhang, Weiwu, Thomas J. Johnson, Trent Seltzer, and Shannon L. Bichard. "The Revolution Will Be Networked: The Influence of Social Networking Sites on Political Attitudes and Behaviour." *Social Science Computer Review* 28, no. 1 (2010): 75–92.

Zhang, Xiaoling. *How Ready Is China for a China-Style World Order? China's State Media Discourse under Construction.* University of Nottingham: China Policy Institute, 2013.

Zhao, Suisheng. "A Neo-Colonialist Predator or Development Partner? China's Engagement and Rebalance in Africa." *Journal of Contemporary China* 23 (2014): 1033–52.

Zhao, Yuezhi. "The State, the Market, and Media Control in China." In *Who Owns the Media*, edited by Pradip Thomas and Zaharom Nain, 179–212. New York: Zed Books, 2004.

Zhimin, Chen, and Jian Junbo. *Chinese Provinces as Foreign Policy Actors in Africa.* Johannesburg: South African Institute of International Affairs, 2009.

王慧卿. "希拉里访非'力不从心'" ("Hillary Clinton's Africa Visit 'Did Not Meet Her Expectations'"). 第一财经日报 (Shanghai), August 7, 2009.

龙周园, [Long Zhouyuan]. "掮客"中基"在非洲" ["China International Fund Broker in Africa"]. 财新 *[Caixin]*, October 17, 2011. http://video.caixin.cn/2011-10-17/100314444.html.

Index

About the Contributors

Aleksandra W. Gadzala is a geopolitical risk and social impact consultant focused on emerging and frontier markets. Her career spans senior roles in geopolitical risk advisory and sustainability at Control Risks, Oxford Analytica, and responsAbility Investments, a Swiss impact investment manager that specializes in microfinance and renewable energy. Aleksandra additionally has extensive experience in international development, having worked with the Global Economic Governance Programme at the University of Oxford, the G8 Research Group, and the United Nations Development Programme (UNDP) in New York. She began her career in academia as a Research Analyst with the Hoover Institution at Stanford University. Aleksandra's writings have appeared in numerous academic and professional journals in the U.S. and in Europe, including *The National Interest*, *Review of African Political Economy*, *Journal of Eastern African Studies*, *RealClearWorld*, *China Review*, and in collaboration with the Atlantic Council in Washington, D.C. Aleksandra holds a PhD in Politics from the University of Oxford, an MPhil in Politics, also from Oxford, and BA in Political Science from Northwestern University.

Lucy Corkin has a doctorate from SOAS, University of London, which was published as *Uncovering African Agency: Angola's Management of China's Credit Lines* by Ashgate in February 2013. Lucy currently works at Rand Merchant Bank (RMB), a South African investment bank. She speaks English, Portuguese, French, Afrikaans, and Mandarin Chinese. She remains a research associate of the Africa-Asia Centre at SOAS.

Joshua Eisenman (马佳士) is assistant professor at the University of Texas at Austin's Lyndon Baines Johnson School of Public Affairs and senior fellow for China studies at the American Foreign Policy Council (AFPC) in Washington, DC. Before joining the AFPC in 2006, Dr. Eisenman served for two and half years as a policy analyst at the US-China Economic and Security Review Commission. He has also worked as fellow at the New America Foundation and assistant director of China Studies at the Center for the National Interest (formally The Nixon Center). Dr. Eisenman's second book, *China and Africa: A Century of Engagement* (University of Pennsylvania Press) coauthored with former U.S. ambassador to Ethiopia David H. Shinn, was named one of the top three books on Africa in 2012 by *Foreign Affairs* magazine. In 2007, he coedited *China and the Developing World: Beijing's Strategy for the Twenty-First Century* (ME Sharpe). Dr. Eisenman holds a PhD in political science from the University of California, Los Angeles (UCLA), an MA in International Relations from Johns Hopkins University's Paul H. Nitze School of Advanced International Studies (SAIS), and a BA in East Asian Studies from The George Washington University's Elliott School of International Affairs.

Iginio Gagliardone is British Academy Research Fellow and a member of the Programme in Comparative Media Law and Policy at the University of Oxford. His research and publications focus on media and political change, particularly in sub-Saharan Africa, and on the emergence of distinctive models of the information society worldwide. In the past few years, he has been leading various research projects, from examining the role of Information and Communication Technologies in peace building and state building in Eastern Africa, to understanding the increasing role of emerging powers such as China in the media and telecommunication sectors in Africa, to analyzing the nature and significance of hate speech online, especially ahead of elections. He completed his PhD at the London School of Economics and Political Science, investigating the relationship between development and destabilization in Ethiopia. He is also research associate of the Centre of Governance and Human Rights at the University of Cambridge and of the Centre for Global Communication Studies (CGCS), Annenberg School of Communication, University of Pennsylvania.

Calestous Juma is professor of the Practice of International Development and director of the Science, Technology, and Globalization Project at Harvard Kennedy School. He is faculty chair of the school's Innovation for Economic Development Executive Program and the Mason Fellows Program. He has been elected to several scientific and engineering academies including the Royal Society of London, the US National Academy of Sciences, the World Academy of Sciences (TWAS), the UK Royal Academy of Engineering, and the African Academy of Sciences. His previous positions include: founding executive director of the African Centre for Technology

Studies in Nairobi; executive secretary of the UN Convention on Biological Diversity; chancellor of the University of Guyana; and Dr. Martin Luther King Jr Visiting Professor at the Massachusetts Institute of Technology. He has chaired several high-level advisory panels for the African Union on science, technology, and innovation. Juma holds a DPhil in science and technology policy studies from the University of Sussex (UK) and has received numerous international awards and honorary degrees for his work on sustainable development. He is author of *The New Harvest: Agricultural Innovation in Africa.*

Mark Kaigwa is a Kenyan author and entrepreneur. He is the founder of Nendo, a strategy and storytelling consultancy working across sub-Saharan Africa impacting digital culture, community, and commerce. He is the publisher and author of *The A to Z of Kenyan Twitter*, described as "ingenious" by the *Mail & Guardian* and the *Nendo Social Media Trend Report*, the East and Central African region's first annual publication on digital media. Kaigwa was recognized in 2013 among *Forbes*'s 30 under 30 Best Young Entrepreneurs in Africa. As a professional speaker and trainer, his repertoire has seen him address over ten thousand people in thirty countries on digital innovation, culture, and business on the African continent.

Ben Lampert is a lecturer in international development based in the Development Policy and Practice Group at The Open University, UK. He is a human geographer, and his research is primarily concerned with the role of migrants and diaspora communities in development in Africa. His most recent work has been on Chinese migrants in Ghana and Nigeria, and this formed the basis of the coauthored volume *Chinese Migrants and Africa's Development: New Imperialists or Agents of Change?* published by Zed in 2014.

Giles Mohan is professor of International Development at the UK's Open University. He is a human geographer who studies African governance and the transnational connections to and from Africa, especially migrants. His recent work focuses on China's engagement with Africa and has been funded by a series of grants from the Economic and Social Research Council. Giles has published extensively in geography, development studies, and African studies journals and has consulted for a range of BBC documentaries on issues of international development. In 2012 he coauthored a book, with Marcus Power and May Tan-Mullins, titled *China's Resource Diplomacy in Africa: Powering Development?* (Palgrave MacMillan). In 2014 Zed Books published his latest book, *Chinese Migrants and Africa's Development*, written with Ben Lampert, May Tan-Mullins, and Daphne Chang.

Barry Sautman is a political scientist and lawyer at Hong Kong University of Science and Technology. He researches China-Africa links, including political economy, labor rights, interactions between Chinese and Africans, and representations and perceptions of China and Chinese in Africa, as well as ethnic politics in China, including ethnic policies and the Tibet and Xinjiang issues. His latest monographic works, with Yan Hairong, are *The Chinese Are the Worst?: Human Rights and Labor Practices in Zambian Mining* (Baltimore: University of Maryland, 2013) and 中国在非洲：话语 与实践 (北京：中国社会科学文 献出版社, 2015) (*China in Africa: Discourse and Practice* [Beijing: China Social Science and Literature Publishers, 2015]).

Ian Taylor is professor in International Relations and African Politics at St Andrews and also chair professor in the School of International Studies, Renmin University of China. He holds a DPhil from the University of Stellenbosch, South Africa, and an MPhil from the University of Hong Kong. Focusing largely on sub-Saharan Africa, he has authored eight academic books, edited another eight, and has published numerous articles and chapters in books.

Yu-Shan Wu is a researcher for the Global Powers and African Drivers Program at the South African Institute of International Affairs (SAIIA), based in Johannesburg. During her time at SAIIA she has worked on emerging country (namely China) public diplomacy in Africa; South Africa–China evolving relations; and media impact on policymaking. Prior to her position she assisted SAIIA's China in Africa Project and worked at the South African Broadcasting Corporation. She has a background in International Relations (MA) from the University of the Witwatersrand, South Africa.